Communicating like dolphins with

Spot-On
Encryption Suite:

Democratization of Multiple & Exponential Encryption.

Handbook and User Manual
as practical software guide
with introductions into Cryptography,
Cryptographic Calling and Cryptographic Discovery,
P2P Networking, Graph-Theory, NTRU, McEliece,
the Echo Protocol and the Spot-On Software.

Scott Edwards & Spot-On.sf.net Project (Eds.)

More about the project:

https://spot-on.sf.net

Communicating like dolphins with

Spot-On Encryption Suite:

Democratization of Multiple & Exponential Encryption.

Handbook and User Manual
as practical software guide
with introductions into Cryptography,
Cryptographic Calling and Cryptographic Discovery,
P2P Networking, Graph-Theory, NTRU, McEliece,
the Echo Protocol and the Spot-On Software.

Scott Edwards & Spot-On.sf.net Project (Eds.)

Bibliographic Information:
Detailed bibliographic data can be found in the Internet under:
https://portal.dnb.de

Edwards, Scott / Spot-On.sf.net Project (Eds.): Communicating like dolphins with Spot-On Encryption Suite: Democratization of Multiple & Exponential Encryption; Handbook and User Manual as practical software guide with introductions into Cryptography, Cryptographic Calling and Cryptographic Discovery, P2P Networking, Graph-Theory, NTRU, McEliece, the Echo Protocol and the Spot-On Software,
ISBN 9783749435067, BOD, Norderstedt 2019.

1. Printed Release.

Editors:
Scott Edwards, Mele Gasakis, Michael Weber, et al.

Manufacturing and publishing: BoD – Books on Demand, Norderstedt 2019
ISBN: 9783749435067
Book-Layout-Template with references to Johann-Christian Hanke.
Recommendations also to Wikipedia, in which a lot of cryptographic terms can be looked up in greater depth.

9 783749 435067

Freidank, Bescheidenheit, 1229

diu bant mac nieman vinden,
diu mîne gedanke binden.
man vâhet wîp unde man,
gedanke niemen gevâhen kann.

Georg Friedrich Benecke; Wilhelm Müller; Friedrich Zarncke: Mittelhochdeutsches Wörterbuch. Leipzig 1854–1866, hier Bd. 1, Sp. 354b-357a, Artikel: gedanc, II, 5.

Content

For all those, who have (or are)
a real virtual friend, have family
far away and regard privacy
and alternative and expressed opinions
as a basic and constitutional element
for human rights and democracy
and try to foster these beliefs
within their communities:
Freedom is the respect
to the other's cipher text!

1 What is Spot-On?

Spot-On Encryption Suite is a
- secure instant chat messenger and
- encrypting e-mail client

that also includes additional features such as
- group chat,
- file transfer, and a
- URL search based on an implemented URL data-base, which can be peer-to-peer connected to other nodes.

Thus, the three basic functions frequently used by a regular Internet user in the Internet - **communication (chat / e-mail), web search and file transfer -** are represented in an encrypted environment safely and comprehensively.

A dolphin is the symbol of the Spot-On Encryption Suite using the Echo Protocol to communicate like dolphins within the sea.

It can be spoken from Spot-On as of an encryption suite. It might be regarded as the most elaborated, up-to-date and diversificated encryption software currently.

The three S: Speaking (by text), Searching and Sending - are now secure over the Internet within one software suite. Open source for everyone.

1.1 Main Functions in Spot-On Encryption Suite

In addition, Spot-On has also implemented a number of useful tools, such as encrypted chat server functionality, proxy-enabled pass-through, text and cipher text conversion pads (and vice versa), a feed-reader and a web-crawler, or dash-boards for the friends of statistics and analysis, and much more.

Communication (chat / e-mail), web search and file transfer are represented in an encrypted environment.

Furthermore, the application also offers next to

The three S:
Speaking (by text),
Searching and also
Sending are now
secure over the In-
ternet.

- chat messaging as well
- decentralized public group chat in IRC style,
- decentralized and encrypted e-mail: The e-mail can be IMAP, POP3 and thirdly, p2p e-mail. Spot-On is thus a fully functional e-mail client. As soon as encrypted e-mails are sent, it is necessary that the friend also uses this (or any other Echo) client. This has the advantage that the encryption key is only to be exchanged once, but then no longer has to be applied to every single e-mail. This function of transferring the key encrypted back in a direct way is called in Spot-On "RE-PLEO" based on the Echo-Public-Key-Sharing Protocol (EPKS) and later on this was also taken over in other projects under the name Autocrypt or KeySync (within an automatic process).
- As in any messaging program, files can be shared and sent. The transfer is always encrypted per sé.
- As said, there is also the function to implement a URL web search in a decentralized database repository: Users can store URLs and the content of a website - as we do it so far with bookmark URLs in the browser and its cache - in a comfortable searchable database in Spot-On. A thematic RSS feeds can import these URLs into the encrypted database, which is based either on SQL or PostGres and is also p2p network able.
- With the tools "Rosetta CryptoPad" and the
- "File-Encryptor" the user can encrypt text and/or files additionally or convert them back. This adds one more encryption layer to the cipher text or file and turns encryption into multi-encryption. These encryption tools can therefore also be used for other transmission paths (such as an unencrypted path outside of Spot-On like uploading a file into a cloud box, sending a message over another messenger or email service or posting ciphertext to any board).

With the use of Spot-On the user can therefore be relatively sure - because of the modern and elaborated encryption techniques and processes - that no unwanted third party can eavesdrop on the conversations or read e-mails or look into file transfers. The URL search also happens on the local machine, so that search queries are protected and secured.

The user-to-user communication via the Internet should remain in private, protected space with this application. Spot-On uses for this purpose strong and hybrid encryption, also called multi-encryption, with different levels of modern encryption technology based on established encryption libraries - such as libgcrypt (known from OpenPGP or GnuPG and OpenSSL) and other.

For example, it creates separate and different public / private keys for encryption and signatures for each function - based on the encryption algorithms RSA, or alternatively Elgamal and NTRU. In addition to NTRU, the encryption algorithm McEliece is open source implemented. These latter two algorithms are considered to be particularly secure against attacks that are known from Quantum Computing and are becoming increasingly relevant in the future because of fast quantum computers.

The RSA algorithm has been officially considered as broken since 2016.

Spot-On is thus one of the first communication suites worldwide to implement these two algorithms, thus initiating the renunciation of - or alternatives to - the RSA algorithm that has been officially considered as broken since 2016 (see NIST cited in Adams/Maier 2016).

Figure 1: The tabs in Spot-On Encryption Suite application

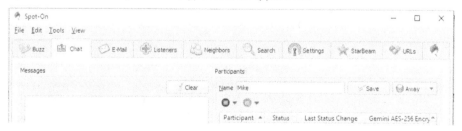

The tabs in the Spot-On software are sorted by default on top (in the north) and provide these functions:

- **Buzz Tab:** Here the group chat in IRC style is found.
- **Chat Tab:** Here the private 1:1 chat messaging takes place.
- **E-mail Tab:** Within the e-mail tab the user can send and receive e-mails. This refers to (1) IMAP/POP3 e-mails which are encrypted (over the POPTASTIC key), (2) POPTASTIC-messages which provide chat over e-mail servers (also with the POPTASTIC key) and third p2p e-mails over the Echo Network connections based on either the C/O function or the VEMI institutions function which provide a postbox in the peer-to-peer network. (3) Also regular @-e-mail is possible, if the receiver uses another e-mail-client (not based on any key as identifier; instead the @-e-mail-address is used).
- **Listeners Tab:** With the term "listener" a chat server software function is described. Within Spot-On it is also possible to operate an own chat and communication server. Several protocols are supported.
- **Neighbors Tab:** The neighbors tab creates the connection to other nodes, friends and chat servers.
- **Search Tab:** This tab provides the search in the local URL-Database.
- **Settings Tab:** The interface of Spot-On requires an active and running kernel. The settings tab is regularly used to start and stop the kernel of Spot-On. Also, the key generation is steered within this tab.
- **StarBeam Tab:** If a user wants to send a file this is possible within the chat pop-up window – Additionally, very detailed information about the sent or received file is provided in this StarBeam tab.
- **URLs Filter Tab:** Here the filters and distillers for the URL exchange with other nodes are defined. This function allows to filter URLs, e.g. from one domain, in case a user wants URLs just from e.g. www.wikipedia.org.
- **Login Tab:** The last tab is the login page to unlock the application with a password.

- **Main Menu:** Above the tabs the main menu is found, where options (e.g. chosen icon set), key import and export and also the further encryption tools are provided like Rosetta Crypto Pad (for conversion of text: from plain text to cipher text and vice versa) or the FileEncryptor (to convert files from a plain file to an encrypted file).

With all its equipment, Spot-On is therefore a so-called "Communication Suite" - a program with numerous functions for secure communication, which realizes the transmission of the encrypted packets mainly with the so-called Echo Protocol (or in addition the later explained POPTASTIC Protocol or EPKS Protocol). The Echo Protocol is particularly secure, as it will be explained in the upcoming chapters.

Spot-On Communication Suite provides multiple, and even exponential Encryption within a network based on the Echo Protocol.

1.2 Why is it important for Internet users to encrypt their communication?

Today almost all wireless Internet accesses are password protected. (So-called "Freifunk.net"-activities are currently trying to reverse this over-regulation through password-free and account-free wireless Internet access). In a few decades plain text messages or e-mails to friends[*] via the Internet should be encrypted as well. In order to consolidate this change, sometimes c-mail (for crypto-mail) rather than e-mail is or should be used as a new term.

The change from plain text to cipher text converts e-mail to c-mail.

Encryption is not a question of having something to hide or not, it is the paradigm of whether we, ourselves control our communication - or whether it is controlled by others, third parties and their communication servers. Users need to have the right to choose an alternative communication server or even create their own with less effort.

Controlling communication is ultimately also a question of attacking free thinking and a question of deleting the

---

[*] In this book all terms always apply to all sex and genders: female, divers and male.

Spot-On is the initial welcome for multiple and exponential encryption.

presumption of innocence ("In doubt for the accused" - if every citizen in the Internet ever belongs to a dock!).

Democracy requires thinking and discussing alternatives in private as well as in public.

The communication and data transmission over the Internet should be protected as parents would also protect their loved ones or a mother bird would protect their young against the unknown: Everyone should protect her or his privacy and human rights with modern cryptographic functions.

Strong multi-encryption (also so-called "hybrid encryption") thus ultimately secures the declarations of human rights in their broadly constituted consensus and is a digital self-defense that everyone should learn and use - to ultimately contribute to democracy and support this processes.

Privacy by default requires e-mail and chat messaging software for users encrypting by default. Communication software without encryption is outdated and obsolete today.

Why it is necessary to encrypt and learn about encryption:

- **Economy** is based on encryption. Securing the data at the heart of our modern economy: Encryption helps businesses to stay compliant as well as to protect the valuable data of their customers.
- **Law and regulations** require encryption: Healthcare providers are required e.g. by the Health Insurance Portability and Accountability Act (HIPAA) to implement security features that protect patients' sensitive health information. Institutions of higher learning must take similar steps under e.g. the Family Education Rights and Privacy Act (FERPA), while retailers must contend with the Fair Credit Practices Act (FCPA) and similar laws. In Europe GPDR/DSGVO requires the protection of sensitive data.
- **Guaranteeing data security**: Providers of data services — storing, managing or transmitting personal or business data — must guarantee to use the best available technology to thwart attacks against that data or the entities and individuals who depend on those services.

- **Old Internet protocols** provide only plain text: It is simply clear that every sent e-mail has to be regarded as a post card everyone can read.
- **Consistent privacy by default:** Individuals have a right to be secure in their public, private and commercial lives and interactions. Encryption by default protects privacy by turning personal information into "always encrypted" messages. Everyone should make sure that e-mails are only being sent over an end-to-end encrypted connection. That means that users are encrypting each message with a shared password or with a public key of the receiver of the message. For the Spot-On software the messages are always encrypted once a key exchange has been done. Privacy by default requires e-mail and chat messaging software for users encrypting by default. Communication software without encryption must be regarded as outdated and obsolete today.
- **Protecting government information:** National, state and local agencies should ensure that the data they hold is secure against threats of domestic and foreign intrusion. All the rest belongs to open data government.
- **Encouraging innovation:** Developers and providers of innovation need digital security. Copy-cats are only kept out with encryption.
- **Defending critical infrastructure:** Providers of essential services, such as banking, health, electricity, water, Internet and other critical infrastructure providers, are to be empowered to provide the best available encryption and security technologies.
- **Hacking and collecting user data** is big business: Hackers aren't just bored kids in a basement anymore. They're big business.
- **The Snowden papers** (2013) demonstrate that all internet traffic is saved as big data for possible analyses. Do not send any plaintext since mid-thirteen anymore!

Law and regulations require encryption.

Encryption is a precondition for human rights and democracy.

The Spot-On Encryption Suite tries to be an elaborated and strong tool for this responsibility. Similar to the development of safety in automobiles, the e-mail & chat and file encryption will also develop: if we initially drove without a seatbelt in the car, today we drive with obligatory safety belts (e.g. since 1968 in the U.S.) and additional airbags or thirdly additional electronic security information systems.

Spot-On is an easy-to-use application, but to some extent also a program, which needs to be learned; it requires - as with the car driver's license - the knowledge of the various controls and options. Similar to a cockpit of an aircraft, there are some control buttons available in this original user interface. As we describe later, there is another interface available, in which these options are reduced a bit. Also, another minimal view is offered for beginners in this software for cryptographic processes. In this respect: We have to learn what is still unknown and - to note that - it is already a reduced scope to applied encryption in software. This handbook and user manual can help readers to understand the individual functions. And users who first read and then try out have - as always - clearly an advantage. :-) Otherwise it might be the inspiration of teachers to provide this reference and knowledge to young learners, if they don't find out by themselves what the needful things and actions are.

Learning about encryption within the Internet is required latest since mid-thirteen.

Spot-On is a practical software suite to learn encryption in a school class with friends.

The unencrypted plain text e-mail or chat message should therefore have actually become obsolete after the Snowden Papers revealed in 2013 that private plain text e-mails are widely intercepted and systematically collected and evaluated by many interested parties worldwide. 2013 was also the year in which Spot-On and the complementary GoldBug User Interface have been released after several years of research. Today, we have to send out cipher text messages only. As one algorithm for encryption might be broken, just use two or several: Spot-On is the initial welcome of multiple and even exponential encryption, as it will be referenced in more detail as well in the further sections of this handbook.

2 Alternatives to RSA encryption: Spot-On as the first NTRU & McEliece Encryption Suite

There are basically two methods of encryption:

First, the symmetric encryption: Both users use the same password, e.g. a so-called AES (Advanced Encryption Standard) with 32 characters, which will be explained in more detail below. And on the other hand, there is the a-symmetric encryption.

Second, in a-symmetric encryption: each user has two keys: a private and a public key. Each user exchanges the public key with the friend and can then encrypt data using the private key in combination with the public key.

Figure 2: How asymmetric encryption with Public Key Infra-structure (PKI) works

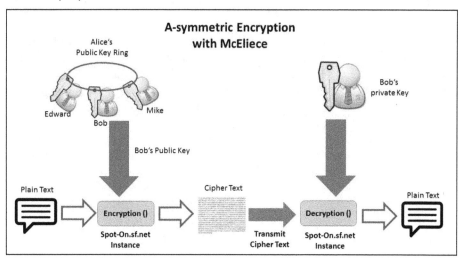

After transmission, the other party is also able to decipher the message with the own keys in combination with the cipher text and the known public key of the friend. This is, mathematically speaking, based on the prime factorization, which requires today years of computational effort. Encryption is only as good as the mathematical calculations cannot be calculated by the automation of computers at lightning speed. The a-symmetric method is also called PKI: Pubic Key Infrastructure, which can be built on different algorithms for key generation, e.g. like RSA.

However, encryption - be it via AES or PKI - is not unbreakable, and the procedures and libraries must also be well-used to be secure. RSA is considered "today as an essential, widely studied and not yet breakable encryption standard - although the further development of fast computers might bring a different future", - it was still 2014 in this (first only online hosted) manual noted. In 2016, the official NIST Institute announced that the algorithm RSA is considered broken in the age of Quantum Computing (see NIST).

The media has barely picked up this announcement, as everyone will probably agree that you cannot buy a quantum computer in the nearest supermarket, so the problem might be not relevant.

Further research is needed on e.g. a SSL/TLS connection based on alternative algorithms like e.g. McEliece.

It has the charm of children who hold their hand in front of their eyes and thus do not let the problem or risk endanger their perception of reality. Nevertheless, it is officially confirmed that RSA can be broken - with special means. The security is gone. This also has an impact on our Internet economy and online banking, because so far, the so called "secure" economic connections are relying on RSA. And a SSL/TLS protocol to secure the connection to online banking or shopping portals based on more secure algorithms like McEliece or NTRU is not yet developed.

2.1 A-symmetric encryption with PKI: RSA, El-gamal and especially NTRU and McEliece in comparison

Therefore, Spot-On encryption suite has already intro-duced additional alternatives to RSA at an early stage - if this RSA encryption algorithm standard would ever be inse-cure: RSA with a correspondingly large size of the key (at least 3072 bytes) might still (or just) be regarded as a time hurdle for non-specialized technical administrative staff.
In addition to RSA Spot-On has implemented the encryption algorithms Elgamal and also NTRU and McEliece. The latter two are both considered to be particularly more resistant to the attacks known from Quantum Computing.

A mix of symmetric encryption (based on passwords) and a-symmetric en-cryption (based on public/private keys – also called PKI) provides hybrid and even multi-encryption.

Figure 3: McEliece's algorithm for advanced protection against attacks from Quantum Computing in the Settings Tab

Spot-On uses the libgcrypt, libntru, and McEliece libraries to create persistent private and public key pairs. Currently, the application generates key pairs for each of the six func-tions during initialization. Key generation is optional. As a result, Spot-On does not require public key infrastructure.

Of course, the desired algorithms can be selected, and keys can be generated.

Spot-On is regarded as one – if not the – first open source encryption suite worldwide which has implemented the McEliece encryption algorithm.

Figure 4: *RSA and its alternatives in Spot-On*

McEliece cryptosystem

The McEliece cryptosystem is an a-symmetric encryption algorithm. It was presented in 1978 by cryptographer and founder Robert J. McEliece. Even with the use of quantum computers, there is no known efficient method by which the McEliece cryptosystem can be broken. This makes it a promising algorithm for post-quantum cryptography.

NTRU Algorithm

NTRU is an a-symmetric encryption technique developed in 1996 by mathematicians Jeffrey Hoffstein, Jill Pipher and Joseph Silverman. It is loosely based on lattice problems that are considered unbreakable even with quantum computers. However, NTRUEncrypt has not been extensively studied so far as more common methods (e.g. RSA). Ntruencrypt is by IEEE P1363.1 standardized (see Ntruencrypt).

Elgamal Algorithm

The Elgamal encryption method or Elgamal cryptosystem is a public-key encryption method developed in 1985 by the cryptographer Taher Elgamal, based on the idea of a Diffie-Hellman key exchange. The Elgamal encryption method, like the Diffie-Hellman Protocol, relies on operations in a finite-order cyclic group. The Diffie–Hellman key exchange method allows two parties that have no prior knowledge of each other to jointly establish a shared secret key over an insecure channel. This key can then be used to encrypt subsequent communications using a symmetric key cipher. The Elgamal encryption method is provably IND-CPA-safe, assuming that the Decisional-Diffie-Hellman problem is not trivial in the underlying group. Related to the encryption method described here (but not identical with it) is the Elgamal signature method (the Elgamal signature method is not yet implemented in Spot-On). Elgamal is not subject to a patent.

Chatting from a RSA-Key user to a McEliece Key user should be tested in practice over the integrated open source McEliece algorithm library.

RSA Algorithm

RSA (after the people Rivest, Shamir and Adleman) is an a-symmetric cryptographic procedure that can be used for both encryption and digital signature since 1978. It uses a key pair consisting of a private key used to decrypt or sign data and a public key to encrypt or verify signatures. The private key is kept secret and can only be calculated from the public key with extremely high expenditure. Clifford Cocks, an English mathematician working for the British intelligence agency Government Communications Headquarters (GCHQ), had developed an equivalent system already in 1973, but this was not declassified until 1997.

Spot-On's encryption is designed so that any user can communicate with any user, no matter what encryption algorithm a user has chosen. Communication between users with different key types is thus well defined when the nodes share common versions of the libgcrypt and libntru libraries: anyone who has chosen a RSA key can also chat and e-mail encrypted with an user who has chosen an Elgamal key. Try it also for a McEliece Key. This is because everyone supports each algorithm and the library supports it. If you want to test the program with a friend, it is best for both to use the latest version of Spot-On.

Well defined and established libraries are the basis for the cryptographic routines in the application Spot-On.

Figure 5: Individual Crypto-DNA: Customizable cryptography, e.g. based on key size and further values

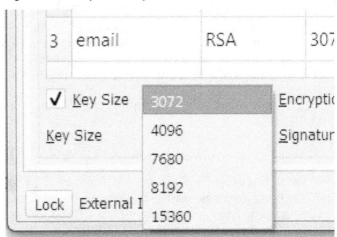

*Spot-On democra-
tizes the choice of
individual Crypto-
graphic DNA for
encryption and sig-
natures by its open
source code.*

Of course, every user in Spot-On can set an own
- "cipher",
- the individual „key size"– e.g. 3072 bit or higher for RSA,
- the "hashtype",
- furthermore "iteration count",
- and the "cryptographic salt length"

.. which are often typical parameters for key creation and encryption.

The advantage is that every user can define this individually and manually according to the own gusto. Other applications - even open source applications - hardly provide for the user this choice, to determine these key values for the encryption process itself. With Spot-On now every user is able to set up an own definition of the, so to say, "Cryptographic DNA" – for the encryption algorithms as well as for the authenticating signatures.

Using a signature means: that the generated encryption key is re-signed with a key to prove that a message is coming from a particular subscriber and nobody else. Signatures provide some authentication. There is also a comprehensive choice of encryption methods available for such signatures: DSA, ECDSA, EdDSA, Elgamal, and RSA.

- **RSA signature:** To verify the origin of a message, RSA can also be used to sign a message: Suppose Alice uses Bob's public key to send him an encrypted message. In the message, she can claim to be Alice but Bob has no way of verifying that the message was actually from Alice since anyone can use Bob's public key to send him encrypted messages. Suppose Alice wishes to send a signed message to Bob. She can use her own private key to do so. She produces a hash value of the message, raises it to the power of d (modulo n) (as she does when decrypting a message), and attaches it as a "signature" to the message. When Bob receives the signed message, he uses the same hash algorithm in conjunction with Alice's public key. He raises the signature to the power of e (modulo n) (as he does when encrypting a message) and compares the resulting hash value with the message's actual hash value. If the two agree, he knows that the author of the message was in possession of Alice's private key, and that the message has not been tampered with since. In Spot-On the OAEP and PSS schemes are used with the RSA encryption and RSA signature respectively.

- **DSA signature:** The Digital Signature Algorithm (DSA) is another Standard for digital signatures, based on the mathematical concept of modular exponentiations and the discrete logarithm problem. Since 1994 the National Institute of Standards and Technology (NIST) adopted DSA for use in their Digital Signature Standard (DSS). DSA is covered by U.S. Patent 5,231,668, filed July 26, 1991 and attributed to David W. Kravitz, a former NSA employee. And NIST has made this patent available worldwide royalty-free. DSA is a variant of the ElGamal signature scheme and works in the framework of public-key cryptosystems. Messages are signed by the signer's private key and the signatures are verified by the signer's corresponding public key. The digital signature provides message authentication, integrity and non-repudiation.

- **ECDSA signature:** The Elliptic Curve Digital Signature Algorithm (ECDSA) offers a variant of the Digital Signature Algorithm (DSA) which uses elliptic curve cryptography. As with elliptic-curve cryptography in general, the bit size of the public key believed to be needed for ECDSA is about twice the size of the security level, in bits. For example, at a security level of 80 bits (meaning an attacker requires a maximum of about 2^{80} operations to find the private key) the size of an ECDSA public key would be 160 bits, whereas the size of a DSA public key is at least 1024 bits. On the other hand, the signature size is the same for both DSA and ECDSA: approximately 4t bits, where t is the security level measured in bits, that is, about 320 bits for a security level of 80 bits.

- **EdDSA signature:** The Edwards-curve Digital Signature Algorithm (EdDSA) is a digital signature scheme using a variant of Schnorr signature based on Twisted Edwards curves. It is designed to be faster than existing digital signature schemes without sacrificing security. It was developed by a team including Daniel J. Bernstein, Niels Duif, Tanja Lange, Peter Schwabe, and Bo-Yin Yang. The reference implementation is public domain software.

- **Elgamal signature:** The Elgamal signature scheme is a digital signature scheme which is based on the difficulty of computing discrete logarithms. It was described by Taher Elgamal in 1984. A variant developed at the NSA and known as the Digital Signature Algorithm is much more widely used. The Elgamal signature scheme must not be confused with Elgamal encryption which was also invented by Taher Elgamal. The Elgamal signature scheme allows a third-party to confirm the authenticity of a message.

Spot-On is regarded as one – if not the – first open source encryption suite which has implemented the McEliece Encryption for a communication application. It is regarded as more secure against the attacks knowing from Quantum Computing.

Quantum Computers could break the PKI of certain algorithms.
McEliece and NTRU are today more secure algorithms in this regard.

Quantum Computers
breaking the security of public key cryptographic systems

Most of the popular public key ciphers are based on the difficulty of factoring integers - if they are the product of few prime numbers - or the discrete logarithm problem, both of which can be solved by Shor's algorithm. Informally, it solves the following problem: Given an integer N, find its prime factors.

By comparison, a Quantum Computer could efficiently solve this problem using Shor's algorithm to find its factors and break the security of public key cryptographic systems: In particular, the RSA, Diffie–Hellman, and elliptic curve Diffie–Hellman algorithms could be broken. These are used to protect secure Web pages, encrypted email, and many other types of data.

However, other cryptographic algorithms do not appear to be broken by those algorithms: Some public-key algorithms are based on problems other than the integer factorization and discrete logarithm problems to which Shor's algorithm applies, like the McEliece cryptosystem based on a problem in coding theory. Lattice-based cryptosystems are also not known to be broken by Quantum Computers. Large-scale Quantum Computers would theoretically be able to solve certain problems much more quickly than any classical computers.

Let's go into more detail about symmetric encryption with an AES password string, which can complement PKI encryption as follows.

2.2 Another method, another layer: Symmetric Encryption with AES

What an AES can do: Encrypting the cipher text once more to cipher text - or defining the next used secure channel (e.g. initiated by Cryptographic Calling).

Symmetric encryption uses often AES - a 32-character password string generated by processes including random. Since all characters are used in the generation, the set of options is also sufficiently large that even fast machines can not try out all variants within a short time. While a-symmetric encryption uses a public and private key pair, in symmetric encryption it is a secret passphrase that both subscribers need to know (hence called symmetric) (- or for Spot-On: in the later discussed Gemini function it is also called "Gemini" (from the Greek term for "twin" derived): Both sides have to exchange and know the secret passphrase).

Figure 6: Example of an AES Password string

```
5847 088B 15B6 1CBA 59D4 E2E8 CD39 DFCE
```

Spot-On thus uses both standards as described above: a-symmetric keys and/or symmetrically encrypted messages are sent through SSL/TLS (i.e. a-symmetric) encrypted connections, and the a-symmetrically encrypted message can possibly also be secured with symmetric encryption (e.g. AES). That means Spot-On could use three levels of encryption like this example of encapsulation shows (simplified, as shown without HASH/MAC or signature):

Figure 7: Example of Encapsulation with three levels of encryption

```
RSA-SSL/TLS (AES (Elgamal (Message)))
```

Translation of this formula: First, the text message is encrypted with the public (a-symmetric) key of the friend via the Elgamal algorithm, then the encrypted text is encrypted again with an AES algorithm (symmetric password) (a second time) (and secured) and this capsule is then sent to the friend through the existing SSL/TLS encrypted (a-symmetric) connection (using RSA). This is though a simplified structure as it does not show the hashes and signatures.

This specific structure to apply different methods of encryption is defining the protocol used in the encryption suite Spot-On: It is called the Echo Protocol, which is just a pure HTTP/S-Transfer and can be seen in a regular browser.

Spot-On uses pure HTTP/S for the transfer of cipher text in the so called Echo Protocol.

Figure 8: Discovering Spot-On's sent cipher text to a localhost HTTP-Listener in a browser

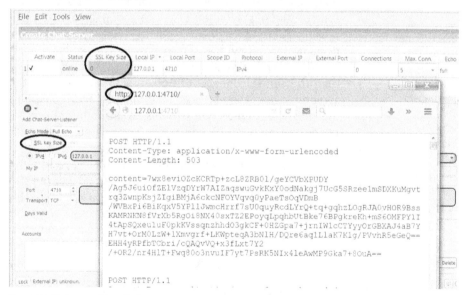

If a HTTP (not HTTPS) listener is set up and the encrypted message capsule is not sent via HTTPS - over the third encryption layer, via a SSL/TLS connection - the cipher text (layer 2) of the message capsule can also be viewed in the browser. It turns out that even with two encryption layers only cipher test is sent (see figure from the practice demo of Adams / Maier 2016).

It is also possible to exchange the symmetric passphrase (the AES) with the remote friend using an established a-symmetric (SSL/TLS) encryption. The passphrase can be automatically generated or manually defined.

This symmetric encryption now can be applied to either to convert plain text or even already converted text, that is cipher text, another time to cipher text (as shown in the message format above) - or the symmetric password can be used to define a new end-to-end encrypted channel (a fast change of the layer 2 credentials in the message example above).

A (symmetric) end-to-end encryption is thus to differentiate from the point-to-point encryption. Therefore, the word "continuous" end-to-end encryption is also added (better still: continuous symmetric end-to-end encryption) - because it's about that only the participant Alice and the participant Bob know the secret passphrase. Point-to-point encryption would be when Alice connects to the server and then the server connects to Bob. This may mean that the server can read the message, so it unpacks and repackages the message, especially if there is an a-symmetric key between the participants and the server located in the middle.

Cryptographic Calling: Superencipherment refers to hybrid and multi encryption.

Instead, Spot-On offers continuous symmetric end-to-end encryption that can not only be manually defined, but can also be instantaneously renewed with automation. This defines the function of "Cryptographic Calling" - a way to instantly renew the end to end encrypting (e.g. symmetric) credentials e.g. within the session (see the Chat Section for a deeper explanation how Cryptographic Calling is defined).

There are hardly any other - also open source - applications that include an end-to-end (e2e) encryption from one participant to the other participant, in which the user can manually and individually define the passphrase (e.g. an AES string).

What now if we mix and serialize symmetric and a-symmetric encryption? We end at hybrid and multi encryption, also so called: superencipherment.

2.3   Superencipherment: Hybrid & Multi Encryption

Spot-On implements a hybrid encryption system, including authenticity and confidentiality. Hybrid means first of all: "both variants are available" and can be combined with each other. Thus, a message can first be a-symmetrically encrypted with PKI shown above and then symmetrically with an AES again. Or the other way around, there is also another variant conceivable: The PKI transmission path transmits with permanent keys again only temporarily used keys, with which then the further communication takes place over this temporary channel. The temporary channel can then again transmit a symmetric encryption with an AES.

Ephemeral Keys are temporary Keys.

Thus, not only in the method change from PKI to AES respective from a-symmetric encryption to symmetric encryption exists one option to build a hybrid system, but also in the switch from permanent PKI keys to temporary PKI keys.

Encrypting often and switching between these methods or using time-limited keys is a strong competence of Spot-On in this hybrid and multiple encryption.

Multi-Encryption

Multiple encryption is the process of encrypting an already encrypted message one or more times, either using the same or a different algorithm. It is also known as cascade encryption, cascade ciphering, multiple encryption, and superencipherment. Superencryption refers to the outer-level encryption of a multiple encryption. Cipher text is converted to cipher text to cipher text and to cipher text...

Spot-On holds even more extensive security especially with multiple encryptions: Here cipher text is either converted another time to cipher text or sent through an SSL/TLS channel.

With these possibilities one can now play and apply it in various ways. Is the permanent or the temporary key applied first, or once again the symmetric and then the a-symmetrical as the second level of encryption? or vice versa? Hybrid and multi encryption have many potentials and offer various research perspectives.

One part of the system in Spot-On generates the key for authentication and encryption per message. These two keys are used to authenticate and encapsulate data (that is, the message). The two keys (for authentication and encryption) are then encapsulated across the public-key part of the system. The application also provides a mechanism for distributing session keys for this data encapsulation (or encryption of the message) as described above, the temporary key. Again, the keys are encapsulated and transmitted via the public key system: an additional mechanism allows the distribution of the session keys over the predetermined keys. Encryption algorithms for the cipher text, signature algorithms and hash values create an encapsulation of the information. As a first example, this format may serve the mentioned message encryption:

Figure 9: Message Encryption Format of the Echo Protocol

```
EPUBLIK Key
(Encryption Key || Hash Key)
|| EEncryption Key (Data)
|| HHash Key (EEncryption Key (Data)).
```

For those who are dealing with encryption for the first time, the above example of encapsulation is a first example to further study and understand the methods; - In any case, one can see how the encryption key is supplemented by the hash key (see MAC) and also the data is embedded in dif-ferent encryption levels.

Next to the modern algorithms also the process innovations are to be mentioned with further examples as follows:

2.4   Further Examples of state-of-the-art encryption & process implementations

Spot-On has not only standardized, forward-looking algo-rithms or numerous details (such as the switch from AES-128 to AES-256 or the use of very high, because necessary key sizes), but also implemented the professional integra-tion of established and new encryption processes.

Spot-On uses CBC with CTS to provide confidentiality. The file encryption mechanism supports the Galois/Counter Mode (GCM) algorithm without the authenticity property provided by the algorithm. To provide authenticity, the ap-plication uses the methodical approach of "Encrypt-then-MAC" (ETM). MAC stands for Message Authentication Code - and means that the order is determined: first encrypt, and then authenticate the message with a code.

Message Authentication Code: Encrypt-then-MAC.

Non-NTRU private keys are evaluated for correctness by the gcry_pk_testkey () function. The public key must also meet some basic criteria, such as the inclusion of the public key identifier.

The authentication of the private key and the encryption mechanism is identical to the method as further discussed in the documentation of the source code in the section on the encrypted and authenticated container. (The documen-tation for the source code for the section of encrypted and authenticated containers contains further technical details.) Another example for innovation is the implementation of the ThreeFish hash, which was available as an alternative to SHA-3 when it was realized that SHA-1 was no longer able to cope with future requirements. Threefish is a block en-cryption developed as part of the design of the crypto-graphic hash function Skein, which participated in the NIST selection process for SHA-3. Threefish does not use S-boxes or other lookup tables to complicate time-side attacks (computing time attacks).

Figure 10: Threefish implementation

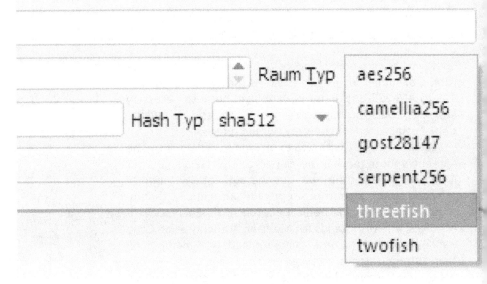

Many more examples can be found, which show that the encryption processes in Spot-On are very state-of-the-art.

Questions and further Research & Development Fields

- Discuss the most important function of Spot-On from your point of view and give some reasons.
- What is PKI? And how is an AES differentiating from it.
- Find literature about multi-encryption and summarize it.
- Why is McEliece more resistant against attacks?
- Describe why it is important to encrypt in the Internet and how to foster the use of encryption.

3   What is the Echo Protocol?

This special way of mixing a-symmetric PKI and symmetric AES, multiplying permanent and ephemeral temp-keys, tying keys from last session to the current one as it is a characteristic for multiple encryption on the way to exponential encryption within a node network, as well as having for the cipher text a transfer via a SSL/TLS tunnel connection in place are referring characteristics of the Echo Protocol, which is to be deepened in this section.

Next to multiple encryption the Echo Protocol contains two further characteristics: one is given by sending messages to the network, the other by unpacking the encrypted capsule and matching its content. So, what exactly are the full specific properties of the Echo Protocol?

With the Echo Protocol is meant - simply spoken – that

- first, every message transmission is encrypted...

Figure 11: Example of message encryption within the Echo

```
SSL (AES (RSA* (message)))
```

*) instead of RSA one can also use Elgamal or NTRU or McEliece.

- ... and second, in the Echo Network, each node sends each message to each connected neighbor. Full Stop. That's how easy the world is. Underlying is the so-called "small-world phenomenon": Anyone can reach anyone somehow over seven corners in a peer-to-peer or friend-to-friend network - or simply distribute the message over a shared Echo-chat server in the circle of friends.

The Echo Match compares two Hashes: One of the original plain text message and one of the converted text message by one key.

- A third criterion for the Echo Protocol can be added, that is a special feature when unpacking the encrypted capsule: The capsules have neither a receiver nor sender information included - and here they are different from TCP packets. The message is identified by the hash of the unencrypted message (compared to the conversion text of all known keys in the node) as to whether the message should be displayed and readable to the recipient in the user interface or not. For this so-called "Echo Match" see even more detailed below.

Figure 12: Graphical depiction of a message within the Echo Protocol

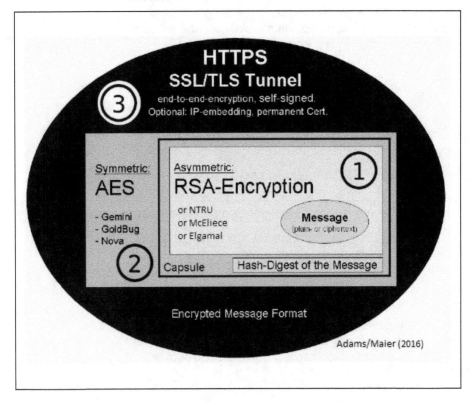

The graphical figure shows from inside to outside the process of how the encrypted capsule is formed in the context of the Echo Protocol:

First level of encryption: The message is encrypted and the cipher text of the message is hashed and then the a-symmetric key (e.g. with the RSA algorithm) can also be used to encrypt the symmetric keys. In an intermediate step, the encrypted text and the hash digest of the message are bundled into a capsule and packed together. It follows the paradigm: Encrypt-then-MAC. To prove to the recipient that the cipher text has not been corrupted, the hash digest is first formed before the cipher text is decrypted.

Third level of encryption: Then this capsule can be transmitted via a secure SSL/TLS connection to the communication partner.

Second level of encryption: Optionally, there is also the option of symmetrically encrypting the first-level capsule with an AES-256, which is comparable to a shared, 32-character password. Hybrid encryption is then added to multiple encryptions (see Adams / Maier 2016:46).

The "Half Echo" mode sends a message only one hop, i.e. from Bob to Alice. Alice then stops sending the message (as is the default with the Full Echo).

Thirdly, in addition to Full Echo and Half Echo, there is the Adaptive Echo (AE). Here, the message is only sent to neighbors or friends, if they know an encryption token, they have previously stored. So if the user does not know the token, the message will not be forwarded to this user.

After all, the Echo still knows Echo Accounts. A kind of firewall. This ensures that only friends who know the account access can connect. So a web-of-trust can be created, which is a network exclusively among friends. It is not based on the encryption key but is independent of it. This means that the user does not have to associate his public key with his IP address or even announce it in the network.

Basically, in the Echo, each node sends a message to each connected node: If a user should then receive a message a second time, it is compared in a temporary cache (based on the hash value for that message) and, if applicable, when the hash is upcoming again, the message is discarded and thus not forwarded. This approach is called "congestion control" and balances the number of messages in the network from multiple nodes or servers.

Assembling Surprise Eggs - An analogy: *The cryptography of the Echo Protocol can be compared with the giving and taking of so called "surprise eggs", a capsule with a to assemble mini-toy in the famous chocolate egg. Bob gives Alice a surprise egg, Alice opens it and consumes the chocolate and bumps inside into the plastic capsule of the surprise egg, trying to open it and assemble the pieces into a toy, a smurf. However, she fails in the assembly, the Smurf cannot be formed and therefore she packs the items back into the plastic capsule, pours new chocolate around and passes the egg to her neighbor, who also tries to assemble some of the pieces. Alice does not know who can assemble the surprise egg or build the smurf successfully, so she continues to copy it (- what a miracle, Alice has a surprise-egg copying machine -) and gives each of her friends a copy. (Unpacking, crafting, evaluating, packing, giving away and unpacking, crafting, evaluating, wrapping, giving away, and so on ...).*

From the point of view of the entities represented in the network (kernels), the network would have become a surprise-egg circulation network in this analogy, if the crafting processes were not reduced again with Congestion Control. Once known, assembling parts are not built a second time together. Alice tinkers many packets until she recognizes a smurf with a red cap, she has received the figure of the Papa smurf intended for her (or as her message).

To exclude time and frequency analyzes in the Internet or Echo Network, there are other functions in Spot-On which increase encryption or make cryptographic analysis more difficult:

For example: with the Spot-On application the user can also send a kind of a "fake" message (from the simulacra function) and also "simulated" communication messages ("impersonated messages"). On the one hand, encryption is here not encryption in the sense of cipher text, but it is a block of pure random characters that are emitted from time to time, and the other is a simulated human conversation, which is also based only on scrambled random characters:

Figure 13: Simulacra, Impersonator, Super-Echo

Simulacra

The Simulacra feature sends a "simulated" chat message to the Echo Network when the checkbox is activated. This "fake" message consists of pure random numbers, making it harder for analysts to distinguish encrypted messages with real and random content appearance like cipher text. Simulacrum is a term that is not unknown from both the movie "Matrix" (https://en.wikipedia.org/wiki/Matrix_(Film)) and Baudrillard's philosophy (Neo uses this name for the repository for software in his home. And the book "Simulacres et Simulation" by the French media philosopher Jean Baudrillard explores the relationship between reality, symbols and society). Several years after the publication of the Echo Protocol, donors to the Tor network have developed a similar software called Matrix Dot Org, which sends encrypted capsules to the network comparable to the Echo Protocol and also addresses a messaging function; an analysis is pending where the Echo over the plagiarism-like architecture offers differences and benefits or offered further open source suggestions.

Impersonator

In addition to random fake messages, the Spot-On program can also simulate a chat with the Impersonator function as if a real person chats from time to time and sends out replies. Also, these messages are filled with pure random data, but they vary – a simulation of a real chat conversation. Thus, analysis of messages can be made more difficult if third-party recorders should temporarily store and record all user communication, which may be assumed. But even more: even the absence of meta-data (see data retention) gives no reason to suspect that a message was for the user. Anyone who has been able to successfully unpack a message normally does not send it back to the Echo Network. A record of metadata could have increased interest in the un-re-submitted messages, assuming that this message could then have been successfully decoded by the user. For this case there is also the option of the SuperEcho:

Super-Echo

The feature of Super-Echo also redirects successfully decoded and readable messages back to all friends. A lack of re-transmitting a message may then no longer indicate - because of the Super-Echo - that the message may have been successfully decoded.

Super-Echo, Simulacra and Impersonation are three options of the Spot-On program, which should make it harder for attackers to understand the messages that are of interest to the user (and apparently others) in the multitude of messages.

Now let's take a closer look at the individual Echo modes of operation:

3.1 Full Echo

The "Full Echo" modus underlies an assumption, as it is also in the so-called "small world phenomenon" given: with hopping over a few friends everyone can send a message to each of them. Somehow, everyone knows everyone about a maximum of seven corners. This is also applicable in a peer-to-peer or friend-to-friend network. Therefore, a user can reach anyone if each node sends each message to all other known nodes.

Small World Phenomenon

The small-world experiment comprised several experiments conducted by Stanley Milgram and other researchers examining the average path length for social networks of people. The research was groundbreaking in that it suggested that human society is a small-world-type network characterized by short path-lengths. The experiments are often associated with the phrase "six degrees of connectedness", although Milgram did not use this term himself.

Guglielmo Marconi's conjectures based on his radio work in the early 20th century, which were articulated in his 1909 Nobel Prize address, may have inspired Hungarian author Frigyes Karinthy to write a challenge to find another person to whom he could not be connected through at most five people. This is perhaps the earliest reference to the concept of six degrees of separation, and the search for an answer to the small world problem.

Mathematician Manfred Kochen and political scientist Ithiel de Sola Pool wrote a mathematical manuscript, "Contacts and Influences", while working at the University of Paris in the early 1950s, during a time when Milgram visited and collaborated in their research. Their unpublished manuscript circulated among academics for over 20 years before publication in 1978. It formally articulated the mechanics of social networks and explored the mathematical consequences of these (including the degree of connectedness).

The manuscript left many significant questions about networks unresolved, and one of these was the number of degrees of connectedness in actual social networks.

Milgram took up the challenge on his return from Paris, and his Psychology Today article generated enormous publicity for the experiments, which are well known today, long after much of the formative work has been forgotten. The small-world question is still a popular research topic (also for network and graph theory) today, with many experiments still being conducted.

In computer science, the small-world phenomenon (although it is not typically called that) is used in the development of secure peer-to-peer protocols, new routing algorithms for the Internet and ad hoc wireless networks, and search algorithms for communication networks of all kinds.

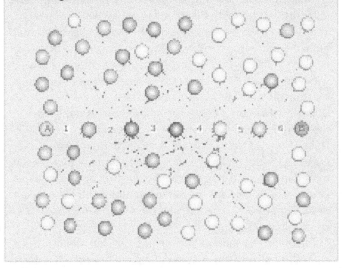

Alternatively, a user can support this decentralized approach or abbreviate the message paths by installing an own chat server based on the Echo Kernel for friends, so that all encrypted messages can be sent to the participants and the server can serve as an e-mail-postbox or intermediate chat server.

The mapping describes sending the message from a starting point to all network nodes across all connected network nodes.

Figure 14: Echo Simulation: Each node sends to each connected node

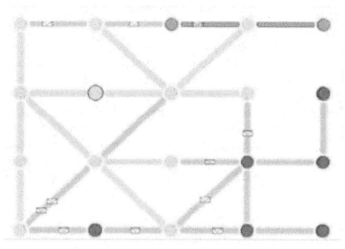

So basically, in the Echo, each node sends each message to each node. This sounds simple: The Echo Protocol is a very simple Protocol, but also has wider implications, that is: There are no routing information within the Echo given and even metadata can hardly be recorded from the individual node or even network. The nodes also do not forward the message. The term "forwarding" is incorrect, because each node actively resends the message to the (its) connected friends, respective neighbors.

This may result in receiving a message (from multiple connected nodes) multiple times - however, in order to avoid this happening and being efficient, the message hash is cached, and the message may be rejected for retransmission if it is identified as a doublet. This called as already indicated above: "Congestion Control".

The message is in a capsule, so to speak, similar to a ZIP file. This capsule is created by a-symmetric encryption with the public key. Added is the hash of the plain text message.

When another node (receiver) tries to decode the cipher text, a new text comes out depending on the used and available key - which can either be decoded correctly or incorrectly, that is to say, it is human-readable - or, if the decoding key was incorrect, out of random characters (the cipher text) became only random characters (wrong decoded text, not readable plain text). This resulting text after the decoding attempt is thus again hashed.

Now, if the hash of the decoded message is identical to the hash of the original message that the sender already attached (readable) to the capsule, it is clear that the deciphering node has used the correct key and this message in plain text is for him: hence, the message is readable and displayed in the user interface. This can be called an "Echo Match". Unsuccessful decoding attempts, in which the hash value between the original message and the message text of the decoding attempt do not match, are not displayed in the user interface, but remain in the kernel of the program for further transmission to the connected neighbors.

The Echo-Match can be regarded as one sustainable innovation and invention in network theory and routing with a direct perspective to Cryptographic Discovery.

The node must therefore try with all the keys of his friends to unpack the message and compare the hash values. If the hash value is not identical, the node packs the ingredients back together in one capsule and sends it to each of the connected friends, who then try the same.

The hash value of a message is not invertible, therefore the encryption cannot be broken with the (enclosed) hash of the original message, it still requires the correct key.

A message that has been successfully unpacked will no longer be sent, unless the user uses the "Super Echo" option, which also retransmits the successfully unpacked messages. Thus, no one who records the Internet packets along the line can identify messages that are not sent again.

Finally, as described above, it is also possible from time to time to send out false messages ("simulacra fake messages") and also "simulated impersonated messages", so that it is difficult for network traffic collectors to find out the message capsule, which has been of interest for the user's own readability. Because it is to be noted that it may be assumed today that all communication data of an Internet user is somewhere stored and recorded on the Internet and in the case of interest also automated and manually evaluated.

Then: This encrypted capsule is again sent over an encrypted SSL/TLS channel that is established between the nodes. This is a decentralized, self-signed p2p connection, a "two-pass mutual authentication Protocol", so the term. The implementation is precisely defined according to SSL/TLS, but it can also be switched off: The network nodes thus communicate via HTTPS or even only HTTP.

Figure 15: Example and Process Description of the Echo-Match

Practical Example and Process Description of the Echo-Match

Sender A hashed his original text to a hash 123456789, encrypts the text and packs the crypto-text and hash of the original message into the capsule (before he adds an AES-Password and sends it out via a TLS/SSL connection). Recipient 1 converts the received encoded text of the capsule to a (supposed) plain text, but this has the hash 987654321 and is therefore not identical to the supplied original text hash of 123456789. This is repeated with all available keys of all friends of the recipient 1. Since all hash comparisons, however, were unsuccessful, he re-packs the message again and sends it on. The message is obviously not for him or one of his friends. Recipient 2 now also converts the received, encrypted text to a (supposed) plain text, this has the hash 123456789 and is thus identical to the supplied original text hash of 123456789, the decoding was apparently successful with one of the existing keys of his friends and therefore the message is displayed on the screen of this receiver (and if Super-Echo is selected, also re-packed again and sent-out again).

However, of course, the transfer becomes more susceptible if one does not use the multiple encryption. Therefore, one should always establish a HTTPS connection to his or her friends and send over this encrypted channel his encrypted capsules in which the message waits, to be kissed awake from the right key (using the "Echo Match" method based on the hash comparison) and to be converted in readable plain text.

No one on the net can see which message a user successfully unpacked, because everything happens on the user's local machine.

3.2 Half Echo

The Half Echo mode sends the user's message only one hop to the next node, e.g. from Bob to Alice. Alice then does not send the message down the path of her connected friends (as it is customary for the Full Echo). This Echo mode is technically defined by the connection to another listener: Bob's Node, when connecting to the node of Alice, notifies that Alice should stop sending the message to her friends. Thus, two friends or nodes can exclude via a direct connection that the message is carried into the wider network via the other, further connection(s) that each node has.

3.3 Echo Accounts

And in addition: The Echo also knows Echo Accounts. An account is a kind of firewall. It can be used to ensure that only friends connect who know the credentials to the account. Thus, a so-called Web-of-Trust, a network based on trust, is formed. It is not based on the encryption key like in other applications, it is independent of it. This has the advantage that the encryption public key does not need to be associated with the IP address (as it is the case with Retro-Share, for example); or that the user must announce the own IP address in the network of friends, for example in a DHT where users can search for it. The Echo Accounts provide a peer-to-peer-(P2P)-connection to a friend-to-friend-(F2F)-network or allow both types of connection. This makes Spot-On suitable for both paradigms.

Figure 16: Account Firewall of Spot-On

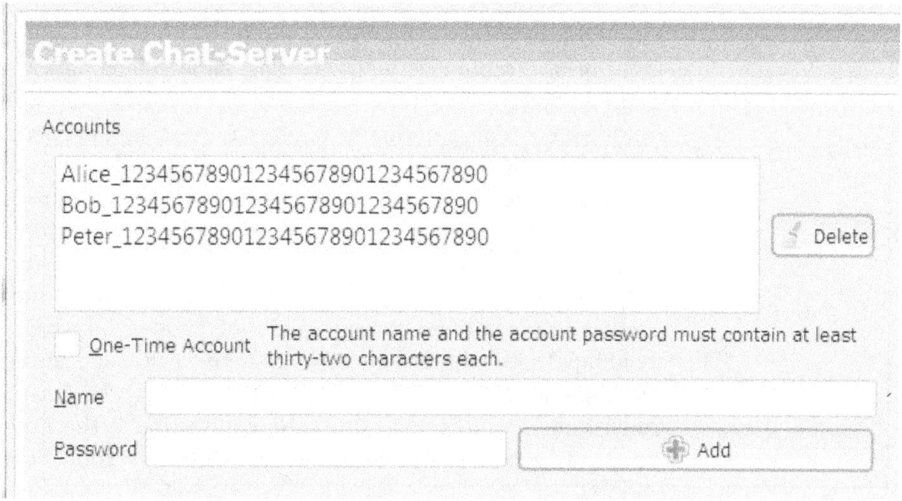

The Echo Accounts work as follows:

Binding endpoints are responsible for defining the account information. During the creation process for an account, this can be defined for one-time use (one-time account or one-time use). Account name and also the passphrase for the account require at least 32 bytes of characters. So, a long password is required.

After a network connection has been established, the binding endpoint informs the requesting node with a request for authentication. The binding endpoint will drop the connection if the peer has not identified within a fifteen second time window.

After the request for authentication has been received, the peer responds to the binding endpoint. The peer then transmits the following information: HHash Key (Salt / Time) // Salt, where the hash key is a concise summary of the account name and also the account password.

Currently, the SHA-512 hash algorithm is used to generate this hash result. The time variable has a resolution of a few minutes. The peer retains the value for the cryptographic salt.

The binding endpoint receives the information of the peer. Consequently, this then processes HHash Key (Salt // Time) for all accounts he has set up. If the endpoint cannot identify an account, it will wait one minute and perform another search. If an account matching this hash key was found, the binding endpoint creates a message similar to the one the peer created in the previous step and sends the information to the peer. The authenticated information is stored. After a period of about 120 seconds, the information is deleted again.

The peer receives the information of the binding endpoint and performs a similar validation process, this time including the analysis of the cryptographic salt value of the binding endpoint. The two salt values must then be clearly consistent. The peer will drop the connection if the endpoint has not identified itself within a fifteen-second time window.

It should be noted, by the way, that the account system can be further developed by including a key for encryption. The additional key then allows even more precise time windows to be defined.

If SSL/TLS is not available during this negotiation, the Protocol may become vulnerable as follows: An intermediate station may record the values from the third step and consequently send to the binding endpoint. Then, the binding endpoint could also grant access to the account to an unknown connection. The recording device could then grab the response of the binding endpoint, that is, the values of the fourth step, and forward the information to the peer. If the account information or password is then accurately maintained, the peer would then accept the response from this new binding endpoint. That's why, as always, it's about protecting passwords and to use HTTPS connections.

In Spot-On, therefore, a server account - if it is specified to be dedicated - therefore requires a password equal to the length of an AES-256: this is a passphrase of 32 characters.

3.4   The Echo Grid

When students talk, or be taught (or teach themselves) about the Echo Protocol, they can simply draw an Echo Grid with the letters E_C_H_O. The nodes from E1 to O4 are numbered and connect the letters with a connecting line on the ground (see figure).

Figure 17: The Echo Grid Template

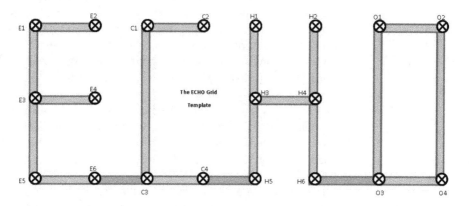

For example, then the connection E1-E2 denotes an IP connection to a neighbor.

If the individual nodes now exchange keys, connections are created that arise as a new level at the level of the IP connections of the P2P / F2F network.

The Echo-Grid to discuss Graph Theory.

With the architecture underlying in Spot-On not only the cryptographic routing/discovery in a kernel program was invented and elaborated, also - as stated above - the term "cryptographic routing" was paradoxically removed from the routing with the Echo Protocol. It is therefore necessary to speak in more detail of the "Cryptographic Echo" instead of "Cryptographic Routing". One further item to differentiate the Protocols is the Protocol of the "Cryptographic Discovery" which will be discussed below in an extra section.

Echo is thus "beyond routing" (Gasakis/Schmidt 2018): Firstly, the message packets do not contain routing information (addressees) and the nodes also do not use "forwarding" in the original sense, because they simply send everything to all connections. And secondly: Even the cryptographic key that tries to decode the message is not an address (which would even be attached to the message package), but only a polarizing glass: it lets us see texts differently and possibly understand. The Echo Protocol therefore also uses the term "traveling" rather than the term "routing". Or just in short: "Cryptographic Echo Discovery".

The Echo node as a sovereign.

From a legal point of view, a different evaluation is then also to be made here, since a node does not forward in the name of an addressee as a middleman, but informs the neighbors independently (see, for example, the forwarding in other routing models such as AntsP2P with its ant algorithm, Mute, AllianceP2P, RetroShare, Onion-Routing or I2P).

As well as spreading an established reputation or news in the neighborhood, the message also spreads in the Echo - otherwise the echoing protocol allows any cryptographic "stuff" to "float" away (by being not decoded or being unreadable).

It seems to be a reminiscence to the Star Trek Borg collective paradigm: everyone has access to all the neighbors' messages (unless half or Adaptive Echo is used and if the message text can be understood (decoded) at all).

In the Echo, the node is more of a "sovereign" for "giving and receiving (non-directional) information"; in other networks, a node could be more referred to as a "postman", "dealer", "forwarder" or "intermediary". Yes, in the Echo the node is a sovereign!

The Echo Grid as a simple network representation is not only used for the analysis of "routing" (or "travel"-ways) to represent Echo modes and encryption stati, but can also be found in graph theory considerations: which path takes a message? depending on the structure of the network? And it also can be used to evaluate the use of Echo Accounts, Half or Full Echo and the Adaptive Echo, as the following examples of the graphs between Alice, Bob, Ed and Maria illustrate.

3.4.1   Examples of key exchanges by Alice, Bob, Ed & Maria

Figure 18: Alice, Bob, Ed and Mary in the Echo Grid - An example of Echo paths and for Graph Theory

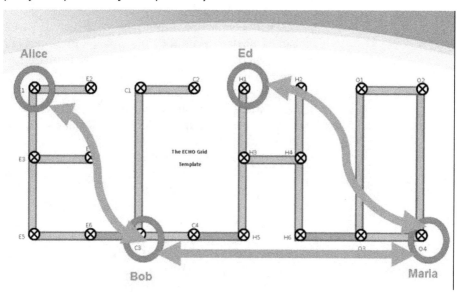

The following examples of the figure can be further discussed (a few vocabulary and processes of functions of the Spot-On client are used, so that in the program inexperienced readers can also skip this section and refer back once the basic functions (installation, chat, e-mail, File transfer or URL search) have been explained – so that these technical examples are understood better at a later stage):

- Alice (IP = E1) and Bob (IP = C3) have exchanged their public key and are connected via the following IP neighbors: E1-E3-E5-E6-C3.
- Bob (C3) and Maria (O4) are also friends, they've also swapped their public keys for encryption: and use their neighbors' IP connections: C3-C4-H5-H3-H4-H6-O3-O4.
- Finally: Maria (O4) is a friend of Ed (H1). They either communicate via the path: O4-O3-H6-H4-H3-H1 or

they use the path of: O4-O2-O1-O3-H6-H4-H3-H1. Since, in the Echo Protocol, every IP neighbor sends every message to every connected IP neighbor, the path that delivers the message fastest will succeed. (The second incoming message is then filtered out by Congestion Control).

- Direct IP connections from neighbors such as E1-E3 can be further secured by the creation of a so-called "Echo Account": No other IP address than E1 can then connect to the so-called "listener" of the neighbor E3. This method can be used to create a web-of-trust - without relying on keys for encryption - nor does it require a friend as a neighbor to exchange their chat or e-mail key.

- So-called "Turtle-Hopping" becomes much more efficient in the Echo Network: when Ed and Alice start a file transfer (via the StarBeam function and using a Magnetic URI link), the Echo Protocol transports the packets via the path H1-H3- H5-C4-C3-E6-E5-E3-E1. Maria is not in the route, but she will also receive the packets over the Full Echo if she knows the StarBeam Magnet. The advantage is that the hopping is not done over the keys, but over the IP connections (e.g. the Web-of-Trust). Basically, everything is always encrypted, so why not take the shortest route on the net?

- A so-called "Buzz" or "Echo'ed IRC Channel" (therefore also short: e'IRC) room can be created or "hosted" by the node O2, for example. Since only the user Ed knows the buzz room name (which is tied into the Magnet), all other neighbors and friends are left out. Advantage: The user can talk to unknown friends in a room without having exchanged a public e.g. RSA key with them. Instead, a one-time Magnet is simply used for this "buzz" / "e'IRC" room.

- Maria is a mutual friend of Ed and Bob and she activates the C/O (care of) feature for e-mails: this allows Ed to send e-mails to Bob, even though he's offline, because: Maria saves the e-mails in her instance, until Bob comes online.

- Furthermore: Alice created a so-called virtual "e-mail institution". This is not comparable to a POP3 or IMAP server because the emails are only cached: Ed sends his public e-mail key to Alice - and Ed adds the Magnet of Alice's "E-Mail Institution" to the program. Now, e-mails from Bob and Ed are also cached within Alice (at the so-called e-mail institution), even if Maria should be offline.

It is helpful to follow the examples on the above graphic or to come back to this at the end of the manual after further explanations of the functions.

3.5 Adaptive Echo (AE) and its AE tokens

In addition to the Full and Half Echo, there is the third: Adaptive Echo (AE). Here, as it will be described below, the message is sent to connected neighbors or friends only if the node knows a particular cryptographic token - similar to a secret passphrase.

Of course, this passphrase must first be defined, shared and stored in the respective nodes. Thus, defined ways of a message in a network configuration can be used. For example, if all nodes in a country use a common Adaptive Echo passphrase, the message will never appear in other nations' nodes if they do not know the passphrase. Thus, a routing can be defined that is not located within the message, but in the nodes. If you do not know the passphrase, one does not get the message forwarded respective further sent out! Adaptive Echo turns messages that cannot be opened into messages that are not known or even exist.

For the explanation of the "Adaptive Echo" another Echo-Grid with the connected letters A and E can be drawn (see following figure).

Natural Evolvement:
The Echo is a natural evolvement. An Echo Server is just a reflector of messages.
First in - First out.
Probably Amazon's Echo (2015) has been derived from the Echo Protocol released since 2013 and earlier. Coincidence?

Figure 19: Adaptive Echo (AE): The "Hansel and Gretel" Example of the Adaptive Echo

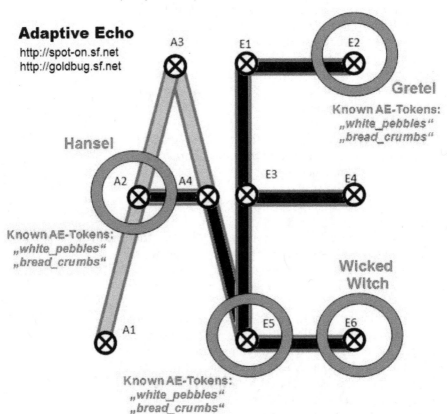

If a user, his or her chat friend, and a configured third node as a chat server insert the same AE token ("Adaptive Echo Token") into the program, then the chat server will only send the user's message to his friend, and not to all other connected neighbors (or users), as it would normally be the case in the Full Echo (server) mode.

The AE token consists, like a passphrase, of at least 96 characters. In the case of Adaptive Echo, the information from the sending node of the encrypted capsule is attached - and all other nodes learn that one is only forwarding (sending) the message to nodes or connection partners, who also know this AE token.

With an AE token, no other node that does not know the passphrase will be able to receive or view the user's message. Thus, potential "recorders" can be excluded: these are possible neighbors, which presumptive record all the message traffic and then try to break the multiple encryption to get to the message core of the capsule.

In order to be able to determine the graph, the travel route for the Adaptive Echo, several nodes must agree with each other and note the passphrase on the way path without any gaps. In the case of the Adaptive Echo it can be spoken of a routing.

3.5.1 Hansel and Gretel - An example of the Adaptive Echo mode

To illustrate the Adaptive Echo, a classic example is the tale of Hansel and Gretel.

In the AE grid explained above, the characters Hansel, Gretel and the evil witch are drawn as nodes. Now Hansel and Gretel think about how they can communicate with each other without the evil witch noticing this. According to the fairy tale, they are in the woods with the witch and want to find out again of this forest and mark the way with bread crumbs and white pebbles.

These fairy tale contents can now also illustrate the Adaptive Echo in the above grid pattern and show at which points of the grid or the communication graph a cryptographic token called "white pebbles" can be used:

If nodes A2, E5 and E2 use the same AE token, then node E6 will not receive a message that node A2 (Hansel) and node E2 (Gretel) will exchange. Because the node E5 learns about the known token "white pebbles", it does not send the messages to the node E6, the "Wicked Witch". It is a learning, adaptive network.

An "Adaptive Echo" network reveals no target information (compare again above: "Ants Routing" et. al.). Because - as a reminder: The mode of "Half Echo" sends only one hop to the connected neighbor and the "Full Echo" sends the encrypted message to all connected nodes over an unspecified hop number. While "Echo Accounts" encourage or hinder other users as a kind of firewall or authorization concept when connecting, "AE tokens" provide graph or path exclusivity - for messages that are sent via connected nodes that know the AE token.

Chat Server Administrators can exchange their tokens with other server administrators if they trust each other (so-called "Ultra-Peering for Trust") and define a Web-of-Trust. In network labs or at home with three or four computers, the Adaptive Echo is easy to test and to document the results:

For an Adaptive Echo test, simply use a network with three or more computers (or "SPOTON_HOME" as the (suffix-less) file in the binary directory to launch and connect multiple program instances on a single machine) and then implement this example flow:

How to test Adaptive Echo

---

1. Create a node as a chat server.
2. Create two nodes as a client.
3. Connect the two clients to the chat server.
4. Exchange keys between the clients.
5. Test the normal communication skills of both clients.
6. Put an AE token on the server.
7. Test the normal communication skills of both clients.
8. Now set the same AE token in a client as well.

Note the result: The server node no longer sends the message to other nodes that do not have or know the AE token.

This example should be easy to replicate.

4 Cryptographic Discovery

Cryptographic Discovery describes the method of an Echoing Protocol to find nodes in an Echo Network. The Echoing Protocol is supplemented with another useful method, if not even more important, than the Echo itself: Cryptographic Discovery is available in existing clients such as the Spot-On compatible chat server for the Android operating system, SmokeStack, and implemented within the code base. The source code and its documentation define the method accordingly. For example, Cryptographic Discovery can replace a Distributed Hash Table (DHT) to find a friend on the network.

On the mobile device, on the other hand, it makes more sense for reasons of efficiency and battery protection to receive and decode only the messages, which are intended for the own use as a participant.

This initial question: how the number of encrypted message packets can be reduced, especially for mobile devices - was the goal of further development of the Echo Protocol.

A response offers the in the meantime developed, and the Echo Protocol supplementing protocol "Cryptographic Echo Discovery" (CRED).

Cryptographic Echo Discovery can be described as follows and can, as we shall see, replace the concept of a Distributed Hash Table (DHT) with its disadvantages.

If a user sends a message to a regular Echo server, it does not know where to send it to and so it sends it to everyone. One of those everyones is the correct one. The correct one will then send the message to the other user. The alternative is to have the peer knowing my peer in a virtual cryptographic software structure. These peers are separate processes. Then the peer of the user could send the message to peer A and peer Z instead of peers: A through Z. Peers would be aware of other peers based on a cryptographic discovery with cryptographic identities. Complex stuff - but already coded in into the mobile client of Spot-On: Smoke Messenger and its Server Smoke Stack.

In its brief form, Cryptographic Echo Discovery is a simple protocol where clients share presence information with nearby and connected servers. Nearby servers, if acting as clients, share their information with nearby servers, and so on. Presence information is shared whenever necessary.

In the following, we look closer at several examples in a detailed explanation. Lets assume, we have a graph as following:

C1 => S1 => S2 <= S3 <= C2.

Client C1 connects to Server S1 and shares some semi-private key material. When S1 connects as a Client to S2, it shares its pool of semi-private material. C2 connects to S3 and performs a similar task as C1. S3, similarly.

In the end, S2 knows both, C1 and C2 through the nearest-neighbor Sprinkling Effect (SE) (see also further below for a further description of the so called Sprinkling Effect):

S1 knows about C1. S3 knows about C2. Also S2 and S3 know each other. And so, C1 can address the message to C2 and these messages can be limited and defined to certain paths.

If knowledge is not known, the Echo controls the data flow.

Let's explain the "Cryptographic Echo Discovery" (CRED) with the "Sprinkling Effect" (SE) over the Echo Protocol with another simple example from the development source:

Figure 20: SECRED – Sprinkling Effect (SE) & Cryptographic Echo Discovery (CRED) via the Echo Protocol

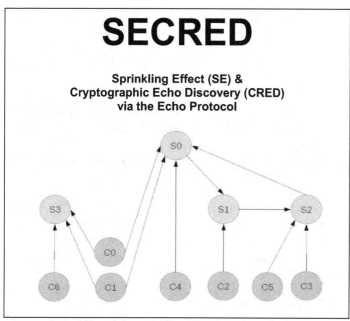

Source: Description of the sprinkling effect based on the Spot-On Project Documentation 07/2016

In the above diagram, the Cs represent clients whereas the Ss represent servers. Servers may behave as clients (see directions of arrows in the diagram). Let C4 and S0 establish a network connection. The connection need not support SSL / TLS. Assuming that a correct connection has been established, C4 will optionally share some non-private discovery details with S0.

The client tells the server any hint: any kind of information. This information may include, e.g., digests of Buzz magnets for a group chat room, digests of StarBeam magnets, digests of personal (not private) public keys, etc.. Some of this information may also be shared later.

That means, the server of the user knows of a means of delivering something to the user.

If the server of the user has other servers, it tells them the hint of the user. If the server does not know another server, the hints end there.

So, such hints are needed to get the message from A to Z.

Also, let's suppose that C1 performs a similar task. As the network contracts and expands, entities such as S0 get informed of some of the virtual materials of C0, C1, C4, and S2.

- Notice that S0 is aware of neither C6 nor S3 within a direct connection, because the paths to S3 are inward within the network.
- Also notice that S0 may become aware of Node C3 and Node C5 courtesy of S2.

So, what's the purpose of Cryptographic Echo Discovery? CRED's primary purpose is to place the performance of data inspection on certain servers. Servers will be able to direct traffic by inspecting packets and delivering them to their correct clients.

Let's assume that the above network is static for the remaining portion of the exercise.

Also it is assumed that the discovery process has established sufficient knowledge with each of the servers in the given chain, a steady state.

Now, suppose C4 wishes to communicate with C3. C4 will deliver a message to S0. S0, having a delicate knowledge database, will deliver the message to S2. Likewise, S2 will deliver the message to C3.

It is therefore clear: Without Cryptographic Echo Discovery, C4's message would spread through the entire network over the Echo Protocol.

The decisive factor is not only the protocol inherent data inspection, but also the pre-existing process of the division of clients representing presence information (for example, one of the above-mentioned hash digest options).

Figure 21: Definition of SECRED

> **Process of the Sprinkling Effect**
> **via Cryptographic Echo Discovery**
>
> The sprinkling effect (SE) can be understood as a watering that can feed and nourish a flower. The collected information is passed on by a node to the neighbors. Each neighbor participating in the Cryptographic Echo Discovery distributes this complementary CRED information to the other neighbors. So, every neighbor is sprinkled.
>
> **SECRED**
> **is an acronym for the term = Sprinkling Effect via CRyptographic Echo Discovery.**

SECRED is the beginning of teaching machines by Cryptographic Discovery and the Sprinkling Effect.

The Echo Protocol then regulates the rest to the respective graph. Clients, e.g. mobile devices, then receive over the SECRED exchange only those messages which are intended for them.

One doesn't always own the server. One also cannot possibly configure it. So, one has to teach it, how to give someone the messages. And the server teaches. Or not.

That is quite simpler than a search for a friend in a Distributed Hash Table (DHT) or the distribution of sender and receiver information.

A Distributed Hash Table (DHT) is a data structure that can be used, for example, to store the location of a file or the precision information in a p2p system: is my friend online and if so, which current IP and which port does the referring friend use?

Thanks to the SECRED and Echo Protocol, a user need not to care what happens up-stream, after the message has been sent on its journey.

That is a big advantage of SECRED even compared to the Adaptive Echo (A.E.): A.E. requires configurations - a token that is based on the user's definition. SECRED does not need a token manually inserted in an intermediate server.

Hence, SECRED is an elegant way to organize, that people, who know the user, can derive messages for the user. And, when the user address others, they can be given the data properly: here is this data for user X.

The criterion for this hint is, that the data is identifying something about the to-be-addressed person in a graph chain. The server sees and knows things from neighbors.

Data is free. Sometimes there are lots of data, sometimes not. So, there will be localized networks. And servers learning and teaching, because one can be a client, a server, or both - and based on own roles, one can learn and/or teach.

If a node doesn't know where to send to, it sends it wherever it can.

Perfection is not required. Nor is completeness required, because the Echo is redundant.

The method of SECRED removes now some of the messages from the network flow, so that mobile devices can be easily addressed and save battery and CPU-capacity.

The default implementation of the "hint" in the "Sprinkling Effect" of the "Cryptographic Echo Discovery" is based on keys. E.g. a cryptographic digest hash is the secret a user tells the server.

And messages to the user will be signed by that digest.

Because friends know the keys of the friend, they can address this specific user over the SECRED Protocol.

The message is not signed in the sense of a digital signature. The hint for the user is just added to the message in this format: D (Public Key) = XYZ. Hash (Message, D).

The Hash () is the product (signature) and the server can compute it.

And then the server knows, that this specific user/neighbor should get it: Message || H(Message, D).

The server computes H(Message, D) and knows this user is D. So, it hands it to this user.

If it doesn't know D, it hands it to everyone.

As an example in other words: Mary assigns the word "Po-pocatépetl" to your presence. And Mary can write you using "Popocatépetl". And if there are two "Popocatépetl"s, both get the message. So, a semi-private construct, while the Hash Digest offers great variety to be unique within your environment.

H(Message, D) is visible to all. D is the hash of the key. D is also a digest of something that the friends know about you.

Need the hash to be shared? Well, users have their public keys. So, a user can compute an ID based on those. A user has the friend's public keys, so this user can process it too. I tell the server that I am so-and-so. I address my message to so-and-so.

The server doesn't know so-and-so, so it echoes it. The server knows only that something from me is being sent to a recipient. The server doesn't know I wrote. In general: the server knows that something from somewhere is sent to another node.

This describes also the programmable functions of the sprinkling effect via the Cryptographic Echo Discovery (SECRED).

The more stable the network is, the more qualitative the mapping will work. Decisive for the stability is not only the online and offline status of friends, or the continuous availability of a chat server, but also the basic (stable) structure of the friends, one wants to address with a mobile chat messenger.

Here it is an advantage that the friend structures are usually relatively stable.

That is, also with the context of a "steady state" the relationship in the SECRED protocol can be compared:

Some communication applications try to find the friend in a Distributed Hash Table (DHT) to obtain updated port and IP information as well as status information about the presence.

However, the mixture of peers and servers in the network means that the SECRED protocol has the advantage that presence information (as in a DHT) is no longer required, as intermediate entities keep the messages ready for the retrieval.

Likewise, binding nodes with stable addresses for the mobile end devices are relieving and fostering security as they do not have to connect to numerous foreign nodes in the DHT for presence and IP or port queries.

SECRED is also a more secure alternative to DHTs (Distributed Hash Tables).

The implementation of a SECRED or DHT is thus not only dependent on the requirement of the battery and the hardware capacity of a possibly mobile device, but also on consideration of efficiency and also demands on the privacy of the data in the network at other nodes.

Questions and further Research & Development Fields

- Describe the encryption layers of the Echo Protocol.
- Explain Half and Full Echo within an Echo Grid.
- Explain Adaptive Echo within a graph.
- What is the Echo-Match? Give a Process Description.
- What's the idea of SECRED & Cryptographic Discovery?
- Describe the Sprinkling Effect in comparison of a DHT.
- Set up in your class a network with several computers and test the Adaptive Echo.

5 First Set-up of the software Spot-On

In this chapter the first setup of the software Spot-On is described before the main functions of the software will be explain each in an own chapter.

5.1 Set up a first installation – e.g. with the wizard

The first initial setup of the software is very simple done in a few steps:

---

1 - Downloading & Installing the Software

The user unpacks the program from the Zip (for Windows) and starts (under Windows) the Spot-On.exe from the path to which the program was unpacked,

- e.g. C: /Spot-On/Spot-On.exe
- or   C: /Programs/Spot-On/Spot-On.exe.

For Linux users a .deb installer file is provided and for MacOS users a .dmg file.

Download the software under:
- https://sourceforge.net/projects/spot-on/files/

or from Github under:
- https://textbrowser.github.io/spot-on/

---

2 - Key Generation with the Wizard

After starting the binary the user interface and a wizard appear, with which the settings can be implemented step by step. Alternatively, the user can close the wizard and create the settings manually in the tab for the settings respective the tab-section for kernel activation. It is recommended to use the wizard.

Figure 22: Initial Wizard of Spot-On

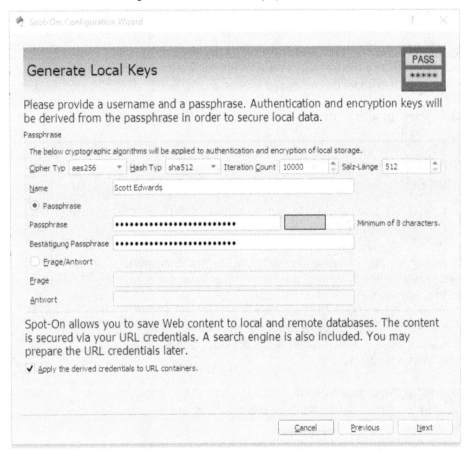

In the wizard, the necessary cryptographic keys are then generated with the user name and a passphrase to be entered twice.

The wizard has the following sub-pages:

1   Initial Welcome,

2   Setting the passphrase for the login: Choosing be-
     tween passphrase and question-and-answer method,
3   Confirmation of creating (default) RSA keys,
4   Launch Kernel upon completion of the wizard,
5   Enable URL-Distribution and set-up a SQLite Database
     for it: Here the user must confirm the check boxes,
6   Button Initialize: The setup will be prepared.

3 - Activating the Spot-On Kernel

After completing the wizard, the kernel must still be activated. That means, the Spot-On Encryption suite has a user
interface (also called Graphical User Interface (GUI)) and a
kernel. Both are given as a binary file (in Windows called
Spot-On.exe and Spot-On-Kernel.exe).

Hence, the user must activate the kernel via the "Activate" button in the tab for settings (section for kernel activation) after each start of Spot-On.exe, which then coordi-
nates the connections to friends or to a chat server. So the
kernel file Spot-on-Kernel.exe will be turned on or off from
Spot-On's program user interface.

4 - Connecting a Neighbor/Server IP

If the kernel is running, the user connects to a neighbor or
server with the appropriate IP and Port in the neighbors
tab.

5 - Key Exchange with a Friend

Then the user exchanges the key with a friend and the encrypted communication via chat or e-mail can begin... if
both have entered the key(s) of the friend.

> **6 – Starting a Chat from the Chat Tab**

If the key has been added, the friend appears in the chat tab, and if a neighbor is connected, kernel running, and the network set up, both friends should be able to chat and communicate.

Let´s close the application after the wizard has been completed and let's start again with this process – not with the wizard, but with the login into the application after the wizard has been completed successfully: and look more into the details and options within this above described process to start a first chat. So let's start again to go through this above briefly proposed process in more detail:

5.2 Passphrase creation within the Wizard: Two login methods & a virtual keyboard

If the user starts Spot-On for the first time, the user enters a nickname in the corresponding box and defines a passphrase for the login into the application (see figure widget box "passphrase" – as explained for the wizard).

The password must be at least 16 characters long. If this is too long, the user can repeat a shorter password three times, such as "password_password_password", but then the password is not as secure as one with a random string.

Figure 23: Set Passphrase - if not the Wizard is used, it is found in the settings Tab for kernel activation - here shown within the GoldBug GUI

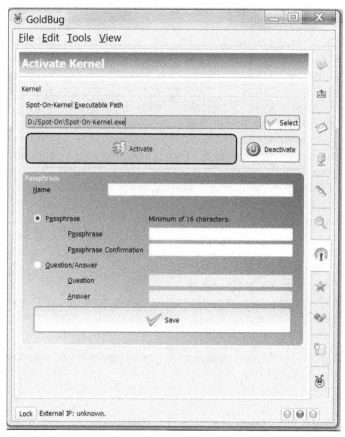

There are two methods to define this: the passphrase method or the question-and-answer method. They can be differentiated as follows:

Passphrase method: When the password is created, it is not stored locally, just the hash of the input. The hash is supplemented by a supplementary string, the so-called cryptographic salt. This complements the hash and makes it safer. The "Salted Hash" is thus defined as follows: hash (passphrase + salt). To achieve that the password is also trained for the user and typing errors are excluded, it must be entered a second time.

Question / Answer Method: This method does not enter a password twice but defines a string as a question and a string as the answer. Both strings will not be checked a second time. Technically, this login method is implemented via a HMAC: Hash (Question, Answer), indicates that an "HMAC" (Keyed-Hash Message Authentication Code) is used. And: neither the question nor the answer is stored on the user's machine and no cryptographic salt is randomly generated by the machine. Instead of the question, the user can of course also enter two passwords without a question mark. It should be noted that here the question and the answer must be entered in subsequent logins exactly as they were defined and here at the first definition no second input check ("confirmation") regarding typing errors is given as in the password method.

Please note, that in Spot-On no password or question and answer is stored on the encrypted hard disc container. Also not via the ciphertext of it.

Figure 24: Authentication: Login to the application Spot-On with a passphrase

Since the hash generated from the login passphrase unlocks the encrypted containers that also store the private key for encryption, it is especially important to protect the login process and login password. Therefore, the above two methods have been taken into account to make it more difficult for attackers: they do not know a) which method a user has chosen and b) the question-answer method is safer, as described above, because neither the question, nor the answer can be stored somewhere and a HMAC may be more complex than a password as a "just" salted hash. Only the user knows question and additionally the answer and only the match of both can open the container.

Virtual keyboard: In order not to reveal information to keypad loggers, there is the possibility to use a virtual keyboard when logging in (see image). The user starts this by double-clicking on the input line for the password. At best, only mouse clicks can be recorded here, but no keystrokes.
In principle, it is important that the private key is kept encrypted in a sufficiently secured container. It is reasonable to suppose that, in particular, access by providers to mobile operating systems would otherwise make it easy to fetch the private key.

This is especially critical for web mail offers to provide the encryption in the browser or with keys that are deposited at and with the mail provider online. Encryption should always take place on the user's machine and for this login procedure purpose. An open source client and no online web application in the browser should be used for encrypting chat and e-mail.

Figure 25: Virtual Keyboard of the Spot-On application

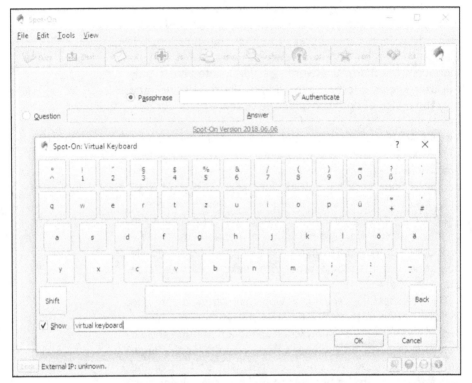

The risk of seizing the possibly insufficiently encrypted private key is far too great. Program audits should also pay attention to capturing passwords for the encrypted container in which the private key is located, as well as to remote accessing the private key over the operating system supplier or Trojan applications.

Even the few open source messengers with encryption that can be counted on one hand for the desktop as well as for mobile devices that have undergone a security audit are hardly sufficient with regard to the security of the encrypted storage of private keys and their processes to access these.

5.3   Generation of 12 Keys for Encryption

When the user launches the Spot-On application for the first time, the wizard asks if the user wants to generate the encryption keys. For key creation the user should choose a key of at least 3072 bits (default for RSA) or larger. The user can also choose other options such as algorithm, hashtype, cipher, salt-length or iteration count, for example, if he re-generates the key. The first setup has a presetting based on RSA ready: So if the user wants to test out NTRU or McEliece as an algorithm, then after the first setup the user has to generate again new keys with one of the then se-lectable algorithms.

The generated keys are stored in the sub-path "/.spot-on". If the user wants to set up a new login with new keys and all user data should be deleted, then this path can simply be deleted and the Spot-On.exe has to be restarted. For Linux and the other operating systems the adequate path specifications apply accordingly. The same can be done in the main menu with "!!! Total_Database Erase !!! ".

Asymmetric keys are generated for the following func-tions (a key for the encryption as well as a key for the (op-tional) signature):

- Chat Key: This is about the 1: 1 chat,
- E-mail Key: This is about e-mail to other users of Spot-On or any other Echo client like GoldBug or other,
- POPTASTIC Key: This is about the chat via e-mail server,
- URL Key: This involves searching for URLs in the URL database (web search),
- Public Library Key: This is a pair of keys reserved for further implementation of sharing public files out of a library,
- Rosetta Key: With the Rosetta encryption pad, text with a-symmetric keys can be converted back and forth from plain text to cipher text and vice versa before the texts are sent. This is recom-mended when other insecure messengers or e-

mail applications are used or the cipher text should be posted anywhere on the web - or the plain text, before it is sent in Spot-On, should again receive an additional encryption level!

That each function uses its own key pair is again a security feature. If the (permanent or temporary) chat key were compromised, the e-mail encryption will not be affected. Furthermore, the user can only pass friends his chat key and not the e-mail key. Thus, the user can decide whom he allows to chat with or just to e-mail or possibly also to exchange URLs for the function of p2p web search in the integrated URL database.

Also a minimal view on the user interface is possible: Via the main menu one can choose between "full view" or "minimal view". If the user is not familiar with computers, one should choose the minimal view because it fades out the possibly unnecessary variety of options. Keep it simple: The GoldBug Echo client is fully compatible with Spot-On and provides an even simpler interface than the minimal view of the Spot-On client.

Qt developers, and those who are looking for an exercise project for their own Qt development or a university project, may even minimize the user interface within their own Echo Client (and are invited to "fork" the Spot-On client).

5.3.1 A posteriori Key (re-)generation: Switching from RSA provided by the Wizard to McEliece and other

During the first setup over the wizard, the option of the maximum view is not available; it will only be shown and set-able at the further logins. The possibility of looking at even more details in the user interface should therefore be addressed briefly here, since many details also refer to the last-mentioned point of the cryptographic values for key generation, which is also contained in the settings tabulator for the kernel activation and generation of encryption keys:

Key-Generation e.g. with the McEliece algorithm is here to be found.

The algorithm and values can be set individually for a new key generation (after and without the wizard). However, if the user is using the client for the first time, the typical setting values are in the wizard automatically available, i.e. the key has a (predefined) size of 3072 bits of the RSA algorithm.

In case of a non-minimal view, for example, the tab "Activate Kernel" shows the following elements in the user interface:

- **Path to kernel:** Here the user can enter the path to the kernel. If the kernel with the "spot-on-kernel.exe" in the path specified correctly, then the path is highlighted in green. Otherwise, the user has to look at the executable file of the kernel or copy it to the executable file of the GUI (Spot-On.exe) or adjust the path accordingly.

- **PID:** The PID number identifies the process ID that identifies the executable file in Windows. The user also finds the process IDs in the Windows Task Manager.

- **"Key regeneration" function:** With the "regeneration" function, the user can also generate individual keys - with new values and options. For this the check box has to be activated, the values have to be set and the respective keys have to be re-generated. This is the way to get e.g. keys of the McEliece or NTRU algorithm. Then the user has to put his new key back to his friends, because the key is a kind of communication ID for the cryptographic Echo-Matching.

Another variety of options can also be found under the main menu / options in a pop-up window, which will be explained later (for example to choose another icon set (e.g. Nuvola instead of Nueve icon set).

Figure 26: Options for Display: e.g. change icon set

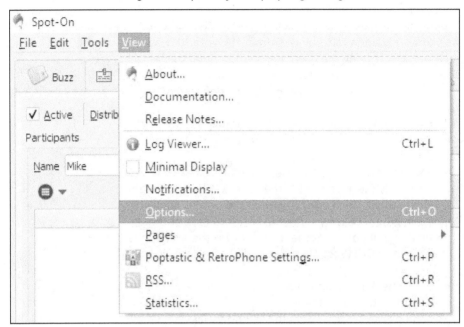

For now, it is more important to start the kernel after the first key generation via the wizard has taken place.

5.4 Activation of the kernel

When the user launches the Spot-On application for the first time, a pop-up window at the end of the wizard asks if the kernel should be activated. Otherwise, the "Activate Kernel" button in the settings tab should be pressed on all subsequent starts after the login. Without a running kernel no communication process is possible.

When the user closes the program interface, a pop-up window also asks if the kernel should continue running. So it's a good idea to first deactivate the kernel and then close the GUI of Spot-On if the user wants to completely close the program.

Otherwise, the user runs the kernel without a GUI, which is sometimes desired on a web server, so that nobody can manipulate within the open user interface. (In addition to the Spot-on kernel, there is also the Spot-on-Lite kernel for this daemon web server purpose, which can be found in the repository of the source code as a standalone repository.)

Figure 27: Lock of the user interface in the status bar

If the user wants to leave the GUI in place, but no one should be able to enter or change anything during the absence, it is also possible to click the "Lock" button on the left in the lower status line: the user interface will close and return to the login tab for the input of the password back, so that the running processes and inputs of other tabs are not visible. To unlock the interface, the user presses the lock button again in the status bar and enters then the passphrase(s) in a pop-up window.

Figure 28: Activation of the kernel in the Settings Tab

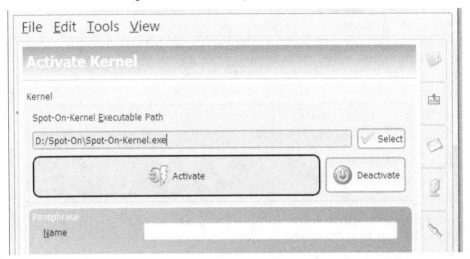

The user can also enable/disable the kernel by pressing the first LED in the status line at the bottom left. If it is green, the kernel is active; if it is red, the kernel is off. The middle LED indicates whether the user has set up a listener / chat server and the third LED indicates whether the user has an active and successful connection to a neighbor / server.

Figure 29: Encryption between kernel and GUI and three LEDs.

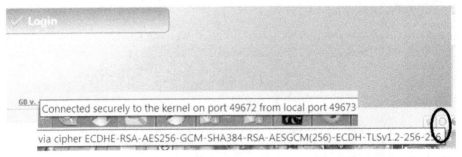

The connection of the user interface (Spot-On.exe) to the kernel (Spot-On-Kernel.exe) is also encrypted, although both run on the same machine of the user. A tool-tip with the mouse-over action over the first LED indicates the encryption.

5.5   Connect a neighbor with the IP address

Upon initial activation, the IP address of the project chat server (or a localhost) is automatically added as a neighbor. This serves as a temporary chat server through which the user can chat with his friend's test-wise until a separate connection node has been created on a web server or at home (or two users connect directly to each other). The test server will not last forever, so far, users will need to first set up a server themselves before they can connect two clients (see chapter server setup).

Up to now, the user has been connected to a chat server directly after activation of the kernel by the provided test server. If the user would like to add another, the tab "Connect neighbor" must be used. Here is an input field for the IP address of the neighbor respective the web server, on which a Spot-On Kernel is running, or a friend also uses a Spot-On instance with an accessible listener/server.

Figure 30: Creating a connection to a neighbor/server

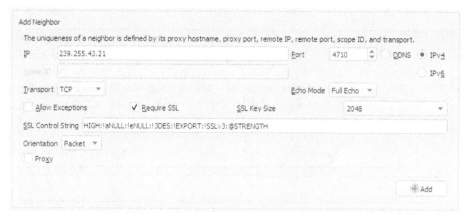

In the field, enter the IP address of the neighbor node. The points are each separated by three digits of the IP address (according to IP-V4). If a block only contains two digits, e.g. 37.100.100.100, then the 37 can be placed arbitrarily in the first block or entered as 37 in the first two positions. Then the user presses the "Connect" / "Add" button. The IP address is then stored on the default port 4710 and appears as a link in the neighbors table.

Figure 31: Connected neighbors/ servers

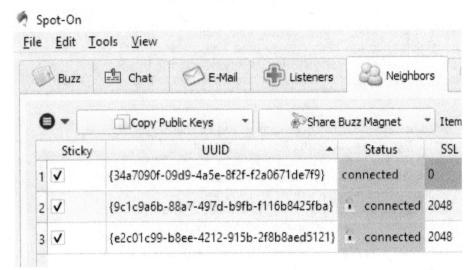

If an error message appears, then this IP address has already been entered. In order to delete all neighbors, the button "Delete all neighbors" can be pressed (via the context menu button or via the right mouse button in the table in which the neighbor appears) and the IP address can be entered again. Optionally, the user can also delete the file "neighbors.db" in the installation path "./spot-on" on the hard disk. It rebuilds immediately and is then empty.

When the kernel is activated (left, first LED in the status bar is green) and the neighbor or server is connected (middle LED is green) everything is successfully installed and online. Entering an IP address and pressing the connect button should be quite easy.

If the user wants to connect directly to another user without a server, one of them must create a so-called listener in the tab chat server (and release the firewall for the port and, if necessary, forward the port in the router to the own machine, see below in the create server section in more detail).

Or: if both users are on the same Windows network, the existing neighbor "239.255.43.21" can be activated, then the Spot-On Messenger is converted into a LAN messenger and finds all other Spot-On participants in the local LAN automatically and connects these as a neighbor. If the users then exchange the keys, the communication can start.

By default, Spot-On uses the port 4710. Furthermore, the program can also be operated via IPv6, as well as to a listener/server which is linked via the dynamic DNS-URL. Then DNS is no number sequence for the IP, but a domain name to be added in a textfield. Please choose then the DNS radio button. Further security options can also be defined, e.g. the connection to the server can be addressed via a proxy (e.g. if the user wants to use Spot-On via the Tor network or behind a firewall).

5.6   Key Exchange

How to copy the own key, how to exchange the key with a friend and to paste the friend's key into the application is described with an example for the chat key within the next chapter for starting a chat, which follows immediately. Let's just pint out the option to use an even more simpler interface for the Spot-On-Kernel, which is called: GoldBug.

5.7   GoldBug: Alternative Graphical User Interface (GUI)

Spot-On is a very detailed, customizable and for some probably also a complex software. It requites some learning about all the buttons and functions, like a pilot in an aircraft also has many options and things to learn.

After the first setup has been done and before all the functions of Spot-On are described at this point the hint, that there is a second Graphical User Interface for the Spot-On kernel, which has a reduced overview. This allows beginners in practical encryption to start with a simplified interface: called GoldBug. GoldBug is an own software compilation based on the Spot-On GUI und code, with the difference, that it provides a simplified interface and the tabs are in right east and not default on the top north like in Spot-On. Thus, users who want to test a simpler graphical user interface (GUI), can also try out the GoldBug client as a further Echo application. GoldBug is quite popular in the web and at download portals and can be found in the source of the Spot-On source tree at Github.com and at the dedicated website of Sourceforge.net:

http://goldbug.sf.net/

Website of the GoldBug software, which has a more simplified Graphical User Interface for the Spot-On kernel than the Spot-On application itself.

The name GoldBug derives from a historical situation: The Gold Bug is a short story by Edgar Allan Poe: The plot is about William LeGrand, who recently encountered a gold-colored ladybug.

His buddy, Jupiter, now expects LeGrand to evolve in his quest for insight, wealth, and wisdom after being in contact with the Golden Bug - and thus goes on to another friend of LeGrand, a narrator not further mentioned by name, who thinks it would be a good idea to visit his old friend again. After LeGrand then encountered a secret message and was able to decrypt it successfully, the three start an adventure as a team.

The Gold Bug - as one of the few pieces in the literature - integrates cipher text as an element of the short story. Poe was thus far ahead of the popularity of cipher texts of his time when he wrote "The Gold Bug" in 1843, in which the success of history turned to such a cryptogram and metaphorically to the search for the knowledge of the philosopher's stone.

The Gold Bug was a much-read story, extremely popular and by the literati the most studied work by Poe during his lifetime. His ideas also helped to promote the writing of encrypted texts and so-called cryptograms.

Over 170 years later, encryption in the Internet age has more weight than ever. Encryption should be a standard when we send communications over the insecure internet -

reason enough to use this name for this application and therefore to remember the origins of the encrypted writing.

The GoldBug GUI is thus a historical tribute, which possibly requires an adaptation to the term, because "bug" is often understood in the IT context as an error correction. Depending on the person, the idea of valuing a golden ladybug as much as another cuddly toy may require a strong cognitive reorganization of a so far dominated worldview or the routinized expansion of the appreciation of bug-finds as interesting research finds.

Those who like exploring new things, openly approaching what is found, will be able to learn and deepen many things in cryptographic processes with this software application, if so far no access to this "new territory" has been made possible. For teachers, the software is therefore an interesting teaching tool that can introduce and test encryption in practical implementation and exercises with playful testing, reminiscent of the beginnings of popular cryptography at the time.

Incidentally: The logo of the GoldBug logo is written in the font "Neuland" (which means translated: new territory) - a font that was developed in 1923 by the typographer Rudolf Koch.

Interestingly enough, the logo has been an allusion to the German "sentence of the year" 2013, when German Chancellor Angela Merkel - in connection with the surveillance and espionage affair in 2013 and the Listening to her personal mobile phone - in a conversation with American President Barack Obama coined the phrase: "The Internet is a new territory for us all." ..

.. - How long encryption for the subsequent student generations will remain a new territory (or "Neuland") or literally 'secret science' - or a kind of "seat belt", which will also convert e-mails to c-mails, decide the learners, teachers and the media and technicians - but in any case everyone (e.g. the reader of this manual) with the own friends with whom this (or other) encryption software is used.

Figure 32: Logo of the GoldBug Crypto Chat Application

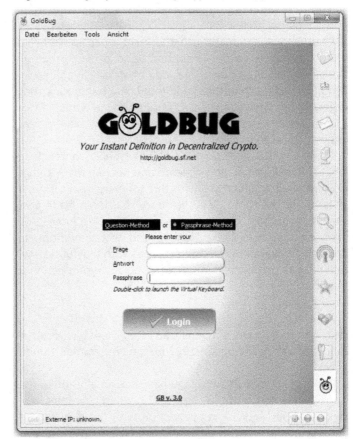

Questions and further Research & Development Fields

- Set up the application without the Wizard and write a description about the process.
- Use Spot-On as a LAN Messenger and try to find other nodes automatically.
- Regenerate Keys with the McEliece algorithm.

6   The chat function with Crypto-graphic Calling

Now that the infrastructure is set up, that means: if login-password is defined, key generated, kernel enabled and a neighbor-server connected - so in the status bar two LED-lights are green - then the user can exchange the own key with a friend and the communication for a defined partici-pant can start. Personal 1:1-chat takes place in the chat tab or in the pop-up window (see figure, opened by a double-click on the friend in the chat tab).

Figure 33: 1:1 chat in the pop-up window

1:1 personal chat has a share button to send files encrypted to a dedicated friend.

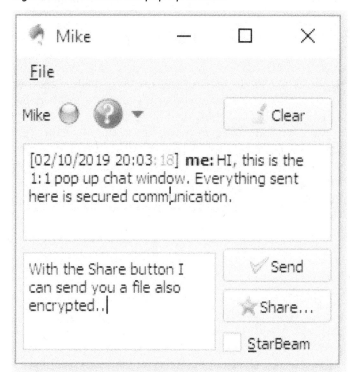

But step after step: if the software is running and server-connected, the key exchange is still the pre-condition to start a secure chat. The key exchange is done over:

- the "Copy public keys" button in the neighbors tab,
- and pasting the key(s) into the pop-up-window for "adding participants" - found under: Main-Menu/Tools/Add-Participant.

6.1 Adding a friend by swapping and inserting the keys

Spot-On uses a public/private key infrastructure, as it is well-known in the case of encryption: The public key(s) can be exchanged with friends and the private key(s) remain(s) on the user's hard disk in an encrypted container that is opened (mounted) by the login password – and used for the application runtime.

The user and the partner, both friends, must first exchange their public key, i.e. copy it out, transfer it and then insert the friend's key: Add participant and confirm (see figure). The friend can send the key via e-mail or another messenger. The user then copies the key into this window and presses the "Add" button at the bottom.

The user finds the own public key in the neighbors tab. The large button ("Copy Public Keys") allows the user to copy all own (or selected) keys to the clipboard. The user copies the full text here and sends it to the friend. Likewise, the friend does the same and the user inserts the friend's key in the "Add Participant"-textbox.

The main menu also provides a menu item to export and import keys.

Figure 34: Add Friend/Key

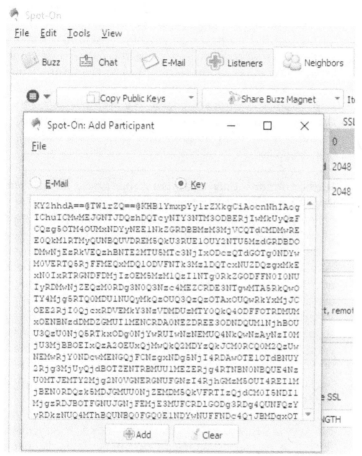

The own chat key consists of ciphertext like data and begins with the letter K or R.

Optionally only as a note – IP transfer of the keys: it is also possible to share a key over the direct IP connection (to a friend or to a server). Then it may be necessary to confirm a new friend as friend with the right mouse button in the context menu of the friends list in the chat tab (make-friend function). If a friend uses the Spot-On client and builds a direct IP connection to another user with a Spot-On client, then it is possible to transfer the key via a direct IP connection instead of copy/paste. The friend appears with his nick name in the chat tab (or e-mail tab) (with a different icon) and can be confirmed as a friend with the right mouse button from the context menu: Make Friend.

This is a further development of the REPLEO function, which is the function of encrypting the own key with the friend's public key (upon receipt) before the return transmission starts. The key exchange over IP is thus automated: a synchronization process follows. The user must agree that the key will be displayed after synchronization via the neighbor connection in their own client respective their own friend list.

EPKS =
Echo Public
Key Sharing,
later also known as
AutoCrypt.

Further option - only as a note - Sharing via Echo Public Key Sharing (EPKS) function: In addition to send the key online via e-mail, another messenger, as a REPLEO or over the direct IP-connection to a friend, the Echo Public Key Sharing (EPKS) protocol, function and tool can also be used (as also further described below). This is used if the friend is not connected to a direct IP-connection (e.g. both partners use a shared chat server or a node is in the middle). Both partners then enter a common password secret in EPKS and send their public keys to the Echo Network via this password protected EPKS channel. See the more detailed information in the section of this tool, which may be a good alternative to the often uncomfortable and insecure usual key servers known from a PGP key exchange.

This innovation by a REPLEO, and the synchronization of the keys via the so-called Echo Public Key Share function (EPKS), or via an existing IP-connection, has later also been taken up (copied) by other projects under the name AutoCrypt or KeySync. These functions are therefore based on the REPLEO, EPKS and the key exchange via IP-connection of Echo nodes. Autocrypt has been invented within the Spot-On Project and been overtaken several years later by other projects under the name AutoCrypt, e.g. using the IMAP protocol for the key exchange.

However, the key sharing problems over PGP-key servers have been avoided and differentiated with some alternatives: The key(s) can be shared by copy/paste, can be exported, copied by menu and buttons, resent by a REPLEO, and shared via EPKS and also shared via a direct IP-connection or an IP-broadcast.

Furthermore, there is an even simpler way to share keys – over the Group Chat function: two people create a Group Chat Room within Spot-On, which is just based on the same group room name. The Group Chat Room is provided in the first tab, called Buzz, and will be explained in the next chapter. The room name is quasi semi-anonymous, if only the two users agree upon a secret room name. In this secret room two users can share their public keys in privacy. As EPKS channels and BUZZ rooms (which work on the same principle of symmetric encryption) will be explained later on, let's have a short explanation of the REPLEO function in more detail first.

6.1.1 Special feature: REPLEO – Encrypting the public key

If the user has already received a key from the friend (e.g. the chat key) and inserted it into the own client, but now does not want to disclose the own public (chat) key to the public, does not want to transfer and store it in an e-mail program (although the public key may actually be public), then the user can also encrypt the own public key with the received key of the friend. This is called REPLEO. Hence, the key is transmitted encrypted as soon as a user has already received a public key of the other party.

This process then has to be carried out for each function or key, i.e. the user can in each case send back the chat REPLEO, the e-mail REPLEO and the URL REPLEO etc.. The friend can also insert a REPLEO in the window for "Add Participant/Key". In older versions, above the insert-box, the user just defines the radio-select-button: whether it's a Key (K), a REPLEO (R), or an e-mail address (E) the user would like to add. Meanwhile, the K and R radio buttons in Spot-On have disappeared because the client automatically de-

tects if it's a (K)ey or a (R)EPLEO. The current versions have an automated recognition of keys and REPLEOs:
The text of a key always starts with a letter "K" or "k" and a REPLEO starts with a "R" or "r". The user still can recognize it if the key or REPLEO is copied out. So the user has in the Add Participant window today the option to add a key or an e-mail address (which is used within the e-mail functionality, explained further below).

6.2   Starting a first secure chat

A user finds the chat friend in the "Chat" tab after a successful key exchange. For getting the chat to work, both parties should ideally use the same and most up-to-date version of the program, generate and exchange their keys, and connect to a network node or chat server (neighbor) on the web. When the first two LEDs in the status line at the bottom are highlighted green and the friend's name appears in the chat tab, it looks excellent.

If the friend's online status turns blue (absent), red (busy), or green (ready to talk), the chat can start. Either the user marks the friend in the table and chats out of the tab, or the user double-clicks on the friend and a pop-up chat window opens for that friend.

The advantage of chatting in the chat tab is that the user can mark multiple friends so that the message reaches all friends. If the user uses the pop-up chat (see figure), then the user no longer needs to look at the marker to select a friend from the friends-list in the chat tab.

And: In pop-up chat modus, the user has the button "Share StarBeam", with which the user can select a file from the hard drive, so that it is then encrypted and securely transferred to the friend (see also the section below about StarBeam-File-Sharing). This feature, which sends a chat friend a file simply by a mouse-click, provides a fully encrypted end-to-end transport. That is not included in many closed or even open source applications. Encrypted transmission e.g. of a ZIP with vacation pictures to own siblings becomes thus quite simple and is possible without the use of a hosting or cloud platform in the Web.

Figure 35: Chat Tab

In the status line at the top of the pop-up window, the user can see the nickname and online status and, for example, launch the Socialist Millionaire Protocol (SMP) to authenticate a friend and test whether the friend knows a common secret and enters it correctly, as it will be described below. Both users will be authentic if they enter the same password within this SMP process.

But before we explain the Socialist Millionaire Protocol (SMP) for authentication - that means if the real friend is in front of his or her machine and not a theft, who has stolen the machine - let's first have a look how to secure the end-to-end encryption with Cryptographic Calling.

Cryptographic Calling sends out - over an already existing secured connection - another temporary key, so that this encryption layer is (solely) used (or additionally used). The temporary key can be a-symmetric (PKI) or symmetric (a password string also known as a passphrase).

Figure 36: Chat in the pop-up window with the SMP authentication option

The figure shows a lock-symbol for a successful SMP-process for authentication.

6.3   Cryptographic Calling - additional security feature invented by Spot-On

In the early development, Cryptographic Calling started with one button. It was called MELODICA and described the Calling over a long distance with multi-encrypted layers of encryption. The MELODICA button performs the Cryptographic Calling function.

Figure 37: The MELODICA Button since 2013

MELODICA Button

MELODICA stands for "Multi-Encrypted LOng DIstance CAlling" – that means: "Multiple-Encrypted Calls over a Long Distance". The MELODICA symbol is therefore a piano keyboard as musical instrument and was first implemented in GoldBug's User Interface of Spot-On.

The Cryptographic Calling has been developed by the Spot-On kernel project and secures the connection via an immediately renewed end-to-end encryption by transmitting the password via the a-symmetric connection of the Echo Protocol. Cryptographic Calling with the MELODICA button means calling a friend like with a phone - only that it creates a secure end-to-end encryption.

Spot-On invented the Cryptographic Calling.

The end-to-end passphrase - also known as Gemini (Greek word for twin) - is mapped through an AES string and should be kept secret between both parties. Therefore, it is important to secure the electronic transmission always very secure with further encryption levels (as here in the Echo Protocol with the a-symmetric chat key and the TLS/SSL connection), as the transmission can potentially be eavesdropped.

In the meantime, Cryptographic Calling has been elaborated in a great way and further methods have been added, so that the term Cryptographic Calling (besides the historical MELODICA button) has established and is used in Spot-On. Other projects even overtook some years later the term, which had been brought up by the Spot-On development many years before, as it is proved by the code commits.

Cryptographic Calling transfers over a secure connection new credentials for a switch to a new secure connection with new credentials. These can be symmetric as well as a-symmetric credentials.

Cryptographic Calling

Cryptographic Calling is the immediate transfer of end-to-end encrypting credentials to secure a communication channel. Cryptographic Calling has been invented and introduced by the Software Project Spot-On. It refers to sending new end-to-end encryption credentials to the other participant through an existing secured online channel.

That means, a "Call" transfers over a public/private key encrypted environment e.g. a symmetric key (e.g. AES). It is a password for the session talk, only the two participants know. With one click a user can instantly renew the end-to-end encrypting password for the messaging. It is also possible to manually define the end-to-end encrypted password (manually or self-defined Calling in the sense of Customer Supplied Encryption Keys: #CSEK). There are some further different ways to call: Asymmetric Calling, Forward Secrecy Calling, Symmetric Calling, SMP-Calling and 2-Way-Calling, which will be explained later below.

The Calling with a-symmetric credentials refers to ephemeral a-symmetric keys, which are used for the time of the call. This could be one session or even a shorter part of time of the session. It depends on whenever a communication partner starts to initiate a call. The asymmetric ephemeral credentials for the call should be transferred over a secure connection, which is either a symmetric key, over a a-symmetric key (PKI) or over an already existent call-connection, in this case an ephemeral asymmetric key. "Cryptographic Calling" can even replace an a-symmetric channel with a symmetric channel.

The following modes of Calling can be differentiated:

6.3.1 Asymmetric Calling

Spot-On has solved the end-to-end password transfer question by encrypting the Gemini (the to be formed string for symmetric encryption, e.g. the AES) a-symmetrically (using the key for chat) and then encrypting again (a-symmetric) the SSL/TLS channel, over which it is transmitted.

As said: Gemini is the Greek term for twin, meaning it refers to both participants who should then know the passphrase.

This function thus generates a "Cryptographic Call", a call in which the password is transmitted, which then later forms the end-to-end encryption. Strictly speaking, the Gemini consists of two keys or components, because the Gemini is authenticated by another process: This further component is also called MAC-Hash, as explained above.

IPFS:
Instant
Perfect Forward
Secrecy

The "Cryptographic Calling" as an executable Protocol with the MELODICA button respective Call menu thus extends the old paradigm of Forward Secrecy as follows:

6.3.2 Instant Perfect Forward Secrecy (IPFS)

The user can now renew the (symmetric) encryption or the Gemini at any time. This means that the paradigm of "perfect forward secrecy" has been extended by two components: on the one hand, one can manually or automatically define the end-to-end passphrase (the Gemini) and, on the other hand, renew it immediately, i.e. "instant" at any time. Therefore, we speak of "Instant Perfect Forward Secrecy" (IPFS).

By comparison, many other applications offer only one key per online session and the user cannot manually and individually edit the symmetric end-to-end encryption phrase.

The Instant Perfect Forward Secrecy (IPFS) here in Spot-On uses a-symmetric encryption (of the chat key), whereby the temporary key could be a symmetric key (the Gemini, an AES string).

6.3.3 Symmetric Calling

Another option is Spot-On's innovative ability to send a new Gemini through the channel of an existing Gemini: Here, the end-to-end key (that is, the symmetrically-encrypting Gemini) is sent through another existing end-to-end Gemini connection (i.e. channel of a symmetric key). The symmetric encryption phrase (the Gemini or the AES password) is therefore not encrypted with a-symmetric encryption (the chat key) (e.g. with RSA, Elgamal, McEliece or NTRU) and then sent over a secure channel (SSL/TLS) from point-to-point, but it is itself encrypted with the existing (symmetric) Gemini and then sent by the described Echo method (again via SSL/TLS).

Compare the double-rachet method of the Signal-Protocol, in which the key of the following message is in the encrypted content of the previous packet: it may have been ajar or derived from Symmetric Calling.

Thus, an A-symmetrical Call and a Symmetric Call can be fundamentally differentiated. Symmetric Calls use an existing Gemini. Asymmetric Calls send the Gemini over the a-symmetrically encrypted connection (namely the permanent chat key) to the friend. Even when Calling over an existing Gemini, the sent Gemini can be instantaneously renewed at any time.

In sum: Secure end-to-end multi-encryption arises in the Echo when an encrypting messenger encodes a manually-defined symmetric key with an existing symmetric key and then encrypts it with an a-symmetric key. And then this package is sent through a secure connection. What's a preferred hybrid concept?

6.3.4 Two-way Calling

Finally, in the context menu (right mouse-click on a friend in the friend list), a third method for a so-called "Cryptographic Call" is added: Two-way Calling. Here, the user sends an AES-256 as a passphrase for the future end-to-end encryption to the friend, and the friend also sends an own generated AES-256 to the first user in response. Now the first half of the AES of the first user and the second half of the AES of the second user are taken, respectively, and assembled into a common AES-256. It refers to the method of 2-way safety.

Make it Fifty-Fifty!

Figure 38: Definition of Two-way Cryptographic Calling

Fifty-Fifty: Two-way Cryptographic Calling

Spot-On implements a plain two-pass key-distribution system. The protocol is defined as follows:
1.   A peer generates 128-bit AES and 256-bit SHA-512 keys via the system's cryptographic random number generator.
2.   Using the destination's public key, the peer encapsulates the two keys via the hybrid cryptographic system.
3.   The destination peer receives the data, records it, and generates separate keys as in step 1.
4.   The destination peer transmits the encapsulated keys to the originating peer as in step 2.

Once the protocol is executed, the two peers shall possess identical authentication and encryption keys. Please note that duplicate half-keys are allowed.

This ensures that no third party - if someone succeeds in compromising the friend's machine - sends a Gemini (or an old Gemini) in the friends name from a third, foreign machine (which is not really possible, since it would mean the unnoticed acquisition of a machine or breaking the existing TLS and RSA (or NTRU or Elgamal) encryption). The ping-pong game of two participants in Two-way Calling ensures that both participants are currently doing their part to agree on a secure end-to-end password: Both define it Fifty-Fifty.

Figure 39: Two-Way Calling in the context menu from the friends-list

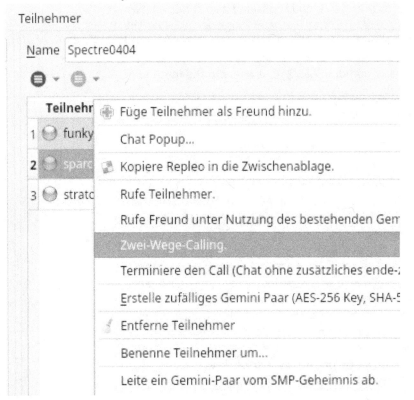

The possibility for the Gemini password
- first, to be edited manually,
- second, to be able to be renewed every second - or within each call,
- third, to send the password through an existing end-to-end encryption,
- and finally, being able to generate the end-to-end encrypting passphrase in a two-way process

makes it very difficult for attackers to break the end-to-end encryption of the Spot-On Cryptographic Calling feature.

Additionally (see below) the SMP-Calling authenticates the sender for the Call.

"Perfect Forward Secrecy" (PFS) has become not only "Instant Perfect Forward Secrey" (IPFS), but (in this feature) even a "2-Way Instant Perfect Forward Secrecy": 2WIPFS. This feature has significantly advanced PFS and the important element of instant end-to-end encryption with this process implementation. The encryption itself is not new, instead the process is sophisticatedly implemented to provide more security by Cryptographic Calling.

6.4   Additional security feature: Socialist Million-aire Protocol (SMP)

While Spot-On encrypts the messages three times -
- on the one hand the message is indeed sent in a secure TLS/SSL channel,
- second, every message is encrypted a-symmetric (e.g. with RSA-, NTRU-, McEliece- or Elgamal-PKI, i.e. with the chat key),
- and third, yes, it is possible to use the "Crypto-graphic Calling" function to send a Gemini to set a symmetric end-to-end encryption passphrase (as seen with different methods to perform the "Call"),
- Fourth, there is an additional security enhance-ment mechanism: it is the "SMP" Protocol: Socialist Millionaire Protocol (a method also described here for off-the-record messaging (OTR): https://otr.cypherpunks.ca/Protocol-v3-4.0.0.html).

The idea behind this is to ask a friend a question like: "What is the name of the city we visited together last year?"; Or, to ask a question like: "What is the name of the restaurant, in which we met for the first time?" etc. (see figure).

Both participants usually sign the messages with a RSA (or other) algorithm to verify that the key used is from the original sender. But for the (possibly unlikely) case that a machine would be hacked or stolen, or if the encryption algorithm were broken, the Socialist Millionaire Protocol (SMP) process can simply identify a friend by entering the same password on both sides. It is important to ensure that the password is not to be sent through the chat, instead both friends should describe a situation that leads to the same password. If the SMP process is tested for the first time, the users can just enter the password "test" on both sides (in lower case and without the quotes).

Figure 40: SMP Protocol in the pop-up chat window

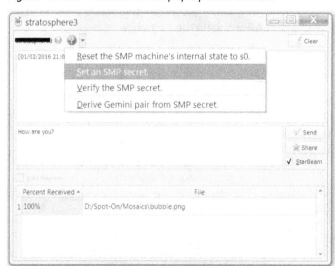

It is practically applied as follows: The user opens a personal pop-up chat window to use SMP and clicks the question mark icon next to the user name on top of the chat window. Then a password is defined with the menu. Then the chat friend is asked to enter the same password. Third, the first user then finally clicks on the Verify button.

If both participants have set the same password - respective the same hash value has been generated from the same password - then the question mark icon changes to a "lock" symbol. The chat friend has now been authenticated and the chat remains safe — in the sense of authenticated. Please note, that the hash or password is not transmitted over the secure connection! The process is based on a so-called Zero-Knowledge-Proof.

SMP is thus another ideal way to authenticate the chat friend with a shared secret in the live process, so it is not additional encryption!

An example illustrates the calculation process of this Protocol as follows: Spot-On describes this so-called "Zero-Knowledge-Proof" during SMP's various data exchange processes. Spot-On also uses the SHA-512 of the entered secret passphrase as the x and y components. Let's assume in an example that Alice begins the exchange:

- Alice:
    1. Picks random exponents a_2 and a_3
    2. Sends Bob $g_{2a} = g_1{}^{a_2}$ and $g_{3a} = g_1{}^{a_3}$
- Bob:
    1. Picks random exponents b_2 and b_3
    2. Computes $g_{2b} = g_1{}^{b_2}$ and $g_{3b} = g_1{}^{b_3}$
    3. Computes $g_2 = g_{2a}{}^{b_2}$ and $g_3 = g_{3a}{}^{b_3}$
    4. Picks random exponent r
    5. Computes $P_b = g_3{}^r$ and $Q_b = g_1{}^r\, g_2{}^y$
    6. Sends Alice g_{2b}, g_{3b}, P_b and Q_b
- Alice:
    1. Computes $g_2 = g_{2b}{}^{a_2}$ and $g_3 = g_{3b}{}^{a_3}$
    2. Picks random exponent s
    3. Computes $P_a = g_3{}^s$ and $Q_a = g_1{}^s\, g_2{}^x$
    4. Computes $R_a = (Q_a / Q_b)^{a_3}$
    5. Sends Bob P_a, Q_a and R_a
- Bob:
    1. Computes $R_b = (Q_a / Q_b)^{b_3}$
    2. Computes $R_{ab} = R_a{}^{b_3}$
    3. Checks whether $R_{ab} == (P_a / P_b)$
    4. Sends Alice R_b
- Alice:
    1. Computes $R_{ab} = R_b{}^{a_3}$
    2. Checks whether $R_{ab} == (P_a / P_b)$

If everything is done correctly, then R_{ab} should hold the value of (P_a / P_b) times $(g_2{}^{a_3 b_3})^{(x-y)}$, which means that the test at the end of the protocol will only succeed if x == y. Further, since $g_2{}^{a_3 b_3}$ is a random number not known to any party, if x is not equal to y, no other information is revealed.

(See also the formulas in the documentation of the source code).

Zero-Knowledge-Proof

A zero-knowledge proof or zero-knowledge protocol is a method by which one party (the prover) can prove to another party (the verifier) that they know a value x, without conveying any information apart from the fact that they know the value x. The essence of zero-knowledge proofs is that it is trivial to prove that one possesses knowledge of certain information by simply revealing it; the challenge is to prove such possession without revealing the information itself or any additional information.

If proving a statement requires that the prover possess some secret information, then the verifier will not be able to prove the statement to anyone else without possessing the secret information. The statement being proved must include the assertion that the prover has such knowledge, but not the knowledge itself. Otherwise, the statement would not be proved in zero-knowledge because it provides the verifier with additional information about the statement by the end of the protocol. A zero-knowledge proof of knowledge is a special case when the statement consists only of the fact that the prover possesses the secret information.

Interactive zero-knowledge proofs require interaction between the individual (or computer system) proving their knowledge and the individual validating the proof.

Research in zero-knowledge proofs has been motivated by authentication systems where one party wants to prove its identity to a second party via some secret information (such as a password) but doesn't want the second party to learn anything about this secret. This is called a "zero-knowledge proof of knowledge". However, a password shouldn't typically be too small or insufficiently random is used in many schemes for zero-knowledge proofs of knowledge. A zero-knowledge password proof is a special kind of zero-knowledge proof of knowledge that addresses the limited size of passwords.

Figure 41: Socialist Millionaire Protocol (SMP) in the chat window to authenticate the chat partner

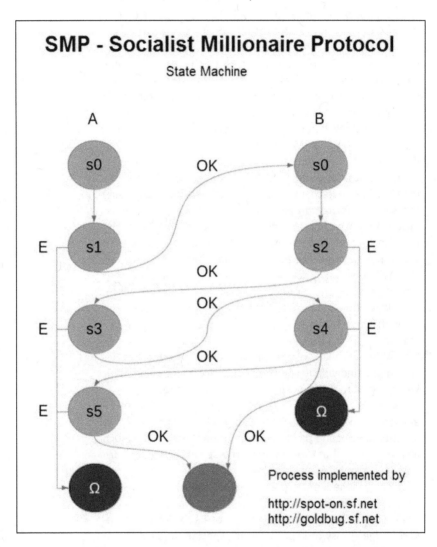

SMP therefore requires sharing a common secret with the communication partner. This is described by SMP-Cryptographic-Calling.

6.4.1 SMP-Calling

Above, we explained the Call function of how to generate and transfer a Gemini. A user can not only define the Gemini manually or through the AES function, but it can also be derived from the password used in the SMP process as outlined above. Thus, the password input from the SMP process is used (not the SMP process itself). It is another way of "Cryptographic Calling" and thus securely transmits to its counterpart an end-to-end password that does not! originate from an AES generator this time - if someone doubts the randomness of a machine number generator. Once the basic functions of encryption in Spot-On are explained in detail, the user can see, for example, the interconnectedness of the individual processes in this architecture and encryption suite, here: how the SMP process is used to create a secure end-to-end encryption. A zero-knowledge proof to derive end-to-end encrypting credentials does not transfer any key over the internet. That is the queen method of Cryptographic Calling. It can be multiplied within so called Secret Streams.

A zero-knowledge proof to derive end-to-end encrypting credentials does not transfer any key over the internet. That is the queen method of Cryptographic Calling. It can be multiplied within so called Secret Streams.

6.5 Cryptographic Calling with Secret Streams

Figure 42: Definition of Secret Streams

Secret Streams

Secret Streams are a dedicated function within the Spot-On Encryption Suite to provide a bunch of passphrases for end-to-end encryption, which are not deriving from an AES based on a random number generator but are built on a zero-knowledge proof provided by the same password entered of two participants within the Socialist Millionaire Protocol (SMP) process. This not only authenticates both users, but also provides derived passphrases on both ends, which are not transferred over the web. The Secret Streams generate a stream of bytes via the secret within the SMP process and the selected friend. The key sharing problem has been solved with Spot-On's invention of Secret Streams based on a zero-knowledge proof method. This way, a random number generator of the machine (which could be manipulated) is avoided, and also a possibly taped connection or keyboard cannot record any end-to-end encrypting password.

Hence, if the SMP password is present, it can also be used as a basis for other and more elaborated functions: The Secret Streams function - relevant for Forward Secrecy not only in chat, but also in e-mail - can be also derived from this SMP process. Secret Streams - a bunch of verified zero knowledge proofs generated by the SMP process - can also be built on the successfully verified SMP password.

Figure 43: Secret Streams based on SMP Protocol

6.6 Additional security feature: Forward Secrecy (a-symmetric)

Spot-On is also supporting Perfect Forward Secrecy within the function as an e-mail client, making it the first e-mail client to offer Forward Secrecy for e-mail, with both, symmetric and a-symmetric Forward Secrecy.

While Cryptographic Calling with a Gemini for the chat function has the "Instant Perfect Forward Secrecy" (IPFS) and refers to a symmetric key (just the Gemini or the AES string), the Perfect Forward Secrecy is for e-mail with temporary, a-symmetric keys defined.

Forward Secrecy means a compromised key cannot reveal the user, as it is a temp-key.

This variant of the use of temporary a-symmetric keys can of course also be transferred to the chat function. And this has been done since the release in 2015.

Figure 44: Definition of Forward Secrecy

Perfect Forward Secrecy
Perfect Forward Secrecy (PFS) is a feature of specific key agreement protocols that gives assurances your session keys will not be compromised even if the private key is compromised. Forward Secrecy protects past sessions against future compromises of secret keys or passwords. By generating a unique session key for every session, a user initiates, even the compromise of a single session key will not affect any data other than that exchanged in the specific session protected by that particular key.

While chat with the permanent chat key is always (a-symmetric) encrypted, a temporary a-symmetric key is now used with this new layer of end-to-end encryption. This temporary a-symmetric key is called an ephemeral key. This key is created by the forward secrecy function in the chat, which is displayed via the context menu (right mouse click) or via the menu button.

A tooltip on the screen (in the systray) indicates when the chat partner in chat has created a forward secrecy with temporary (ephemeral) a-symmetric keys, so that the user can confirm this in his client in a pop-up window. The user looks at the bottom of the status line for the newly appearing icon, clicks on it and can then confirm the forward-secrecy process in the appearing pop-up window. Then, the (temporary) chat key is no longer used, but the new, temporary a-symmetric keys. The permanent chat key is thus complemented by the temporary chat key.

Only few software applications understand end-to-end encryption as a-symmetric and build forward secrecy via a-symmetric encryption.

6.6.1   Forward Secrecy Calling

Thus, the Cryptographic Calling can be extended again: The symmetric Gemini is sent in the Forward Secrecy Calling (FSC) not as described above by the permanent (a-symmetric) chat key or by an existing (symmetric) Gemini, but by the new ephemeral, temporary and a-symmetric chat key.

While sending a Gemini over an existing Gemini defines a "symmetric" "instant perfect forward secrecy", sending a Gemini over the ephemeral keys of the initiated "forward secrecy" in the chat function may be considered an "a-symmetric" one of "Instant Perfect Forward Secrecy".

(While sending a Gemini via the permanent chat keys is also called an a-symmetric "Instant Perfect Forward Secrecy").

While "Forward Secrecy Calling" and "Call by a Gemini" already have a "Forward Secrecy" and then define the renewability of the end-to-end key at any time (Instant Perfect Forward Secrecy), the other Calling Types are not with Forward Secrecy given in advance. Instant Perfect Forward Secrecy is generated here only by a call as a result of the call.

The continuation of Forward Secrecy is called – to abstract a bit more from MELODICA and Instant Perfect Forward Secrecy (IPFS) - Forward Secrecy Calling.

6.6.2   Fiasco Forwarding & Fiasco Calling

Fiasco Forwarding should be mentioned here only brief: Forward Secrecy has been developed to Instant Perfect Forward Secrecy (IPFS, or even 2WIPFS) and this paradigm has already been extended by Fiasco Forwarding (FF) within the mobile Echo Client: Smoke. Here Fiasco Calling – as a another further development of Cryptographic Calling - has been introduced, which sends a bunch of keys to the friend with one Call.

Cryptographic Calling with Fiasco Forwarding has been implemented in the Mobile Echo Client of Smoke and the referring Crypto Chat Server Smoke-Stack.

Then the recipient must try out over a dozen keys which are sorted and tried out from newest to oldest.

This Fiasco Forwarding has not been yet implemented in Spot-On Echo Client, as it was developed for the Smoke Echo Client. It should be mentioned here in this context, that even another Calling Feature could be established structurally and is already coded into the Smoke Client, which is also compatible with the Listeners/Servers from Spot-On.

This is especially of interest to be compared with the Signal Protocol, which is more schematic and determines the (one) key for the message in the last message sent out before and is not able to be steered by a manual action of the user to send out a new ephemeral key or even a bunch of these. A Fiasco for old-fashioned protocols? Multiplied potential Keys for a Message.

6.7   Overview of the different Calling types

End-to-end encryption in Spot-On is as simple as making a phone call - simply by pressing a button: just pick up or hang up the phone. At any time, the communication remains a-symmetric encrypted and the symmetric end-to-end encryption can be easily added - and also renewed by a-symmetric or symmetric encryption (within a TLS/SSL channel). This is a new architectural implementation standard established by these methods of Cryptographic Calling, invented through the development of the software application Spot-On.

From the methods described to transfer an end-to-end key to the friend, the following overview can be created, which highlights the different methods with their respective specific characteristics (see figure).

The call information - that is the end-to-end encrypting passphrase (if not ephemeral PKI is used) - can of course also be transmitted manually, e.g. verbally or by telephone. If one adds the above-mentioned existing call types, it concludes then in total in seven different ways to be able to implement a call. For the first time, the Spot-On architecture has spoken in the cryptographic discipline of "Cryptographic Calling" in regard of the transmission of end-to-end passwords. Later concepts have borrowed this term.

Figure 45: Overview of the different types of Cryptographic Calling with respective criteria

Criteria	Asymmet-ric Calling	Forward Secrecy Calling	Symmetric Calling	SMP Calling	Secret Streams	Fiasco Forwarding	2-Way Calling
TLS/SSL-Connection	YES	YES	YES	YES	YES	YES	YES
Permanent asymmet-ric Chat/E-Mail Key	YES	YES	YES	YES	YES	YES	YES
Symmetric AES as Gemini	NO	NO	YES	NO	NO	NO	NO
Half AES + Half AES	NO	NO	NO	NO	NO	NO	YES
Secret SMP Password	NO	NO	NO	YES	YES	NO	NO
Ephemeral/temp. Chat/E-Mail PKI-Key	NO	YES	NO	NO	NO	NO	NO
Forward Secrecy as Pre-Condition	NO	YES	YES	NO	NO	YES	NO
Instant Perfect Forward Secrecy as result	YES	YES	YES	YES	YES	YES	YES
Several keys as a result	NO	NO	NO	NO	YES	YES	NO

Please note the following explanations:
- Each of the presented methods results in Instant Perfect Forward Secrecy (IPFS).
- Only Symmetric and A-symmetric Calling requires no action on the part of the other party.
- Forward Secrecy Calling and Symmetric Calling require an existing status of Forward Secrecy.
- 'Symmetric Calling' and 'Forward Secrecy Calling' have triple encryption layers (TLS/SSL, Permanent

Chat Key, as well as a temporary symmetric or a-symmetric key through which the new Gemini will then be sent).

- 'SMP Calling' and '2-Way-Calling' break AES generation by replacing parts of the AES phrase and creating a new password string.
- Secret Streams and Fiasco Forwarding provide a bunch of potential temporary future keys.

The message formats with the encryption levels then look simplified - since signatures, HMACs and hashes are not included - as follows:

- Asymmetric Calling: (TLS/SSL (Permanent Chat Key e.g. RSA (message is an AES string)))
- Forward Secrecy Calling : (TLS/SSL (Permanent Chat Key e.g. RSA (ephemeral keys RSA (message is an AES string))))
- Symmetric Calling: (TLS/SSL (AES (Permanent Chat Key e.g. RSA (message is an AES string)))
- SMP Calling : (TLS/SSL (permanent chat key e.g. RSA (message is a string formed from the SMP)))
- Two-way-calling: (TLS/SSL (Permanent chat key e.g. RSA (message is an AES string that is 50% modified with friend's AES)))

From this variety of options in securing end-to-end encryption or even defining and manually entering the end-to-end encryption passphrase, the slogan, claim or headline has emerged: "Your Instant Definition in Decentralized Crypto" (as provided in the GoldBug GUI). The encryption is thus not only a user-specific, which can be renewed (instant) at any time, but also a decentralized at the user's place and machine - defined and designed by him- or herself.

A simple litmus test compared to other software applications is the simple question of whether the user can enter the end-to-end encrypting password himself; or, if the user can send a bunch of keys; or, if the user can use a zero-knowledge-proof to create security besides the random of the number generator of the machine. With Spot-On the user can do all this (as well as with the mobile version of Spot-On: Smoke Chat currently for Android).

6.8 Emoticons aka Smileys

Spot-On offers a variety of different emoticons - also called smileys - for chatting (see figure).

Figure 46: Emoticon list in Spot-On Encryption Suite

To use the emoticons, the user clicks twice on a friend, so a pop-up chat window opens for private chat. If the user now moves the mouse over the Send button, the smileys are displayed in a tooltip that appears. By entering the ASCI code, the emoticons are then displayed in the chat.

In settings, the options also allow the user to turn off the graphical display of smileys in general.

6.9 File transfer in the chat pop-up window

The Qt menu allows to remove individual menu parts from the regular user interface and to create a pop-up window for certain settings.

Figure 47: Tear-off / hook-up of controls

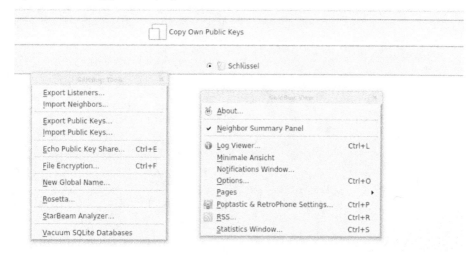

Likewise, the file-sharing function in particular is integrated in a pop-up menu: In the 1:1 chat window. So if a user wants to send a file to a specific friend, the user can simply click the button "share" within the pop-up chat window for that friend.

The shared file as well as the text is transmitted securely and encrypted to the friend. The file transfer feature is called StarBeam and also has its own tab but is already built into the 1:1-chat-window for easy and direct usability. Just another little hook-up menu.

Figure 48: File transfer in the pop-up chat window

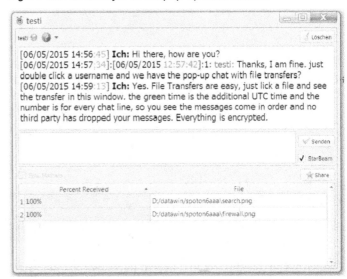

File Sharing in an encrypting messenger is based on friend-to-friend (web of trust) connections. No one can investigate the file, which is sent to a friend. That's encryption.

In general, the chat is easy to use with several ways for Cryptographic Calling and end-to-end security of the connection. The user can be authenticated with SMP and a file can easily be shared over the secure connection within the chat. In which other application can a file be sent over instantly renewable end-to-end-secured connections over an own encryption handling chat server?

Questions and further Research & Development Fields

- Describe one method for Cryptographic Calling.
- What`s the difference between Secret Streams and Fiasco Forwarding?
- Describe the zero-knowledge proof in the SMP process.
- What's the advantage of IPFS?

7 Group chat in IRC style

In addition to chat and e-mail and transferring files to the communication partners, Spot-On Encryption Suite also has also a group chat feature. This works like an IRC chat. The transmission of the messages to all group participants is again fully encrypted via the Echo Protocol. The encryption is symmetric, similar to a password string. Finally, in the p2p network or via the chat server, all subscribers can read a group chat who know the particular symmetric end-to-end key that defines the chat room. The group chat is also based on the Echo Protocol.

Figure 49: The e'IRC group chat

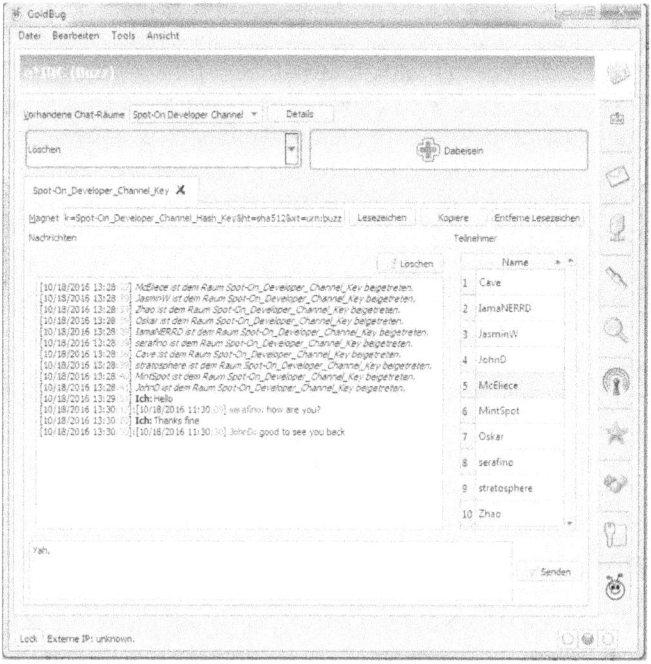

It is therefore spoken of Echo'ed IRC (or in short e'IRC). That opens new options for the IRC chat, since the transport routes of the e'IRC chat are also encrypted.

As normal POP3 or IMAP e-mails today also have at least one transport encryption, e.g. with TLS 1.3, IRC can also be understood as an encrypted group chat. Also, the traditional IRC chat can therefore learn from such security models and improve: The e'IRC chat can represent a model of a new group chat generation. Echo introduced and provides a kind of transport encryption for IRC group chat.

The encryption details of the group chat are again defined via a Magnet URI link (see below) (defined in the link with extension &URN=buzz). Buzz is the technical name in the source code for the e'IRC group chat.

Buzz Group Chat is based on symmetric encryption: The room name is the passphrase.

To start the Spot-On group chat, open the as preset given community chat room, which can serve as an example. Here, the user can ask the other present users questions about the program or just use this channel with a friend (e.g. to exchange their public keys).

To join an own channel, the user simply enters a room or channel name or uses the Magnet link method above. The Magnet link has embedded additional values for encryption in addition to the room name, such as key, hash or cipher for the encryption type.

If the user enters only the room name and does not use a Magnet URI, the additional encryption details are set to the value 0000 and the encryption of the room is based on the room name only. If the user has entered all the values or the room name (or pasted the Magnet link), then the "Join" button is just to be pressed.

If the user has inserted a Magnet as link, then in the pull-down menu the command "de-Magnetize" should be used first. The Magnet is then broken down into its individual components and the room is created and entered based on the encryption values embedded in the Magnet link.

If the room is open, the user can also save the room as a bookmark or copy the corresponding Magnet-URI at any time from this chat room as a bookmark and send it to friends to invite them to the room.

Figure 50: IRC-style group chat within the e'IRC buzz channel

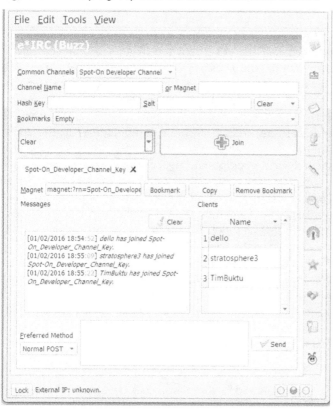

In order to send a message, the user then enters a text in the chat room and presses the send button.

The Buzz or e'IRC chat room can be public or private, depending on how much the user announces the Magnet or the individual encryption values. As a public e'IRC chat room, the user can post or link the Magnet-URI on the own website and everyone knows how to get into that chat room: with "de-Magnetize".

Ultimately, it works for these news channels like an IRC chat, only with the difference that the Internet provider and other rooting servers cannot look into the communication, since it is encrypted - as a connection in online banking too.

So it does not make any difference whether a user is talking to friends or to the online bank advisor.

If the user wants to use the chat room as a private room, the user can secretly share the Magnet-URI only with the own friends and they stay on their own privacy. This is a convenient feature of the Spot-On program: the user can simply chat encrypted without first exchanging a-symmetric (PKI) keys. The user simply tells his friend verbally that he should come in Spot-On on a certain server in the room "Amber Room" and both participants can very easily and securely chat encrypted using a common chat server.

A One-Time Magnet is a link to a chat room (or to a file), which is randomly composed and used only once.

Tip: The user can create a one-time Magnet for a room. This is used to protect his public chat key when exchanging the key with the communication partner through the (self-defined) IRC channel. It requires that the Magnet-URI is only known to the friend.

With the REPLEO, with EPKS and the key exchange via an one-time Magnet (OTM) for a private e'IRC group chat room, Spot-On offers several methods for a secure key transfer. Thus, public keys no longer have to be public! (compare: Kerckhoffs's principle, Shannon's maxim). Let's foster and re-define or re-define and foster!

Questions and further Research & Development Fields

- Define a Magnet for the Group Chat and let a friend demagnetize it.
- Program a bridge in Qt, so that in Spot-On also regular plaintext IRC channels can be read.
- Try to bring a group chat window into the browser with a Spot-On-Kernel connected to Python, Apache and further tools like PHP or JavaScript.

8 Smoke Mobile Chat Client

While Spot-On is a desktop client that is compiled and deployed on numerous operating systems as well as platforms such as Raspberry Pi, the mobile client of the Echo Protocol is called "Smoke Chat" and developed in Java.

Spot On is coded in C++ wit Qt and used on Desktops.

8.1 Smoke Android Client

Smoke offers a direct 1:1 chat to a friend as well as a group chat. The group chat in Smoke is called FireChat and it is similar and compatible to the Buzz/e'IRC group chat in Spot-On.

The Android mobile version is called Smoke and uses Java.

The 1:1 chat of Smoke on the mobile device does not use the phone number of the participants as an identifier, but a short string, a so-called SIP hash, is used as an identifier.

Smoke users connect to a common server - this can be a Spot-On, GoldBug, Spot-On-Lite, and SmokeStack server listener - and then swap their public key over the SIP hash connection, which is used for symmetric encryption of this channel. SmokeStack is a chat server for Android and can serve around 500 users on an Android device - ideal for a workshop group, family or within school.

8.2 Fire chat to Buzz chat

Since Java and C++ programming do not know common key formats from the crypto libraries, it is usually not possible to use an open source Java client to chat encrypted to a C++ client.

Group chat from both clients is possible over FireChat (of Smoke) and Buzz-Chat (of Spot-On).

Smoke, however, has innovated and implemented a way to do so: the so-called FireChat in Smoke can also be used to reach a user in Spot-On and vice versa. This is based on a symmetric encrypted chat (like a symmetric Crypto Call).

Other applications mostly use the Java Script Crypto libraries for the browser or connect to a central server, but these methods are generally considered to be less secure.

So if a user wants to use a mobile version of Spot-On for the chat, this can be found in Smoke Chat and under the concept description MOMEDO (both at Github: https://github.com/textbrowser/smoke).

Offline Messaging in Smoke uses so-called Ozone-Postboxes on the SmokeStack Server for Android. These offline messaging postboxes will be also described in the next chapter about e-mail and p2p e-mail postboxes.

Figure 51: Mobile Smoke Messenger with left-right chat layout

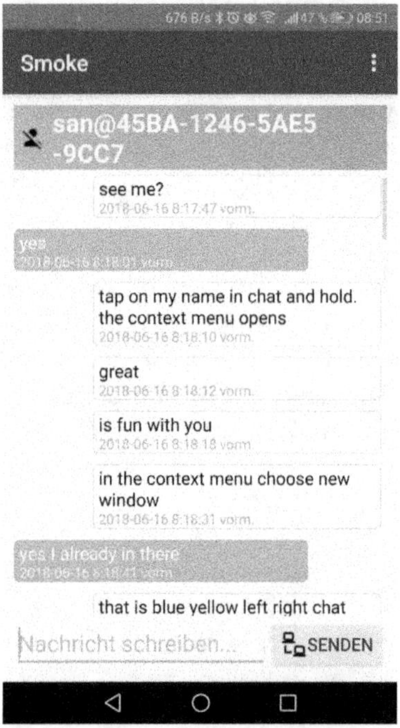

Essential for mobile encrypted Messaging is not the GUI of the client, but the option to set up an own server.

Smoke uses the App SmokeStack as Server on Android or a Spot-On-Listener.

Questions and further Research & Development Fields

- Define a Group Chat from FireChat of Smoke to a Group Chat of Spot-On.

9 The e-mail function

Spot-On is a fully functional e-mail client.

Not fully - like e-mail applications that have existed for decades - here it still needs further programming from the community, but fully functional in the sense of a fully usable e-mail client. The advantage: the reading and writing of e-mails is shown very efficiently in the user interface on one page respective in one tab (see figure). And: the emails to other Spot-On users are always encrypted.

Spot-On uses technically the library CURL and supports POP3, SMTP and IMAP. Finally, Spot-On's special feature is that it also supports p2p e-mail and p2p hosted mailboxes: Here the e-mail is stored in the distributed network of the participants and not at a central provider. With Spot-On, users can very easily provide an e-mail server and communicate with it. The infrastructure is not only easy to install but can also be created by the user.

From a future perspective, this is also the (necessary) progress, that users of the Internet organize the Internet again more on their own and use cryptography within their own encrypted mailboxes that are not deposited at central hosters, but on their own network of participants.

Figure 52: E-Mail - read view (shown here in the GoldBug GUI)

After all, centralization is always followed by decentralization, even though only the users, who recognize and value this freedom, will pay attention to decentralization necessities and such remaining opportunities in the future.

Here's how to set up the three ways to load own emails:

9.1   POP3

The Post Office Protocol POP3 is a transmission Protocol that enables a client to pick up e-mails from an e-mail server. POP3 allows you to list, retrieve and delete emails on the e-mail server. For sending e-mails, additionally the Simple Mail Transfer Protocol (SMTP) is usually implemented in clients and servers as a complement to POP3.

The POP3 Protocol is thus integrated in all popular e-mail programs, including Spot-On. How it is set up next to IMAP is explained below and also further below in the description of the window of POPTASTIC (see the following pages).

9.2   IMAP

The Internet Message Access Protocol (IMAP) on the other hand was designed in the 1980s with the emergence of personal computers to resolve the e-mail storage on individual client computers in the mail communication.

That is, the (PC) clients instead access the information online on the servers and, if necessary, receive copies of it.

While a user of POP3 has lost all e-mails after losing his or her PC (if e-mails on the server are not kept), a mail client at IMAP only copies the requests to the server for the information currently required.

For example, if a user wants to see the content of the inbox folder, the client will get an up-to-date copy of the message list from the server. If the content of an e-mail is to be displayed, it is loaded as a copy from the server. As all data remains on the central server, a "local storage of the data" is unnecessary and extended possibilities such as the search of mails are also performed only on the server side.

This also makes a local taking-over of the data - by taking it away from the server - mostly impossible, as the configuration of IMAP by default is not geared to it. At the same time, the issue of confidentiality and security of data that is outsourced to IMAP servers comes to the fore in the case of unencrypted e-mail. The question arises as to whether the recipient of an e-mail has jurisdiction over the confidentiality and storage of the e-mail itself, e.g. has the right not to show it to anyone or to delete it in secret, or if the recipient only has one copy, gets a "right of view" of the own mail.

However, and however the central delete of POP3 or IMAP e-mails on a central server is defined, with regard to the findings from 2013 – to better encrypt emails fundamentally - IMAP is to be judged particularly critically in this light: The storage of emails is not made at IMAP as in POP3 in the mail client on the machine of the user, but the personal data remains mostly still unencrypted on the server of the provider. With IMAP the cloud, which is widely used today, was invented in the field of e-mail in the 1980s. POP3 is more likely to enable on-premises handling of e-mail storage on the local machine.

Still it is better to store even encrypted e-mails in the local repository on the own machine, in case the algorithm can be compromised. Don't leave e-mail copies on central servers, even if they are encrypted, if you want to have exclusive ownership or privacy of it.

Spot-On supports both standards and makes it possible to receive and send plain text messages via IMAP and POP3. If data is encrypted in IMAP or POP3 postboxes, it does not matter, which of both is used. Here's how to enter the settings for an e-mail account in Spot-On.

Detailed description of POP3 / IMAP setup options:
Via the main menu "View" of the Spot-On Encryption Suite the own e-mail address and the POP-3 or IMAP server details are stored. These are the same details that are also entered, for example, in the Thunderbird e-mail client or Outlook, for example:

- "Incomming Server Server:" pop.gmail.com Port: 995 TLS Username: mygmailname@gmail.com Password: ** **
- "Outgoing Server Server:" smtp.gmail.com Port: 587 TLS Username: mygmailname@gmail.com Password: ** **

The user can press the test button to check the functionality of the server input. With the "OK" button then the inputs are stored.
(If the value "Disabled" is used in the selection menu instead of POP3 or IMAP, the program no longer sends e-mails: the mail function is completely switched off.)

Users who want to use the chat function described below via the POP3/IMAP e-mail server (that is the POPTASTIC protocol, see below) should therefore not deactivate the e-mail information.

Figure 53: POPTASTIC: chat via e-mail server

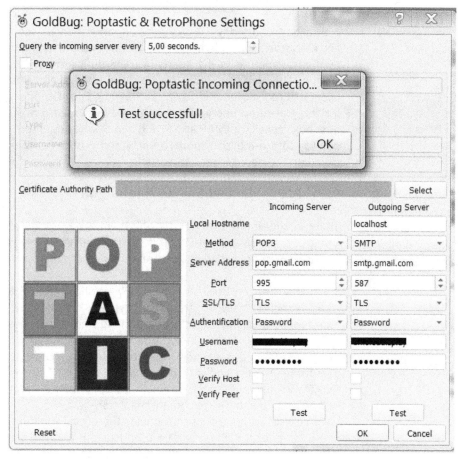

According to the above security considerations, a user should always load own e-mails right from the server onto the own machine and delete the e-mails on the server, if they are not encrypted. So, there seems to be much to talk about using POP3 instead of IMAP, as IMAP is more focused on keeping emails on the server. A central repositorium.

In general, e-mails in this light do not belong to a remote server, not into the cloud, not into a browser-based web service - they are stored on the user's own machine - or they are in any case to be encrypted for such a temporary postbox cache.

But the trend today is exactly the opposite: Central servers that store the messages, without encryption, without own infrastructure in the hands of users define the mainstream. This will last, until the trend reverses again, and users will rediscover their own sovereignty. Spot-On offers for this transition encryption for the old-fashioned e-mail-post box caches (of IMAP and POP3) and also several methods to store e-mails in modern encrypted postbox caches based on the peer-to-peer network.

To e-mail a friend, use the e-mail key, the POPTASTIC key or the @-e-mail address.

9.3   P2P E-Mail: without data retention

Third, in addition to IMAP and POP3, there is the option of using p2p e-mail in Spot-On. This means that the e-mails are not stored or cached in a central server, but in the client of a friend.

Regarding encryption, it has already been shown that the e-mail function uses a different encryption key than the chat function. So the user can add a friend to the chat, but refuse the e-mail or vice versa. It makes sense, however, to copy all the keys as a whole, then the user has his friend present in all functions (so e.g. in addition the URL key, the POPTASTIC key and the Rosetta key - several functions that will be described in the upcoming chapters).

Of course, with the key transfer for the e-mail function, the security of a REPLEO can be used again, if a user does not want to reveal the own public e-mail key to the public.

No matter which e-mail method a user chooses, whether POP3, IMAP or P2P, outgoing e-mails to cryptographic keys in Spot-On are always encrypted, there is only one exception, that is if the user in the Add Participant Window does not adds a Key (or a REPLEO), but chooses the selection:

Add E-Mail-Address. Then the e-mail program of Spot-On sends unencrypted text from @ -mail to @ -mail.

Note: Anyone entering a POPTASTIC key will also see the @E-Mail address in the contact list for e-mail, but it is color-coded and also has a padlock icon, which means it will be a POPTASTIC e-mail address (a key) — just used for encrypted emailed - and also chat. After all, a key is inserted for POP-TASTIC (and not an @-e-mail address). Only e-mails sent to @-e-mail addresses that do not have a lock symbol remain unencrypted.

To clarify again:
The user can use the following ways by e-mail

- The e-mail key: This can send e-mails via POP3, IMAP and P2P.
- The POPTASTIC KEY: This can send chat via POP3 and IMAP.
- The @mail address: This can send unencrypted emails from regular @mail addresses via POP3 and IMAP to @mail addresses (not to keys).

Therefore, two Spot-On users can exchange encrypted e-mails with normal @Mail, e.g. via the major e-mail providers such as Ymail, Gmail, GMX, Outlook etc. without any further technical knowledge: either unencrypted via @-mail addresses or encrypted as chat over the POPTASTIC key, which will be explained later. And thirdly, the user can always use the e-mail key to send encrypted e-mails, including p2p.

This is very comfortable in that it is enough to exchange the keys once. So, it is not every single e-mail that the user writes, to encrypt each time again individually (as previously practiced in other software procedures). Each @-mail provider can now be exempted from viewing the user's e-mails by simply pushing encrypted cipher text over the central server to the communication partner. What is needed is the agreement with the friend that the friend also uses Spot-On or one of the other Echo clients as an e-mail client to exchange the keys only once.

E-Mail attachments can also be attached to an e-mail as a file and are automatically encrypted regardless of which encryption e-mail method is chosen. This is also possible with several attachments.

In addition to the discussion for the encryption of e-mails, the meta-data is still stored in many countries, i.e. when and how often a user retrieves the messages from the own mailbox. Here is the alternative method of p2p e-mails interesting: Spot-On also makes it possible to store e-mails on the subscriber network (or on its own server) and decentralize the corresponding e-mail inboxes, which also exclusively and automatically handle the standard of encrypted e-mails.

The e-mail client thus also contains a peer-to-peer-based component, i.e. the e-mails are sent over the network of the encrypted connections and buffered in the nodes of friends. This network is provided by the integrated architecture of the Spot-on kernel. The advantage of p2p e-mail is that the e-mail inbox does not reside with a central host and public e-mail provider but can be set up in the decentralized network of the user's own friends.

3 ways to store e-mails in the p2p network:
- *C/O-function,*
- *VEMI Institutions,*
- *OZONE Postboxes.*

With Spot-On everyone can easily set up an e-mail inbox for own friends. Nobody can then log when and how often a user retrieves own e-mails. The Echo Protocol also helps to minimize metadata that reveals who has read which e-mail and who is storing an e-mail for whom (since the opening of the encrypted messages occurs exclusively on the user's machine and each node - according to the Echo Protocol - sends each message to everyone).

How to set up a mailbox for friends is shown in the following section:

9.4 Setting up C/O: e-mail postboxes at a friend

The interesting thing about the Spot-On e-mail feature - and here it may differ from other p2p e-mail implementations - is that it's also possible to send e-mail to friends who are offline.

There are three different methods for doing this:

9.4.1 Care-Of method (C/O)

One method is to use a third, common friend to temporarily store the e-mails there with this dedicated friend. So, if Alice and Bob set up a common chat server on the web on their web infrastructure, and all three of them have swapped their keys, the web server (as common friend) acts like an e-mail inbox, as we know it from POP3 or IMAP.

Figure 54: P2P e-mail from the postbox to a friend: C/O function (shown in the GoldBug Interface)

Basically, the e-mails do not need central servers; it can also be a third friend or a small Raspberry Pi computer at home, which remains online. It therefore makes sense to have more than one friend in the own list and to network friends with other friends who can act for a caching. Since all e-mails are encrypted, the friends who provide a cache function cannot read the user's e-mail either.

Also, the e-mails are stored in encrypted databases. The figure shows that even cipher text is displayed even when viewing the structure of the database file.

Figure 55: Database encryption – file email.db

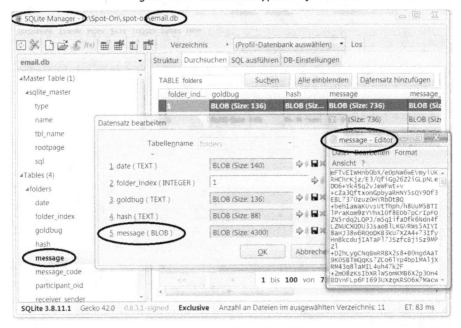

In order to activate this Care-Of (C/O) caching function, the check-box "Care-Of" must be activated in the sub-tab "E-Mail Settings". If two friends are then connected to each other and to the third friend and want to enable the caching of e-mails in their own clients, then all have just to insert the other two friends in the own e-mail contact list.

The Spot-On user can also choose to have the e-mails sent authenticated or unauthenticated in the p2p e-mail network, so they can simply be sent encrypted without evidence that the key belongs to a particular user.

The Care-Of P2P e-mail feature is one of the simplest in the software landscape for P2P e-mail at all. If three users share a common Echo server and have added each other as a friend, only the C/O feature needs to be activated, and the e-mails are stored in the friends of friend's cache, in case they are offline. Nothing is simpler than this architecture: The user only needs a few friends who want to participate in this process for internal communication within a group.

The second method is the establishment of a virtual e-mail institution. This is great for people who like to equip an entire community of friends with an e-mail inbox. It requires a bit administration but the VEMI method for postboxes could replace IMAP postboxes in the future, as it handles only encrypted e-mails.

9.4.2 Virtual E-Mail Institution ("VEMI") method

For this it is also necessary to activate the C/O function with the check box as described above.

Then the user can create a so-called "Virtual E-Mail Institution" (VEMI).

For the text and definition fields "Name" and "Address" of the institution, the user can freely get creative and choose any name. Then the public e-mail keys of the friends who want to save e-mails in this institution are still to be copied into this node.

Finally, the user can then copy out the created Magnet-URI-link and make it available to friends who then temporarily store in that mailbox. (For the Magnet-URI standard and what that is, see also below in the file transfer section with "StarBeam"). In addition, please remember: the node that sets up the e-mail institution must always also add the public e-mail key of the user for which it is to save the e-mails.

The advantage over the first method is that the public e-mail key of the node setting up the institution need not be disclosed to anyone. With the C/O method, however, the public e-mail key must be exchanged. Therefore, one can easily say that in the small friends network a common node with the C/O function is ideal and the VEMI method of setting up Virtual E-Mail Institutions tends to focus on vendors who want to set up mailboxes for a larger number of subscribers.

Settings example:
Here is an example of how the C/O function and the VEMI function, i.e. the creation of a virtual e-mail institution, are implemented step by step:

- The user activates the C/O function in the e-mail settings tab.
- The user creates an institution and chooses a name and address for the institution.
- Example: Institution-Name = "p2p mailbox" and address = "Dotcom"
- The user inserts the e-mail key of a friend into the own client. The user then copies the available e-mail Magnet from the own e-mail institution and has the friends to paste it into their program.

The user recognizes an e-mail Magnet at his ending: URN = institution. Then you know that the Magnet is not a buzz-group chat Magnet nor a StarBeam Magnet for file sharing - they would have the suffix "URN = buzz" or "URN = starbeam". The Magnet for an institution will look like this one:

Figure 56: URN = Institution (VEMI Method)

URN = Institution
Magnet: in = p2p mailbox & ct = aes256 & pa = Dotcom & ht = sha512 & xt = urn: institution

So, after adding the Magnet-Link for an Institution the referring node will cache the e-mails of the friends in the established institution - if necessary especially for participants, which appear to be offline.

The user (as creator of an e-mail institution) does not need to exchange his own e-mail key with the friends or "subscribers" of this institution. The creator of an e-mail institution can also exchange the e-mail keys of the friends in a group chat room via e'IRC/Buzz. The exchange process of key & e-mail Magnet does not have to impart any further identities.

9.4.3   Ozone Postbox

Ozone Postbox is a method, which should be just mentioned here, as it is implemented in the application Smoke and Smokestack Server, the first Echo applications for Android. SmokeStack provides a Postbox for all users of this mobile Echo Messenger, which is also compatible with the Servers/Listeners of Spot-On. Currently Smoke is workable with a Spot-On Listener/Server, but Spot-On has currently no Ozone Postboxes, as they are only provided for the Smoke Messenger Client in relation to the mobile Smoke-Stack Server.

Individual, customer-oriented and further research is needed for the best method to reach other offline users over own communication servers in a p2p federate-able network.

> It will be up to **further research** based on customer and case needs to compare the three messaging methods to offline users: C/O, Institutions (VEMI) and Ozone Postboxes in their optimal functionality and probably also add the IMAP/POP3 postbox method for the POPTASTIC Protocol (which might have probably a bit of a delay in comparison to presence messaging servers and their postboxes for offline appearing users).

Next to IMAP and POP3 Postboxes now also further methods exist like C/O, Institutions and Ozone-Postboxes, which are more related to encryption than the old storage options.

9.5 Additional Encryption: Put a "Goldbug" on an e-mail

If you like it, put a Goldbug on It.

Regardless of which transmission and cache method a user chooses, whether POP3, IMAP or p2p, the e-mails are always encrypted using the public (a-symmetric) e-mail (or POPTASTIC) key and the Echo Protocol for transmission.

This is also the case if e-mails are cached in an intermediate station such as a provider mailbox or a virtual institution or an intermediate node of a friend. Transport encryption and end-to-end encryption is consistent throughout.

As additional security for the e-mail function there is - similar to the so-called "Gemini" for Cryptographic Calling in chat-, now for e-mails the option to set a password on the e-mail: Not only the alternative GUI for the Spot-On Kernel is called GoldBug, but also the function in the e-mail client to set an additional password on the e-mail is called "Goldbug" (please note the different writing).

E-mails that have a "Goldbug" password set (see below the description of the file transfer function "StarBeam", here the additional password is "NOVA") can only be read by the recipient if they have the appropriate "Goldbug" - so the user needs to know the golden key as a password. The user should therefore inform the friends about the password to be entered if the user sends them e-mails that still require an additional password in order to be opened.

Symmetric Encryption:
- *Gemini for chat,*
- *Goldbug for e-mail,*
- *Nova for file transfer.*

This can be, for example, in the e-mails to the own wife, that the user always encrypts the e-mails with the name of the city in which the wedding or the wedding holiday took place.

Again, as with the chat with the Gemini, and as we will still see with file-sharing with the NOVA, the Goldbug Password is an important feature of symmetric and end-to-end encryption for e-mail that the user can individually and manually create for an end-to-end encrypting password.

In addition to the reminiscence of the short story by Edgar Allen Poe about a cryptogram and his work for cryptography in the early years of the beginning of industrialization - the Goldbug on an e-mail is a new idea, next to automatically encrypted e-mail created by the key exchange. It is a-symmetric encrypted e-mail, but also with a symmetric encryption: the Goldbug on an e-mail. It is another, hybrid and multi-encrypting layer per single e-mail, as this process, to touch each individual e-mail, is so far the standard (elsewhere by PGP, but here additionally symmetric).

This process is done without additional encryption software, which elsewhere must be additionally installed e.g. as a plugin. Here, integrated within the e-mail client.

9.6   Forward Secrecy for e-mail

Using the included architecture of the Spot-on kernel, Spot-On is one of the first e-mail programs in the world to offer Forward Secrecy encryption, which can be both, a-symmetric and symmetric for e-mail – so both methods within one e-mail Program are supported.

Spot-On is one of the first e-mail programs to offer FS Encryption with both encryption methods.

Forward Secrecy means – just to remember - that temporary keys are used to transmit the end-to-end encrypting password, so that if later an analysis should be made in regard of the communication and the encryption, not the regular (permanent) key for the communication is affected.

The user now sends the e-mail partner a session-based, symmetric (forward secrecy) key via the usual a-symmetrical encryption of the e-mail key (see figure).

Figure 57: E-mail with forward secrecy

If the partner confirms the request and returns his tempo-rary key, then both parties can use session-based a-symmetric keys to further secure the e-mail communica-tion. Incidentally, this method of a-symmetrical end-to-end backup was not only integrated for e-mail, but also for the chat function (see above: Forward Secrecy (FS) Calling).

The permanent public key is then used only to transport the session-based keys - not to transport the message (or: the previous message becomes the new key to the follow-ing message). That is, the ephemeral (temporary) key is shared with the partner via the permanent public e-mail key. Then, if the ephemeral public key was correctly accept-ed by a recipient, said recipient also generates an ephem-eral session key (symmetric), which is then sent back to the user via the user's public key as well.

The initiator then deletes its a-symmetric ephemeral keys as soon as the temporary session has ended.

So, when a user writes an e-mail, Spot-On has four forward-secrecy modes available to encrypt the e-mail:

- **Normal encrypted:** The e-mail is sent as usual within the encrypted system (Echo or POPTASTIC), that is, the regular permanent symmetric e-mail key is used to encrypt the message.

- **Forward Secrecy Encrypted:** Regular encryption uses session-based forward secrecy keys - that is, the user sends session-based keys over the permanent e-mail key channel and then encrypts his message with the temporary keys. So, this adds to the message another a-symmetrically encrypted level to the already existing e-mail encryption.

- **Pure Forward Secrecy Encrypted ("Pure FS"):** The message is encrypted and sent only through the user's session-based (ephemeral) e-mail key. The permanent e-mail key is thus not used in the "Pure FS": This can therefore also be called the "instant" option within the e-mail process, that means it is immediate (in the sense of volatile) and a kind of one-time e-mail. This generates quasi mail-addresses and mailboxes in the sense of encrypted data packets - which can be deleted after the session. This creates one-time e-mail accounts thanks to Pure Forward Secrecy.

- **Goldbug encrypted:** A Spot-On node sets as described above a Goldbug password on the e-mail (e.g. with an AES, symmetric encryption) and the user must inform the e-mail partner about the password, ideally verbally. Just another layer: The thus symmetrically encrypted message is then also sent via the a-symmetric e-mail encryption (permanent e-mail key).

If the user selects the checkbox option "plain" next to the e-mail text, the e-mail is not written in HTML rich text mode, but in plain text mode. Word plain text has nothing to do here in terms of an antonym to cipher text.

Again, with the following attention to understanding: through the permanent (a-symmetric) key (for e-mail (or so in chat) ephemeral keys (as a-symmetrical keys) are exchanged, which are then the basis for the use of end-to-end encryption. That means, the ephemeral keys can be deleted at any time after use and the communication is not tied to the identities in the sense of permanent keys.

One should not be confused here, because even the end-to-end encrypting symmetric passphrases are ephemeral keys. But it becomes more apparent if only the a-symmetric temporary keys which are pushed through the permanent a-symmetric e-mail keys are initially referred to as ephemeral keys (so that this is not confusing to those who are dealing with the forward-secrecy process or the word "ephemeral key" for the first time).

The encryption levels in Forward Secrecy in the Spot-On e-mail program can be described simplified as follows:

- External encryption level: SSL/TSL connection,
- Possible, additional encryption level: permanent a-symmetric e-mail key (not with "Pure FS" - otherwise: first-ephemeral-then-permanent),
- Further level, which may later be deleted: Ephemeral, temporary a-symmetric key (used only to transfer symmetric keys),
- First encryption level via Forward Secrecy: Symmetric key,
- Alternative first encryption level via a Goldbug Password on an e-mail: Symmetric key via a manually defined Goldbug on the e-mail. The message format is thus: (TLS/SSL (AES-Goldbug (e-mail message)).) According to Encrypt-then-Mac, this can be called "Goldbug-then-Permanent." The Goldbug on an e-mail encrypts the text in the envelope.

Temporary keys are not derived from permanent keys and have no relation to them in the generation. Session periods are defined manually by the user. This means that unlike other programs, the session is automatically defined by the online coming and going back offline, but the user himself determines when he wants to use new session-based keys. Again, this can be anytime and "instant" (see above: IPFS).

The process or Protocol for forward secrecy within e-mail can be described as follows with this example:

1. I send you my postal address. This is public.
2. You also send me your postal address. This is public.
3. Our addresses are permanent. These addresses change only when we move.

  • Days later -
4. I make a unique envelope, an ephemeral envelope.
5. I send you, and only you, my unique envelope. Of course, I use your postal address to send you this. We assume, only you can read the written sentences. I could also sign the draft with my signature.

  • On the same day -
6. You will receive my unique envelope and you will also verify it by my signature, if you like.
7. You create a special letter.
8. You bundle the special letter into the unique envelope I sent you.
9. Once you have sealed it, only I can open it.
10. You send the unique envelope back to my postal address. Optionally you can of course also sign the created bundle again.

  • Still the same day -
11. I receive your bundle. In this bundle is my unique envelope.
12. In my unique envelope that only I can open is your special letter.
13. We use the special letter as often as we want ... Once, twice. Etc.

A set of session-based keys is sent back via the ephemeral key. The first bundle is transported via the permanent keys.

Permanent bowls do not have to be, but they do exist (because the SSL/TLS connection is still there). That is, the user sends the ephemeral key (one way) over the permanent key, and the partner returns the set of session-based (symmetric keys) via the ephemeral key.

At the end - after the log is completed - the ephemeral keys are deleted and only the set of session-based keys remains.

9.7 Secret Streams for e-mail

It has already been described as innovative in an e-mail client, offering both a-symmetric and symmetric forward secrecy. The new and so far uniquely implemented function of the Secret Streams can be further appreciated as even more innovative: Secret Streams are, so to speak, a list of temporary keys generated by the password in the SMP authentication of the Socialist Millionaire Protocol. The SMP process has been extensively described above in the chat section and can also be used for Cryptographic Calling.

Mathematically breathtaking: Spot-On's Secret Streams as a bunch of keys based on a zero-knowledge process and therefore not transferred over the internet - but derived within the elaborated SMP protocol.

And now, this breathtaking new feature of the Secret Streams has not seen the world like this yet, is satisfying users and getting used to companions within the market - if that phrase is allowed - because it solves the key transfer problem fundamentally: both users receive a password known only to them in the SMP process through reciprocal contextual clues or just on commonly known secrets. Once this authentication has taken place, this password can also be used to derive numerous temporary, ephemeral keys that are the same in both clients, without them having to be transmitted - because SMP authentication is the responsibility of a so-called zero-knowledge process, we already know.

The purpose of the SMP filter is to generate key streams from a secret. The secret is mathematically negotiated through the SMP process without it being transmitted as such. Thus, the keys of the Secret Stream function are derived from a zero-knowledge proof!

The function of the Secret Streams is available for chat, e-mail and also POPTASTIC: Temporary keys, which do not have to be transmitted anymore! Secret Streams should represent a small revolution in cryptography, because the password transmission problem would be partially solved. Only the SMP secret - that was previously used for authentication, not yet for encryption - is required.

Figure 58: Implementation of Secret Streams here for e-mail

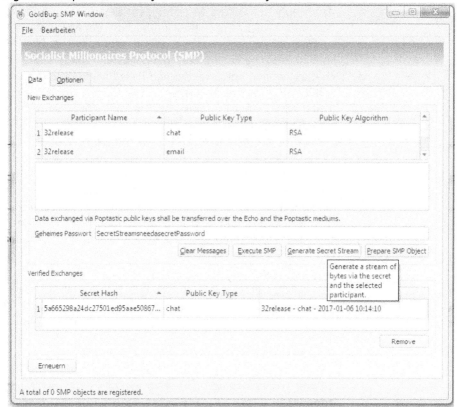

9.8   Further research perspectives

It should be remembered that the permanent (or additional) keys are transformed into transport keys, if temp-keys should be used. If these are compromised, the encryption becomes recognizable with still the other encryption layers. This concept creates a creative research area within the Echo Protocol environment. Here are some concept suggestions that could be further incorporated:

Participants could consistently generate ephemeral (a-symmetric) key pairs and exchange session-based (symmetric) keys over the ephemeral keys. Participants would be notified if there were not enough keys left. Replacement (from ephemeral keys to permanent key or session-based (symmetric)keys to (session-based) ephemeral (a-symmetric) keys would then be automatically regulated ... similar to exchanging status messages via online status in chat exchanged only over session-based keys in the Echo or POPTASTIC Protocol. This is what Echo Client Spot-On established with Secret Streams and the Echo Client Smoke established with Fiasco Forwarding:

Instead of exchanging one set of private session keys, multiple sets of private session bowls could be exchanged for supplies. Retaining data differently for a variety of anonymous e-mail addresses with session-based keys.

The OTR concept (so far for chat) could be applied within the permanent keys and also for e-mail. POPTASTIC in a different way, if chat goes via e-mail, then the chat key with OTR can also be sent via e-mail. Now keys or a bunch of keys mix functions.

By using unique keys, information transfers in a session can be ideally protected - even if there are attempts to compromise it. That means, forward secrecy offers a substantial improvement in the protection of encrypted transmissions for little effort and no cost.

After describing e-mail and its numerous options for improved and innovated encryption, we come to the already announced term POPTASTIC - the function of chat over e-mail servers. As e-mail and chat is possible with this POPTASTIC key, temp-keys can here also be shared for chat and for e-mail.

10 POPTASTIC Protocol - Encrypted chat (and e-mail) utilizing POP3 & IMAP Servers

POPTASTIC is an innovation in messaging: encrypted chat over e-mail servers.

With the POPTASTIC function all e-mail accounts, e.g. from Gmail, Outlook or Yahoo!-Mail can be encrypted a-symmetric end-to-end with Spot-On - and additionally hybrid symmetric. The clou: every POP3 or IMAP server can now also be used for encrypted chat. And that also through firewalls when e-mail is given and going out.

Figure 59: POPTASTIC Protocol Graphic

Let's take a closer look at the POPTASTIC protocol here at the desktop client of Spot-On.

10.1 Chat over POPTASTIC

So why should a user still use a dedicated chat server or a secure chat protocol with plug-ins for encryption, if the user can just use the own e-mail address for e-mail and also for chat at the same time? The multi-decade old POP3 or IMAP Protocol and numerous e-mail servers can now be used for encrypted chat with Spot-On. The e-mail server is simply converted to a chat server. That's an invention by the Spot-On development.

For this, the chat message is converted into an encrypted e-mail, sent via POP3 or IMAP, and the recipient is converting it back into a chat message. Since the Spot-On Messenger is also an e-mail client at the same time, the encrypted message exchange also works via e-mail. The program will automatically detect if it is an e-mail via POP3 or a chat message via POP3 (or IMAP).

Chat and e-mail through POPTASTIC are proxy enabled and can therefore be operated from work, the university or behind a firewall, even through the Tor network. If the users logs in to the own e-mail account with a web browser, one can see what the encrypted chat message looks like among all other e-mails.

The additional symmetric end-to-end encryption via POP3 can - as with the Echo Protocol - not only be used as forward secrecy, but can also be renewed "instantaneously" every second. Therefore, here too (as above) of Instant Perfect Forward Secrecy (IPFS) is spoken, which is now possible via POP3 and IMAP for the POPTASTIC chat! Finally, there is also the option in POPTASTIC of making a call for the transmission of a Gemini using the methods differentiated above.

This option variety of the chat encryption with POP-TASTIC is not given so far also with the architectural derivatives for mobile devices.

However, for users surely an interesting and easy way to chat encrypted via this special e-mail POPTASTIC Protocol.

10.2 E-mail over POPTASTIC

Just as there is e-mail utilizing the e-mail key and as to chat over the POPTASTIC key, it is also possible to e-mail via POPTASTIC. Since POPTASTIC is a key which the friend is adding to the own client (via the Add-Participant-window), the POPTASTIC contact or the e-mail address is provided with a lock symbol and additionally marked with a background color to indicate that the message exchange here always happens only encrypted.

If the user adds an e-mail address in the Add-Participant window, that contact will also be added to the contact list in the e-mail tab - but without the locked icon and background color. This indicates that the e-mail messages are unencrypted with this contact (as it is @-e-mail). This is the case if someone does not use the Spot-On client. Then the mail program will send the e-mail unencrypted to the @mail address (from the own @-mail-address – as long as AutoCrypt is not applied).

POPTASTIC encrypts data over the unencrypted SMTP Protocol.

The program knows: if the users mails from the POP-TASTIC key to a POPTASITC key, then this is always encrypted and can also be chat. And if the user mails from the own @-mail-address without the POPTASTIC key to an @mail address, then the message is unencrypted. This is the only and rare case that the client leaves the message unencrypted, since it does not use the Echo Protocol, but the regular e-mail Protocol SMTP!

In any case: if the contact also uses Spot-On, both can permanently e-mail encrypted when the POPTASTIC key is entered in the Add-Participant window.

E-Mail via POPTASTIC is then a simple permanent encrypted e-mailing, by simply swapping once the POPTASTIC key at the beginning.

10.3 Setting up POPTASTIC

A detailed description of the configuration options of the e-mail server can be found above in the section on POP3 and IMAP (see also figure).

Figure 60: POPTASTIC Settings: Encrypted Chat and Encrypted E-Mail over POP3 and IMAP

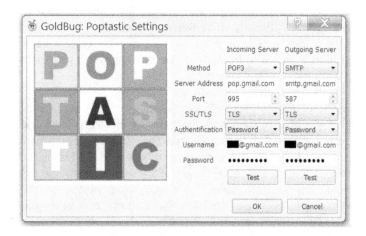

Short Note for setting e.g. Gmail up for POPTASTIC

Note: In Gmail the user should set the option on the Web that retrieved POP3 messages are deleted from the INBOX. To connect, it's also a good idea to set the security setting in Gmail so that the user can connect to all local e-mail clients (Gmail should allow unknown clients):

Settings / Forward and POP & IMAP / POP Download: Enable POP for all Mail

Settings / Accounts & Import / Change Account Settings: Other Settings / [New window] / Security / Access for less secure / unknown Apps: Enabled.

It may be advisable to set up an extra e-mail account for a first test and further use: It may be important to note that new e-mail accounts, e.g. for Gmail, may be limited to the first 30 days for the sending of e-mails (e.g. Gmail for max. 500 chat messages or e-mails per day). This should be sufficient for a test or normal need if necessary.

Otherwise the user can set up an own e-mail server with Spot-On and the user is no longer dependent on the @Mail accounts of the major providers, if it is a small internal user groups that use the Echo mail - represented here with its own server need.

10.4 Further development of the POPTASTIC protocol

This idea of the POPTASTIC architecture has been developed by the Spot-On development team, published and described also in the study "Big 7" by the auditors of the program (op. cit 2016). Then this idea has been taken over by the mobile application Lettera-Chat, though the encryption there also should runs soon via PGP and exclusively only via IMAP server. Also, the Delta-Chat project has taken it over. Commits show, that these projects have started years later than the POPTSASTIC idea was published in the Spot-on and GoldBug Software. The original commits and publication data show the historical origins to these references, and credits could be made in order not to seek the proximity of any meaning of plagiarizing the POPTASTIC architecture of this encrypted communication by following projects[†].

However, a fork and a progression of the POPTASTIC protocol idea (encrypted chat over e-mail servers) that is to be welcomed (and referenced) if it's in a mobile chat client with an appealing user interface.

[†] (See the release of POPTASTIC in 2014 and further publication in mid-2016 and its derivatives with first commits a few years later: https://sf.net/projects/Spot-On/files/bigseven-crypto-audit.pdf (p134, 2016), https://sourceforge.net/p/Spot-On/wiki/release-history/ (2014), Lettera under http://gitbub.com/textbrowser/lettera and https://delta.chat/en/blog (2016)).

Figure 61: MOMEDO Analysis Report

The MOMEDO Analysis report:
Comparing Lettera E-mail & Chat Client

The MOMEDO Analysis Report (2018) has analyzed the benefits of Lettera, Spot-On and Delta Chat in regard of their architecture. While Lettera is pure Java development on Android and uses the Java e-mail-lib by Oracle, Delta-Chat is not only relying on many different libraries, which have to be compiled, it also exists of one core and a GUI, which differentiate with Java and C/C++. So, for developing it is more difficult to choose such a complex application, in case it should be forked. Lettera offers here a cleaner coding and library use and will provide chat as well. The MOMEDO report analyses the need to find a successor of WhatsApp in consideration of the European Law of GPDR / DSGVO and recommends several criteria to compare the first new mobile applications based on the POPTASTIC protocol for chat over e-mail servers.
Found at: http://momedo.github.io/momedo

Further development of the POPTASTIC protocol could be in adding file sharing over it: As the e-mail friends in the client found a friend-to-friend network (a kind of web-of-trust) there is no malicious peer which can interfere. As the connections are always encrypted, the idea is near the concept of a mobile Retroshare.sf.net.

If Lettera would implement a kind of Turtle hopping known from RetroShare over the POPTASTIC Protocol and would send files over encrypted postboxes on e-mail servers from friends to friends of friends, then this results in a secure way to revive a f2f Gnutella over e-mail servers. As this is addressing the mobile world in the future, let's focus first on file-sharing within messaging on desktop clients, using the Echo Protocol with Echo server and listener beside e-mail servers.

Figure 62: GUI Screenshot of the Lettera Application (Android) with also intended chat over e-mail servers

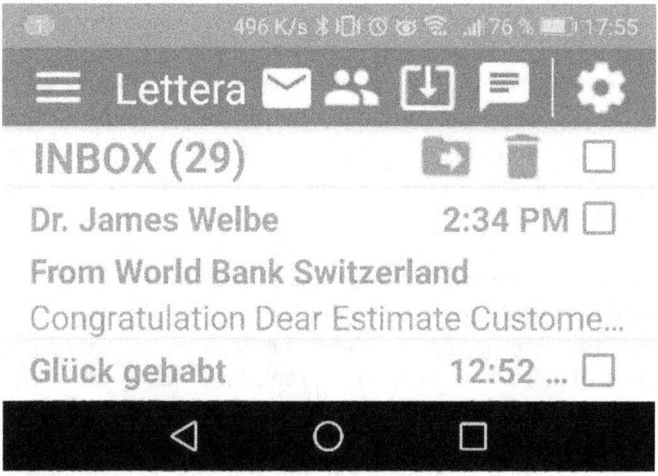

Source: https://github.com/textbrowser/lettera

Questions and further Research & Development Fields

- Set up Spot-On as e-mail client and send an e-mail to either the e-mail key, and the POPTASTIC key of a friend.
- Look up an encrypted POPTASTIC chat message in the regular e-mail client or web interface.
- Test and develop the chat of two Lettera clients.
- Investigate how file sharing in Lettera can be designed and realized. Make a concept for a file sharing protocol based on Turtle Hopping over POPTASTIC.
- Discuss pro and cons of C/O, VEMI, Ozone Postboxes in comparison and compare it also to IMAP/POP3.
- Describe the concept of Secret Streams.
- Encrypt an e-mail attachment with File-Encryptor.

11 File-Sharing: with StarBeam

As in any messenger, a file transfer in Spot-On is also possible and in general this file-sharing function is always encrypted between two defined friends or even multiple people. This happens in the tab "StarBeam". The term StarBeam (SB) implies that File-Sharing should be as simple as the light of the stars projected or "beamed" through the galaxies.

While traditional file-sharing programs such as EMule or BitTorrent have initially relied on specific links such as the ed2k link or the torrent link, file transfers today have to do with the linking of files using the Magnet-URI standard, which is known from both, torrents and nearly all of the more advanced Gnutella clients, even for the Edonkey network it is established in the Shareaza client.

The elaboration of Spot-On and the Spot-On-kernel has developed the architecture of this Magnet-URI standard further and added cryptographic values to the Magnet-URI.

If the user now wants to download a file via Spot-On from others, the user has to copy a Magnet URI link into the program. And accordingly: If the user wants to prepare an upload of a file, a Magnet-URI has to be created for this file.

This process includes encryption and is considered as simple as possible: If the user is chatting with a friend in a pop-up chat window (see images in the chat section), there is a button "Share StarBeam". The user can simply click this, then select the file to be sent from the hard disk and it is already securely encrypted transmitted over the Echo connection to the friend.

Figure 63: Spot-On 1:1-chat pop-up window with file transfer

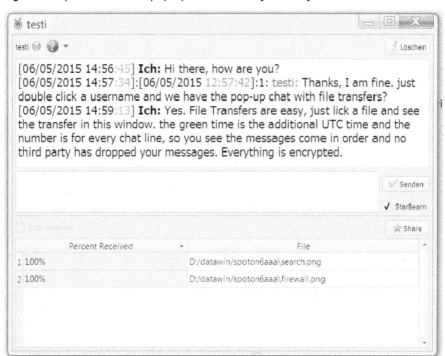

With this integration the user can easily and securely transfer a ZIP with confidential contract documents to family members or business partners via the chat window or the StarBeam tab.

To send a file to an entire group, the user can also post the Magnet-link into the group chat. This will then be automatically added to the downloads (see checkbox in the menu options: Buzz / e'IRC-Chat: accept Magnets).

Because of the Echo Protocol, the individual packages are also "swarmed", i.e. the encrypted packets that pass by the user, are even shared with friends and neighbors. They can unpack and read it successfully if they have the right key.

The file-sharing StarBeam tab consists of three sub-tabs: one for uploading, one for downloading, and one for creating or adding StarBeam Magnets.

Figure 64: StarBeam with its three sub-tabs

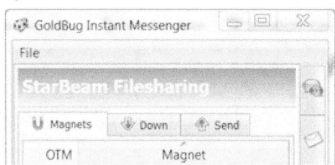

11.1 Creating StarBeam Magnets with crypto-graphic values

A Magnet-URI is a standard known from many file-sharing programs (many in the Gnutella network) or for torrent links and also corresponds to eDonkey / Emule ed2k links (e.g., as given in the Shareaza client).

The further development of the Magnet-URI standard by the Spot-On Encryption Suite lies in the design of the Magnet-URI with cryptographic values. Magnets are used to create or hold together a bundle of cryptographic information.

Between the nodes in the Echo Network is thus created an end-to-end encrypted channel through which a file can then be sent. However, any further file can be sent as well. The Magnet is thus not associated with a particular file. The StarBeam-Magnet is like a channel through which an instance can continuously and permanently send files - or there is a one-time Magnet created, which is deleted immediately after the single use.

This architecture does not allow a Magnet to be associated with a single file or IP address. Also, a filename does not appear in the StarBeam-Magnet (as it is the case even with the also more advanced links, for example, from OFFSystem or RetroShare compared to Gnutella, Emule, and Torrent links). Thus, it becomes clear that no specific file is exchanged in StarBeam, but only encrypted channels are exchanged. A "wormhole", so to speak, to stick to the popular concept of the "Star Trek" movie. And this channel is defined by a Magnet-URI link and its cryptographic values.

Figure 65: Magnet-URI standard with cryptographic values for file transfer

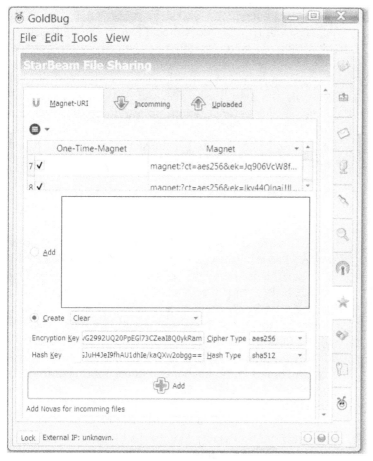

While many opinions see the linking of Gnutella, Edonkey, and Torrent links on the Web as critical, there is no reason to scrutinize those values in a collection of encryption values. A homepage or independent portal with StarBeam and Magnet-URI links present an advanced concept. In addition to the conceptual choices of selecting a link standard, the usage aspect is also about the security of the file transfer between two private users.

In summary: To send a file, an encrypted channel must be created. This works with the creation of a Magnet, marked at the end by the suffix "URN=StarBeam". Then the file is transmitted encrypted - packet by packet - over this channel using the HTTPS Echo Protocol (which can be based on TCP, UDP, DTLS and also SCTP or even Bluetooth connections). It is therefore an interesting question for a practical test, whether a transfer of a large, encrypted file via Star-Beam via the Echo Protocol based on SCTP, TCP or UDP connections is ceteris paribus transmitted error-free and fastest?

For the process of private file transfer from friend to friend some more notes:

11.1.1 Option "NOVA": Encrypt the file before transferring the file!

Before the user sends a file, the user can consider whether he simply attaches it to an e-mail within the Spot-On e-mail function. This is the variant of choice if the file is smaller than 10 MB. Larger files should only be transferred to a friend via the StarBeam feature or in the 1:1-chat window.

Before transferring, the user may also consider encrypting the file on the hard disk (further encryption layer). To do this, the Spot-On Software provides a tool for file encryption, found in the main menu under tools (see the section below: Spot-On-File-Encryptor). A double passphrase encodes the file in it.

Of course, this tool, the Spot-On-File-Encryptor can also be used if the user wants to upload a file somewhere to an online-hoster within the cloud or transfer it via another path, another messenger or any e-mail.

However, as these online hosting sites like Dropbox may control files and mark encrypted files with a question mark, even though it should be an exclamation mark, it makes sense to transfer the encrypted file from point to point, from friend to friend, directly via Spot-On and to use no external or foreign intermediate caches as a host.

Some pack the files in a zip and encrypt it before sending or uploading. However, zip encryption is very easy to crack with 96 bits, so the user should use a key recommended for RSA - today for RSA with at least 3072 bits, better even more bits. And the user can also use the McEliece algorithm instead of RSA, which is regarded more secure despite the attacks known from fast Quantum Computing.

No matter how the user prepares and transfers the file: (1) as a plain binary file, or (2) encrypted with the Spot-On File-Encryptor tool via StarBeam or (3) as a file with an additional NOVA password (see below) as a protection method in the Star Beam process - in any case, it will in turn be encrypted several times using the Echo Protocol. However, this architecture provides an optimum of encryption and a variety of options, which cover numerous requirements.

Just like a user can put an additional password on an e-mail (see above, called "Goldbug" in the e-mail function), the user can also set another password on the file - respective on the used Magnet-URI for the file transfer: This is called "NOVA".

Figure 66: NOVA Password on file transfers

The NOVA Password on file transfers

Optional: A NOVA password for the additional encryption of the file: Finally, the user can still decide whether he wants to put on the transfer an additional password - as described above: a "NOVA". The friend can open the file only if he enters the NOVA password. It is an additional symmetric encryption to secure a file transfer.

Then the user presses the "Transmit" button.

(Tech Note: Since the Echo is transmitted as HTTPS Post or HTTPS Get, the transfer is the same as a web page. The chunk size can be left as predefined, as it is in the minimum view Spot-On interface hidden. In case the pulse size is made larger, the web page being transferred becomes longer, so to speak.)

Even if the file transfer is successful or even a third un-known party could crack the previous multiple encryption (which is not to be assumed), the NOVA password introduc-es end-to-end encryption, which is secure as long as the shared password is exclusive to both partners.

Because, if the transmission of the StarBeam-Magnet should be intercepted - the user somehow has to transfer the Magnet online to his friend - then anyone who knows the Magnet can also receive the file as well. Therefore, it makes sense to protect the file with a "NOVA" - a password that both friends have exchanged, possibly orally, in the past or via a second channel.

The NOVA is also built on the end-to-end encryption standard AES (that means the password string is generated by the computer, if the user does not think up his own passphrase).

As mentioned, the ability to create an own end-to-end encrypting password yourself and manually enter it – is known in the science as "Customer Supplied Encryption Keys" (#CEKS) – it is so far implemented only in a very few applications such as Spot-On Encryption Suite or Smoke Mobile Crypto Chat.

And please note: The NOVA must have been deposited in the node of the recipient - before - the file transfer begins!

11.1.2 Using a one-time Magnet

Ideally, the user has his own Magnet-URI for each file. That would then be a one-time-Magnet (OTM), a Magnet that is used only once for a file. (OTM is the same as the idea of an OTP - a one-time pad: a string that is used only once.) OTP is often considered essential in cryptographic processes to provide security.)

The user can also use a Magnet permanently, then it is like a subscribed video channel in which, for example, a new file is sent every Monday.

This also opens completely new possibilities for torrent portals, for example: there does not even have to be a web portal in which thousands of links are linked! The portal itself needs only a single Magnet in a decentralized network, then consecutively, one by one, it is possible to send one file after the other through the wormhole. (It would be even possible to send a magnet (in a text file) through the channel of a file-transfer magnet. This would add forward secrecy to file sharing.)

As soon as the user has transferred a file via the Magnet, the user can delete or retain the Magnet-URI. If the user creates the Magnet as an OTM and activates the checkbox for OTM, it deletes itself after file transfer. This is similar to the movie Mission Impossible or apps for pictures where messages and pictures destroy itself - The Magnet is, so to speak, a StarBeam wormhole that closes again after a single use.

11.1.3 Overview of Magnet-URI standards for crypto-graphic values

The following overview explains the usual cryptographic values in the Magnet-URI standard.

Figure 67: Cryptographic values for the Magnet-URI standard

Abbreviation	Example	Description
rn	&rn=Spot-On_Developer_Channel_Key	Roomname
xf	&xf=10000	Exact Frequency
xs	&xs=Spot-On_Developer_Channel_Salt	Exact Salt
ct	&ct=aes256	Cipher Type
hk	&hk=Spot-On_Developer_Channel_Hash_Key	Hash Key
ht	&ht=sha512	Hash Type
xt=urn:buzz	&xt=urn:buzz	Magnet for IRC Chat
xt=urn:starbeam	&xt=urn:starbeam	Magnet for filetransfer
xt=urn:institution	&xt=urn:institution	Magnet for the virtual E-Mail-Postbox

This standard is used to exchange symmetric keys for group chat or e-mail institutions or even file transfers with Star-Beam.

Figure 68: Example of a Magnet-URI with cryptographic values (here for a group chat channel)

Magnet-URI with cryptographical values
Magnet:?rn=Spot-On_Developer_Channel_Key &xf=10000 &xs=Spot-On_Developer_Channel_Salt &ct=aes256 &hk=Spot-On_Developer_Channel_Hash_Key &ht=sha512 &xt=urn:buzz

The Magnet-URI standard has been further developed into a format to pass on encryption values similar to a blood count sheet. Encryption with very individual DNA-values provide the highest possible security. They are bundled in the Magnet-URI.

11.1.4 Rewind function

If a recipient has received a file packet, a chunk (or in the Spot-On kernel also called "link"), the user is able to upload it again - even in other Magnet-URI channels. - Or the file can be sent again into the same URI channel. This is similar to a rewind function: the file is simply played again via the Echo Network - like on a cassette recorder or MP3 player. The file can also be sent many hours or days later. Anyone who has received a copy via the Magnet-URI channel becomes a satellite, and can re-import the data into the defined channel, or better, via a StarBeam Magnet.

11.1.5 Comparison with Turtle-Hopping

The bottleneck in a Turtle Hopping chain is a user with low bandwidth.

Turtle-Hopping (see Glossary and: Popescu et al. 2004, Matejka 2004, as implemented in RetroShare) will pass the file packages from friends to friends until they reach a defined destination. It is a transformation of a peer-to-peer (P2P) network into a friend-to-friend (F2F) network. However, it might have the consideration that friends with little upload speed to the next friend in the chain form a bottleneck and slow down the transport:

The Turtle-Hopping Protocol is first connected only to nodes that have been defined as friends and here in this chain of friends can be a friend, which performs only with a small bandwidth. This then could act as a bottleneck and senders and recipients of the file must necessarily send through this bottleneck.

The transmission of a file in the StarBeam function via the Echo Protocol is therefore probably (to be practical measured) also more effective than using a Protocol similar to "Turtle-Hopping" (currently only implemented in the

RetroShare program), because here, depending on the design of the Echo Network (Full Echo, Half Echo, Adaptive Echo) the nodes with low bandwidth do not have to act as a bottleneck, they optimize the desired download speed via other Echo paths.

When sending files via the Echo Protocol, therefore, other nodes such as peers or paths via other graph-options can be included in the hopping over intermediate stations if there is a faster route somewhere:

The Echo Protocol automatically creates the flow in the network of nodes (simply by allowing each node to send encrypted file packets to each linked node) and therefore also chooses the fastest path of all possible graphs to the desired node. A practical measurement must be defined and tested though.

11.2 StarBeam upload: transferring a file

As described above, sending a file from the chat window to a single friend is very simple: with the Share-StarBeam button the user just have to choose one file and it will be transferred to the referring friend.

In the following, we now look at the upload process with its technical details in the sub-tabulator "Uploads" of the StarBeam tab.

If the user has defined and generated a Magnet-URI, it will appear not only in the sub-tab for the Magnets, but also in the table in the sub tab for the upload/seed.

Hence, from here the upload of a file can be started. To do this, the user selects with the check box a Magnet in this sub-tab for the upload. Likewise, the file is selected.

Figure 69: Starbeam file transfer: uploading files

Finally, the user copies the Magnet-URI and sends it to his friend. The user can copy the Magnet URI via the context menu button.

If the other friend has pasted the Magnet into the own instance, the user can start the transfer by deactivating the pause function (check box "Pause" in the table).

Then the file is transferred to the friend.

11.3 StarBeam downloads

As written above - it's the other way around from the per-spective of the receiver of a file: To load a file with Star-Beam, the user needs the StarBeam Magnet of the file. The user receives this from the friend, who wants to send a file.

The user then simply copies the Magnetic URI into the sub-tab for the Magnetic URIs. Before that, the user should activate the checkbox "Receiving" in the download sub-tab. This is deactivated in advance by default, so that no un-wanted files are received.

The user then tells the friend that he has inserted the Mag-net URI and then the friend can start the transmission. The download starts as soon as a transmitter sends the file via the Echo and through the cryptographic channel of the Magnet.

With the additional settings on this tab for the upload, the user can still define the size and the path for the down-load area.

Successfully downloaded parts are called "Mosaic"s with-in StarBeam and stored in the same path of the installation on the hard disk. Similar to a puzzle, the mosaic pieces are assembled into a full mosaic, the resulting file.

The still-to-be-transferred file parts are called "links" in StarBeam (see also the term "chunks" in the old EDonkey network or the term "blocks" in the Gnutella network, which was coined by the use of the then there used Tiger–Tree-Hashes).

Figure 70: StarBeam File Transfer - Incoming Files

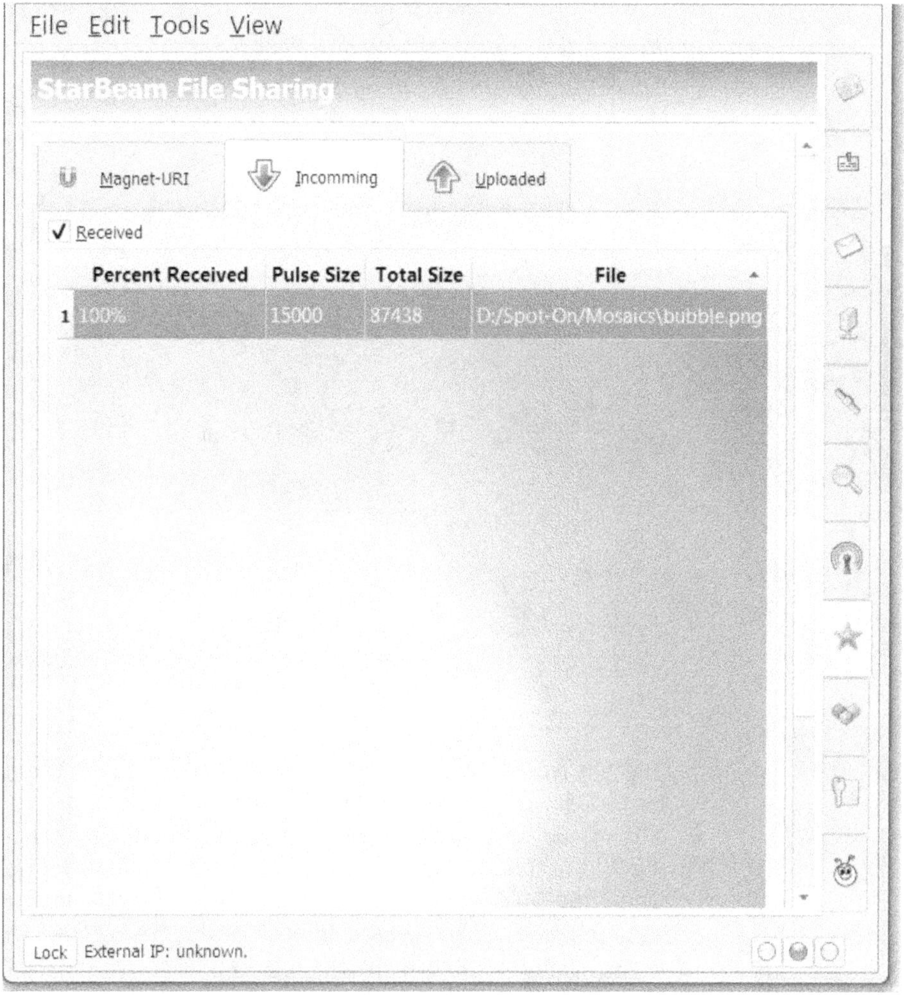

11.3.1 Tool: StarBeam Analyzer

If a file was not successfully transferred 100%, it can be checked with the StarBeam Analyzer tool. This determines if all mosaic parts are present or if any links / chunks / blocks or packages still to be transferred are missing. If any links are missing, the SB Analyzer will create a Magnet URI that the friend can re-enter in his upload tab. Then only the missing links or mosaics are sent again.

Figure 71: File transfer using StarBeam: Analysis tool for the chunks

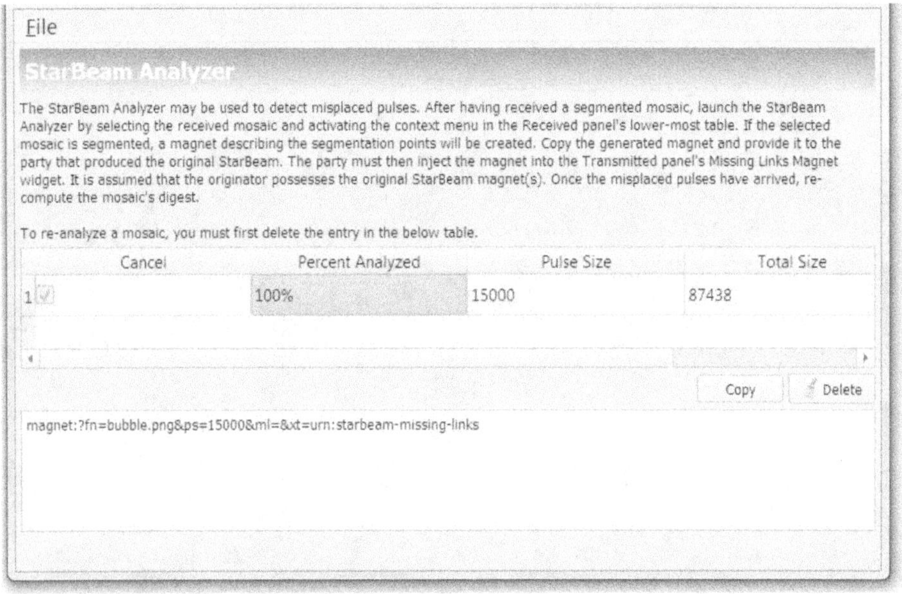

The file would also complete if the sender sends it three times a day over the Echo with the "Rewind" function.

It should be noted that a Magnet is a channel, and existing files in the local mosaic path will then be renewed if no One-Time-Magnet is used and they are sent again in the same channel. A renewed shipment of the file by the uploader will thus overwrite the file received by the user again - if the user has not set a lock option in the transfer table. The checkbox "Lock" then would not allow to delete the file that the user received.

11.3.2 Outlook for Cryptographic Torrents

Because of encryption, nobody can see what file a user is downloading, because nobody knows if the user was able to successfully decrypt the package - and even if, nobody knows if the user created or saved the file in total from it.

The upload is similar. The upload is only visible from a neighbor IP, if this neighbor knows the Magnet of the file. In this case, if the user wants to load public StarBeam Magnets, it is best to connect only to neighbors or chat servers that the user trusts or has define as friend through account access.

Cryptographic Torrents are based on the Magnet-URI-Scheme with cryptographic values.

Also, the above-mentioned variant of setting a NOVA password on the file and the distribution of the physical blocks in time before granting the access rights to the NOVA password in a second process can offer new perspectives in technical, procedural or even legal considerations.

This means e.g. that the transfer of the file takes place in the past and the transfer of the decryption option with the NOVA password takes place in a future, separate and downstream process.

Then, using the Echo Protocol, StarBeam Magnet-URIs can play a role in new ways of thinking about developing and using "crypto-torrents" discussed in the file-sharing community.

Encryption basically means that unauthorized persons do not know what is in the encrypted packet and that the owner of the key decides himself when to perform the decryption. That is, encryption has been logically applied to the file transfer and the sovereignty of the user.

Questions and further Research & Development Fields

- Test the speed of a file transfer over TCP versus SCTP.
- Transfer a file with a one-time Magnet.
- Compare Cryptographic Torrents to regular tracker-based Torrents.

12 Open Source web search engine with encrypted URL database

With the integrated function of a web search Spot-On is also an open source p2p web search engine due to its used architecture of the kernel.

Spot-On is the only (and so far) one of the few handiest p2p distributed search engines like YaCy, Arado.sf.net or Grub (which was once known by Wikia-Search), which is able to handle the transfer of the URLs over encrypted connections into a distributed F2F or P2P network.

Spot-On Websearch is not only open source for the search engine code, the sorting algorithm, but also the URL-Database.

The idea of the web search function in Spot-On is not only to offer an open source programming of the search engine or the sorting algorithm, but also to handle the repository of URLs open source, so that each participant can download the entire URL-Database. Third, finally, transfers and database storage take place in an encrypted environment. An innovative and exemplary model for search in encrypted databases (that means within cipher text).

Website titles, keywords and the URL itself are stored encrypted in a SQLite or PostgreSQL database and linked together via the Echo Protocol (or via the PostgreSQL networking and cluster function).

A user can use a crawler or RSS feed to store own web pages and URLs in a searchable database repository and share them with other nodes.

Figure 72: Web search with Spot-On in the URL database

The user can now design an own search engine: for example, with 15 GB of URLs in the database on the own machine, the user can certainly achieve interesting search results for new websites that a friend finds interesting and has received via the p2p network.

But also, as a local database for own bookmarks or an own crawl of a dedicated domain, the URL database can be used.

The web search in the URL repository remains anonymous, because the Spot-On URL search generates in other nodes no announcement of the search words, so-called "query hits".

Spot-On converts the search words into a hash and searches the local databases to see if it contains this hash. Then there is also the hash of the URLs that contain this keyword. The URL database is then searched for the hash of the URL.

Search in encrypted databases with cipher text is a young research field.

The databases are also encrypted, so that after the search process also a decryption process is connected. Finally, the search results are generated and shown to the user. The UI currently sorts the results for one or more search words for simplicity, such that the most recent URLs are displayed first at the top.

If the user wants to create an open source search algorithm for sorting URL results, Spot-On will provide the open source code base for this function in order not only to develop an own algorithm model, but also to subject it to a practical test.

The distribution of website URLs does not happen via central servers, but is organized via the encrypted Echo Protocol decentralized between the participants: Two or more users exchange their URL keys and then take part in the p2p exchange of website URLs, such as own bookmarks, with all friends. The online exchanged URLs are first collected in main memory and then written to the local database every 10 seconds.

There is also the option of manually importing new URLs into your own local database. This requires the web browser Dooble.sf.net. The first icon in the URL line of the browser allows storing a single URL in an intermediate database: Shared.db. This is then imported by Spot-On with just one click. The Shared.db must be in the installation path of Spot-On and both programs, Spot-On and Dooble, must define in the settings the path of this file.

In order to import an URL of the web page that a user is currently reading from the Web Browser Dooble into Spot-On's own URL database, the user simply has to click on the first icon in the URL line of the browser to start the URL to be stored in the URL-DB: Shared.db. Then, in Spot-On, the user clicks on the tab "Import" in the tab of the web search.

However, the newer version of the browser Dooble (Dooble 2.0) no longer supports this import function of a single URL in Spot-On. Because the new version of the browser Dooble represents a complete reprogramming. which became necessary due to the change in Qt regarding the Webkit module.

In the still available source code of the old Dooble Browser, however, this option can be reactivated with an own compilation. This option should only be mentioned here for a short sentence since other developers may also want to import an URL from a (or any) browser into an encrypted bookmark database and look at this model.

The idea of making bookmarks shared with friends searchable and locally storable for own history thus remains current.

More efficient, however, are the other methods to import numerous URLs using a crawler (Pandamonium Crawler) or the RSS feed in Spot-On.

But first let's look how to setup the URL database in Spot-On.

12.1 URL Database Setup

The URLs can optionally be stored in a SQLite or PostgreSQL database. SQLite is the automatically configured database that is also recommended for users with less experience in setting up databases. More advanced users can also contact a PostgreSQL database facility. This has advantages in the network access, the administration of user rights and the handling of large URL data stocks. Spot-On is therefore suitable for creating an own web search, even for teaching purposes, in case those learners are interested in setting up databases.

The URLs are stored in 26x26 or 36x36 databases (2 (16 ^ 2) = 512 tables), which are encrypted. This means that the search takes place in an encrypted database (URLs.db). Searching in encrypted databases is a field of research that has so far received little attention.

12.1.1 SQLite

SQLite is a program library that contains a relational database system. The entire database is in a single file. A client-server architecture is therefore not available.

Figure 73: Installing the URL database for the URL/Web search

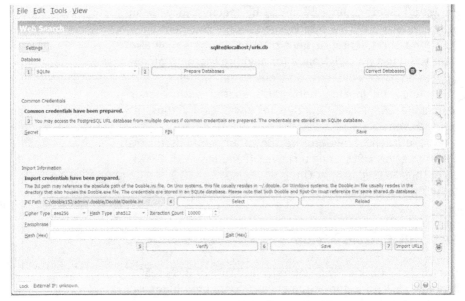

The SQLite library can be directly integrated into appropriate applications so that no additional server software is required. This is also the ultimate difference from other database systems. Integrating the library extends the application with database functionality without relying on external software packages.

SQLite has some special features over other databases: The library is only a few hundred kilobytes in size. A SQLite database consists of a single file that contains all tables, indexes, views, triggers, and so on. This simplifies the exchange between different systems.

12.1.2 PostgreSQL

PostgreSQL - also known as Postgres - is a free, object-relational database management system (ORDBMS). Its development originated in the 1980s from a database development of the University of California at Berkeley, since 1997, the software is developed by an open source community.

PostgreSQL is largely compliant with the ANSI SQL 2008 SQL standard. PostgreSQL is fully ACID compliant, and supports extensible data types, operators, functions, and aggregates.

Most Linux distributions contain PostgreSQL - Windows and Mac OS X are also supported. Since the setup process of the PostgreSQL database is more extensive, it should also be referred to the manuals of this database also regarding its own p2p capability outside the p2p Echo Network.

12.2 URL-Filter

If the user now participates in the p2p process of URL exchange with friends and peers, the user gets all the URLs that others have added to the system. To exclude malicious URLs, the user can also delete URLs in the web search with a single click - or else the user uses the URL filter right from the beginning, which can be found in its own tab.

URL filters - so-called distillers - can filter incoming, outgoing and imported data with a blacklist or whitelist. For example, the user can define that only URLs from the domain www.wikipedia.org are allowed or that uploads of URLs to friends only take place from the domain of his university. Also, the user can specify that he does not want to receive URLs of a particular country domain.

In case the user does not want to receive URLs, he just sets the distiller filter to "http: //" with the value "Deny" for the downloads, then these URLs will not be accepted.

Figure 74: URL Options: Import and Export Filters: URL Distiller

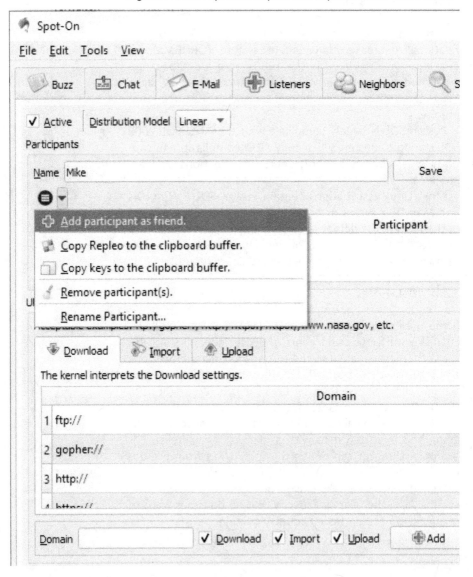

Very important: To have the filter active, the filter should be set to "Active" with the check box at the top.

12.3 URL-Community: Open Source URL-Database

To be able to exchange URLs and letting the own database grow for web search, the user can either manually paste the URL key at the tab "URL Filter" into the participant table; or, the second option is to send the own URL key to a community. *EPKS offers automatic key sharing. Hence it is AutoCrypt.*

If the user's friend is also online, and the user uses the "EPKS" tool - Echo Public Key Share - to send his URL key to the "Spot-On URL Community" defined there, his friend receives the URL key of the User automatically transferred online.

This transfer is encrypted using the Echo Protocol and uses the name of the URL community as symmetric encryption. It is similar to a group chat room (e'IRC/Buzz function) where the URL keys are then sent out and automatically integrated (see as already described AutoCrypt as a derivation from this invention). How EPKS works is described in more detail below in the tools section.

Figure 75: Echo Public Key Sharing (EPKS)

12.4 Pandamonium Webcrawler

Another import option for URLs is to use the crawler "Pandamonium".

The Christmas release 2015 of Spot-On was the "Pandamonium Web crawler release" and referred to the web crawler named Pandamonium, which has been added as a tool to the URL database feature.

The web crawler scans a domain for all linked URLs and can then index new URLs on the discovered websites and add these to the crawl or index. Pandamonium works (as well as the import from the Dooble Web Browser) via an intermediate Shared.db. The web crawler Pandamonium is also open source and can be downloaded from this URL: https://github.com/textbrowser/pandamonium

It is also pre-compiled for Windows in the GoldBug Zip for Windows under http://goldbug.sf.net.

Figure 76: Pandamonium Web Crawler

The URLs added in this way are then also shared with the friends via encrypted connections or stored encrypted in the own local database as well.

For example, the Pandamonium crawler offers the possibility of importing large amounts of web pages of desired domains for a web search in the client Spot-On.

In addition to the URL, Pandamonium also stores the website as rich text (that means without images) in the database and these database entries can also be shared with friends. Web browsing in Spot-On enables the user to browse web pages locally without having to contact the Internet or the domain to reveal own IP information.

It is almost a new kind and advanced idea of the anonymization network Tor: No longer the website is contacted live via a p2p proxy network, but the URL is searched in a p2p web search or database and the same website can be loaded as rich text, browsed and read locally, such as from a browser cache or proxy.

Java scripts, images and referral URLs as well as IP information are not included. The user is thus protected from the disclosure of own data and can still read the desired web page of an URL if it is present in the shared data. While web pages can also call additional links or leave traces on the anonymization tool Tor - due to Javascript, it is preferable for the web crawler Pandamonium to avoid such security risks and provide only rich text in ascii.

Various revisions of web pages at different call times of the website (Memento) are also supported – for both, in the crawler as well as in the web search of the Spot-On client. The page viewer of the web search in Spot-On displays various revisions of the web page, if they exist. That is like having a kind of GIT added to a new kind of Tor.

The setup of the SQLite database for importing the URLs from the Pandamonium Web crawler via the shared.db is done in a few steps:

The user creates a SQLite database in the Spot-On program under Web Search / Settings.

The user now enters a password for "Common Credentials". This is a password feature in case third or further applications provide URLs for import.

Then the user verifies all inputs and starts the import from shared.db, into which the user has previously stored the URLs collected by the Pandamonium Webcraler: The import process retrieves the URLs from this file and adds the URLs to the URL database in the Spot-On client (URLs.db).

Any imported URLs may be shared with the user's friends online peer-to-peer. To do this, the friend's URL Key has to be entered by the user in the Add Participant window (subset from main menu), or the user should use the URL sharing community as described above to swap the URL key.

12.5 RSS reader and URL import

The RSS function extends the Spot-On client to a RSS reader. RSS 2.0 feeds are supported. News-URLs are displayed in a timeline so that the most recent message is always on top.

In addition, the news-URLs are indexed, i.e. prepared for local web search in Spot-On. The import of the encrypted RSS database into the encrypted URL database can be done automatically periodically, or even via a manual import button only on action of the user.

Spot-On is a RSS-Feed-Reader which has a search engine for all received and read URLs.

The RSS feature not only makes it easy to read selected news portals on a news page, but also manually or automatically import the new URLs into an own local URL database.

Even more: The Website respective full message can be read from the database cache.

As far as known, Spot-On is the only News-Feed-Reader with an encrypted database, which enables the user to search in own News-Feeds and provides also a searchable index for the full news website even with revisions.

The indexing of the website uses the 50 longest words of the website-text (or even more according to the user's setting) to prepare these words for the search index of the URL database during import.

For the timeline, the titles of the RSS-messages are provided with a hyperlink only when indexing has taken place. The status line shows statistics on how many RSS feeds are subscribed, how many URLs are already indexed, how many URLs from the RSS database were imported into the web search URL database - as well as the total readable messages or URLs in the RSS window.

Figure 77: RSS feed reader for importing URLs into the URL database/web search

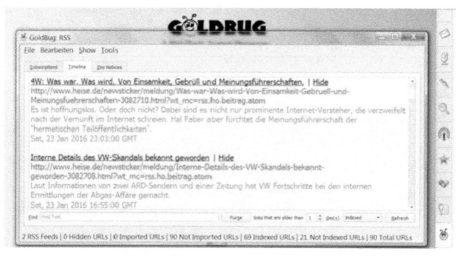

The messages are read in a Page Viewer, which does not display the messages in a browser, but for reasons of safety only in text form. As already indicated: Java scripts, images and advertising are removed from the pages, it will be displayed only the ASCII characters of the website and the hyperlinks to other websites. With the context menu, URLs and hyperlinks can be manually copied out for a view into the (external) browser.

The RSS reader is proxy-capable and can therefore also preserve the content of the websites behind restrictive environments and then make them available for storage and searching in Spot-On.

A feature that today certainly is also offered by some browsers: to look up or offer the URL history and web pages searchable from the cache of the user. Spot-On provides this in an encrypted and p2p environment for local storage in a dedicated URL repository.

As a simple use case a user can be described, who wants to crawl all websites with the key word e.g. "Falun Gong" (a kind of meditation practice, which has been censored later on by the Chinese regime). If the user wants to have an own saving and indexing of all these websites, then Spot-On is the right instrument to create such a database containing public websites, and an URL- and keyword-index for it with a p2p sharing option for this database to friends over encrypted connections.

Questions and further Research & Development Fields

- Define RSS feeds into the feedreader of Spot-On.
- Share URL-Key with your friends over EPKS.
- Provide a URL.db based on SQLite with Wikipedia URLs and pages.
- Try to measure the speed of an URLs transfer over an Echo Connection compared to a PostgreSQL direct connection to another instance.
- Test the revision function of webpages included in the database based on Wikipedia page entries, which have been updated.
- Crawl a website of a school or university with Pandamonium Webcrawler.
- Describe pro and cons for the use of SQLite and PostgreSQL
- Compare Spot-On websearch with YaCy in regard of encryption and Queryhits
- Program an import / export from YaCy to Spot-On or vice versa or program a query of Spot-On in the YaCy Network with saved results in the Spot-On database.
- Create a web interface to URLs.db - using Python, Apache, Javascript, PHP etc. and set up a website for it.
- Develop an algorithm to sort and display Spot-On URL results.

---

13 Setting-up an own server – for chat and p2p e-mail

Secure Chat is not about the Client and its GUI, it is about an easy to install open source chat server in own hands.

Setting up a chat server or Spot-On kernel means setting up a so-called "listener", according to this technical term.

If the user is in the minimal view of the user interface, a chat & e-mail server or listener is set up as quickly as the tab further above shown establishes an IP connection to a server or neighbor.

The user does not need advanced server administration skills to run a Spot-On node on the own web server, to set up a chat server, or even to set up an e-mail inbox for friends and own purposes.

In Spot-On only a so-called listener at a defined port must be defined. And that's possible with just a few clicks. Probably the simplest chat server administration ever compared to other server setups.

Comparing Chat Apps is partly non-sense.
Open Source Server Software for encrypted chat must be compared.

13.1 Set up the chat / e-mail server via a listener

As a reminder, on the Connect tab, the user connects the own Spot-On to another node or neighbor, and with the chat server listener tab, the user creates a server or listener so that others can connect to it. No matter which method, messages can always be sent if the second or third LED in the status line is green and a neighbor is connected: Either to the other user as a server/listener or, the user as a client to the neighbor which offers a listener.

The right (third) LED in the status bar thus indicates that the user has set up an own chat server on the own computer.

To do this, the user must enter the local IP address of the own machine in the "Chat Server" tab. This is not the (external) IP address of the router, but the local network IP address of the device where Spot-On is installed. Again, the user gets over the pull-down menu a selection, the IP is displayed directly, and the user can then select the local IP. The port 4710 is then automatically defined again.

Then the user presses the button "Set" and the entry of the listener was successful when the third LED of the status bar is green. Just make it reachable over your router by port forwarding and probably DynDNS.

13.1.1 Server broadcast

If the user has a client connected to his listener, or the user in the "connect-neighbor" tab is connected to another chat server or friend on his own, then the user can also right-click the command in the table "Publish information".

Thus, this chat server address is communicated over the existing connections to the friends and neighbors as well as friends of friends. "Publish server" means "Broadcast IP + Port" of the own chat server to its (connected) friends and neighbors. Then the friends can also automatically connect to this chat server. In this case, the user no longer must communicate an IP address or needs to let the friends enter the dedicated IP address manually. Everything runs automatically, and the user's server is available as a peer to the friends and their friends. It's that easy to create a chat server and communicate it to others on the network.

The listener or chat server is set up by default for the TCP Protocol, furthermore Spot-On is also equipped to set up a listener via the UDP, DTLS or even the SCTP Protocol. Both latter Protocols are ideal for VOIP or streams. Further, a chat server/listener via Bluetooth is possible, see the sections below.

Therefore, the connection options can also be used to define whether the user's client should connect to the TCP neighbor or another server via UDP, SCTP or Bluetooth.

The neighbor or listener of the server can do without SSL connections, then the transmission is regulated not over HTTPS, but only over HTTP.

Figure 78: Setting up a chat server

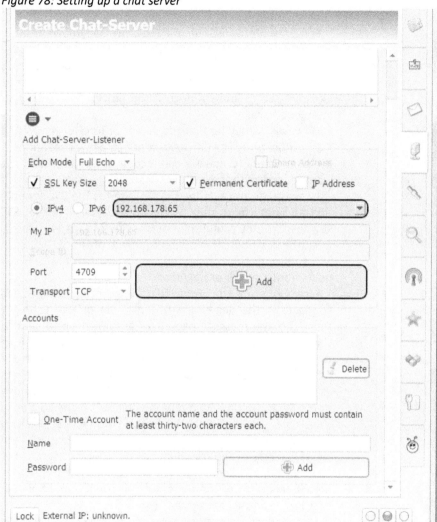

This means that an encrypted layer is not required, the encrypted Echo capsule is not sent through the HTTPS tunnel, but via HTTP - and still remains encrypted because the Echo capsule itself is already encrypted.

13.1.2 Security options

For sure, there are further setting options:

For example, a listener may set the security option to generate a permanent SSL certificate. Thus, the Diffie-Hellman key exchange or negotiation process existing in SSL is not renegotiated in every session, but an attacker would already have to know a negotiation process in the past to intervene here.

However, it may be that the server or listener renews its SSL certificate, so it may make sense to allow exceptions if the user wants to make a connection easier and does not want to perfect that extra level of security.

Likewise, one can define the key size for the SSL connection and determine that connections below a certain SSL key size are not established at all. One time it is defined, what the neighbor should offer in regard of the SSL key size, and the other time is defined, which key size the user expects from a server or neighbor.

Finally, there is the option that the client determines if it connects to the neighbor with Full Echo or Half Echo. At Half Echo, the message packet is - as known - only sent to the neighbor one hop over the direct connection. Assuming the user's friend has the web server set up and sitting in front of it and the user does not want the own Echo packets to go to third parties and their friends, then the user can define with the Half Echo that own packets received by the server are not be distributed further. In practice: The two users chat via a direct IP connection. Both participants see the IP address of the friend and of the chat partner at Half Echo. In the Full Echo, the chat friend does not have to be an administrator of the node but can connect multiple clients like a central chat server.

Further security options allow the user to define the SSL key size when creating a chat server/listener, as well as maintaining a permanent SSL certificate.

Also, the user – if there is a permanent, stable IP address – can integrate this into the SSL certificate.

These three measures make it harder for attackers to exchange or "fake" the SSL certificate - because it would be immediately recognized if a different certificate was to be used as the original one: for example, the client would expect not be a new, but the old permanent certificate. Or the IP address is missing or inconsistent within the SSL certificate. The SSL key size also defines additional security.

13.1.3 Proxy and firewall annotations

If the user wants to run Spot-On as a client via a proxy in the company, behind a firewall or a proxy of the university or via the anonymization network Tor, the user can insert the proxy details for the neighbor.

As a client, the user can connect to any IT environment thanks to the HTTP Protocol if the user is able to surf in that environment with a browser.

That's the advantage of the Spot-On program, which means that wherever users can surf with their browsers, they can also e-mail and chat with Spot-On Encryption Suite because of the HTTPS or POPTASTIC Protocol they use. Many other programs cannot do this, depending on the firewall settings – e.g. from the workplace or in the student residence.

If the user wants to use or test out a proxy e.g. in the company or university with the Spot-On Encryption Suite, then this is uncritical, because a SSL/TLS or HTTPS connection is established - which is hardly different for the proxy administrators like any other SSL/HTTPS connection to an HTTPS website when doing banking or logging into a web e-mail provider.

It is just essential to address a listening node in the web with the own Spot-On, which may not be limited by the port through a firewall or the proxy. If so, the user may ask the friend to set up the Spot-On chat server on port 80 or port 443 instead of 4710 and provide it with login information for an Echo Account, if available and deliverable.

Encrypted traffic remains encrypted traffic, and any Spot-On friend or chat server can be reached on the web through ports 443 or 80 or ports, which are regularly opened in the firewall.

Since the Echo Protocol only requires a simple HTTP connection to a neighbor (and not necessarily a Stun server or a DHT etc.), and thus ideally can be mapped through a proxy, through a firewall or over the Tor network, it's a very simple architecture to operate chat securely through a proxy or a proxy network.

If the user wants to define an additional feature, a further often-used function is that of the Echo Account.

To do this, the user in the table marks the listener that was created and then enters the account credentials, i.e. the name and password. The user then tells the friend what the account name and password are, and when the friend establishes the neighbor contact, the friend will be asked via a pop-up window to enter these credentials. In case not everyone should be able to address to the Echo Server (e.g. behind Tor), then the Echo Account can authenticate a dedicated user.

Furthermore, the user can also choose between IPV4 and IPV6 if he wants to create a listener/chat server. Also, multiple chat servers can be created by choosing a different port. The user can create different listeners with port 4710 or 80 or 443 and decide whether he wants to define these listeners for friends with an Echo Account (friend mode), or for easier to build connections that runs in peer mode without account login.

Echo Accounts thus define whether the user builds an F2F network or a P2P network, because with the account credentials the user creates a web-of-trust with which only his trusted friends can connect with the defined login password. (A SmokeStack server on Android by the way also provides the feature of a private server for defined friends).

13.1.4 Spot-On as LAN Messenger

If the user operates a peer, for example, at a LAN party of a closed network with the IP broadcast function, he can inform all participants that his node has opened a listener for the guests. Thanks to the UDP Protocol, however, the Spot-On Messenger also works directly like a LAN messenger within a closed user group of the LAN.

For this, the LAN listener is already defined as a neighbor in the neighbor table (defined IP: 239.255.43.21). This has just to be activated and other Spot-On installations in the same Windows network are then automatically found for a connection. Besides the many options the original Spot-On client offers, it is a nice Qt-Exercise for a university task to code an own simple LAN messenger with this architecture and a compact GUI as own client for the university or students home LAN.

13.2 Server / Listener Creation at home behind a router / Nat

If the user does not have his own server on the web or does not find a general neighbor with a listener on the web, it is also recommended to set up an own chat server at home behind the own router and to forward the port in the router. The friends then can connect directly to this defined listener as a client.

However, one of the friends has to create a listener if both friends sit behind a firewall or do not use a chat server on the web. So, if the user wants to create a server behind his router/Nat at home, as mentioned the local IP address of the machine for the listener is to take, e.g. 192.168.121.1. Then the user must also forward the port in his router, i.e. port 4710 must be forwarded by the router to 192.168.121.1: 4710. Furthermore, the kernel - Spot-on-Kernel.exe - as well as the Spot-On.exe should be allowed as an exception in the (Windows) Firewall. If the user has forwarded everything correctly, the friend can connect to the client's (external) IP address (see, for example, www.whatismyip.com) and port 4710.

It is only important that the router of the user forwards the contact attempt from the Internet at the defined port to the own local machine. This is a common and secure procedure and does not open any access to a computer, but over the port and the application is defined (as with many other programs that only packages in this sense are allowed).

The user can and must define this by himself and Spot-On does not contain any code that automatically forwards ports in the router or opens or even automatically sets up a listener!

Thus, in Spot-On it is more secure, as there are more options to be decided by the user than in other applications, which configure itself in the interest of user-friendliness and reduce the effort and provision of background automation. – Convenience appears as a security risk for those users, who know the technical details of port forwarding within the own router and for the creation of a listener, and need no automatic definition, opening and forwarding of ports. Once known and done, the own listening server at home is quickly administered.

13.3 Use of Spot-On in the Tor network

If the user wants to operate the own Spot-On chat through the Tor network, this will also be worth a test. The Tor exit node should only see the cipher text of the communication. Here, the chat server is again in the normal web outside the Tor network.

So far, Tor cannot establish HTTPS connections at the exit node of the Tor network, but a pass-through of encrypted packets from two Spot-On instances should be possible: Spot-On -> Tor -> Internet -> Tor -> Spot-On. A HTTP listener can also be set up for the TOR network. This is an ideal test environment of both applications. So far no one has published about Echo over Tor (while Tor is being the overlay network for it). Also, other networks can be tested, e.g. like the Matrix.org.

Figure 79: Testing Proxy and Pass-Through capabilities

Testing Proxy & Pass-Through capabilities

Messaging through a Proxy
Spot-On => Proxy (Entry) => Internet [=> Proxy (Entry)] Spot-On

Messaging over Tor
Spot-On => Tor (Entry) => Internet => Tor (Exit) => Spot-On

Echo through the Echo
GoldBug => Spot-On => Tor (Entry) => Internet => Tor (Exit) => Spot-On => GoldBug

Gopher passing through the Echo
Gopher => Spot-On (Pass-through) => Internet => Spot-On (Pass-through) => Gopher

Compare:
Gopher over Matrix.org is untested and assumed to fail
Gopher => Matrix (Entry) => Internet => Matrix (Exit) => Gopher

Next to a proxy it is also possible to use the pass-through functionality of Spot-On, here Spot-On is not connected to a proxy, but is becoming a proxy on localhost, to which other applications can be tied. That means one can send from a Gopher App to Spot-On and to the network and then from Spot-On at the other end back to Gopher. This is possible as the function is not tied to a special protocol or library (compare a test with Tor or the Matrix network, which require special protocol/library implementations).

13.4 Spot-On Kernel Server

As currently described, the software to set up a chat server is currently described according to the application Spot-On. As an alternative User Interface to Spot-On, there is also the

GoldBug interface and server software. A chat server listener can be set up with both applications referring to the Spot-On Kernel. But there are even some more ways, applications and methods to set up a server for communication:

13.5 Spot-On Lite Server as Deamon

If the user wants to administer a chat server without a user interface, thus using the chat server as a kernel daemon on a web server, one can view at the other Lite server software for Echo clients at: github.com/textbrowser/spot-on-lite.

Figure 80: Bluetooth chat server architecture model

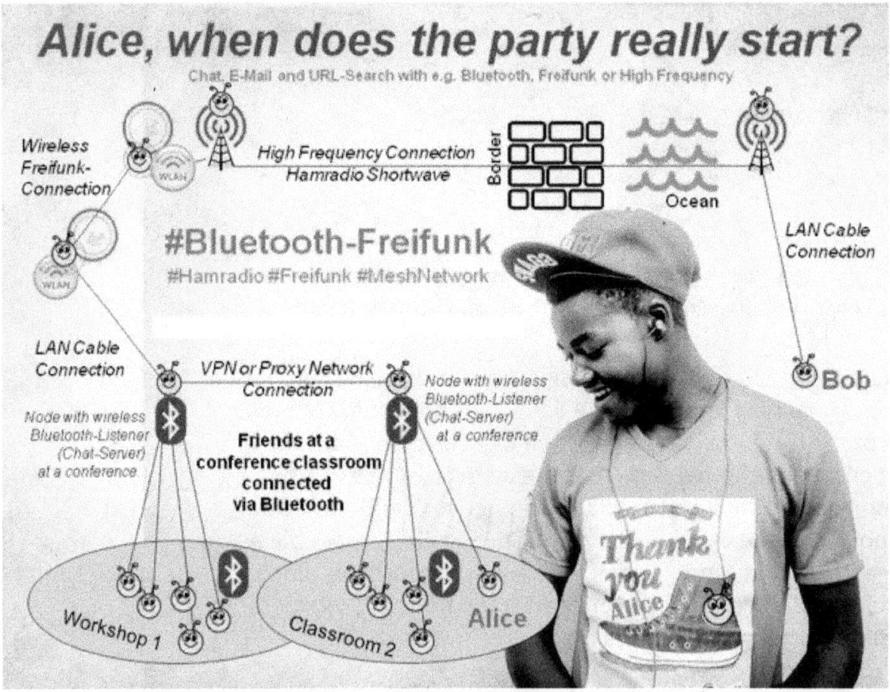

13.6 SmokeStack Server on Android

The simplest option at home in the LAN or even with port forwarding in the router to set up a chat server is to install the App SmokeStack on an Android device. This Android server can also forward the Echo packages of Spot-On Echo clients. Available at: github.com/textbrowser/smokestack.

SmokeStack is an elaborated Chat Server for encrypted chat for the Android operating system.

13.7 Spot-On Bluetooth Server

Finally, a chat server/listener via Bluetooth is also possible (depending on Qt currently only for Linux). With Bluetooth, it is possible, for example, to connect the devices BT-wirelessly via the Echo Protocol at a LAN party. This option can be very crucial if there is no Internet or infrastructure left.

13.8 Spot-On UDP Server

The User Datagram Protocol, UDP for short, is a minimal, connectionless network Protocol that belongs to the transport layer of the Internet Protocol family.

The development of UDP began when a simpler Protocol was required for the transmission of speech than the previous connection-oriented TCP. A Protocol was needed that was only addressing, without securing the data transmission, as this would cause delays in voice transmission.

A three-way handshake, such as TCP (the Transmission Control Protocol) for establishing the connection, would create unnecessary overhead in this case.

UDP is therefore a connectionless, non-reliable and unsecured as well as unprotected transmission Protocol. That is, there is no guarantee that a packet once sent will also arrive, that packets arrive in the same order in which they were sent, or that a packet arrives only once at the receiver. An application that uses UDP, therefore, must be insensitive to lost and unsorted packages or even provide appropriate corrective measures and, if necessary, safeguards.

For the Echo Protocol an interesting basis, since the packets are indeed rather undirected in the flow of the network and lost UDP packets are then not lost because of the multiplication and redundancy within each node.

13.9 Spot-On DTLS Server

A DTLS Server is also possible: Datagram Transport Layer Security (DTLS) is a communications protocol that provides security for datagram-based applications by allowing them to communicate in a way that is designed to prevent eaves-dropping, tampering, or message forgery. The DTLS proto-col is based on the stream-oriented Transport Layer Securi-ty (TLS) protocol and is intended to provide similar security guarantees. The DTLS protocol datagram preserves the se-mantics of the underlying transport—the application does not suffer from the delays associated with stream proto-cols, but because it uses UDP, the application has to deal with packet reordering, loss of datagram and data larger than the size of a datagram network packet. As DTLS can be used also for audio streaming, this is a basis for encrypted voice and audio over Spot-On (e.g. Spot-On-Sender (Analog Audio) => Amazon Echo => Internet => Amazon Echo => (Analog Audio) Spot-On-Receiver).

13.10 Spot-On SCTP Server

The Stream Control Transmission Protocol (SCTP) is a relia-ble, connection-oriented network Protocol. As a transport Protocol, SCTP is at the same level of the TCP / IP reference model as TCP and UDP.

SCTP realizes the concept of an association: Here, a con-nection is set up in which several message data streams are transported in order-preserving (with each other but poten-tially non-order-preserving). In addition, individual, for ex-ample, urgent, datagrams may be sent separately and out of line, possibly "overhauling" the in-order data streams.

Also, to use this Protocol for the transmission of Echo packets is very interesting for the research, since the rather undirected Echo packets may experience a more secure transmission with this Protocol compared to UDP.

This Protocol can also be used to set up a chat server within Spot-On.

13.11 Spot-On Ncat connection

While other applications always require a server that may be difficult to replicate, install or manage, Spot-On also can do without any dedicated server software. For this purpose, Ncat can be used as follows:

In one exercise, two devices are connected to Spot-On through a RaspberryPi running Debian using NCat. It requires a working network, a RaspberryPi and two devices each with Spot-On.

(1) First, ncat will be installed on the Pi:

sudo aptitude install nmap

(2) Then some SSL material is generated:

openssl req -new -x509 -keyout server-key.pem -out server-cert.pem

(3) Then ncat is called:

ncat -broker -ssl -ssl-cert server-cert.pem -ssl-key server-key.pem -k -l 192.168.178.130 4710

(4) Now the user visits the neighbor / server tab in Spot-On and defines the remote server at 192.168.178.130.

If the neighboring devices have been activated and the kernels are turned on, the connection already exists.
A nice exercise to test a network and Ncat for encrypted communication.

Questions and further Research & Development Fields

- Setup an own Spot-On-Listener at home with DynDNS.
- Connect a Spot-On client with a SmokeStack server on Android.
- Define a Half Echo Listener for Spot-On.
- Use the Debian Installer for Spot-On on a RaspberryPi as a server.
- Setup the SmokeStack server on an Android TV-Box from Ebay.
- Test a Bluetooth Server with Spot-On under Linux.
- Compare a Spot-On Listener or Echo Server creation with the setup of a Matrix or XMPP or Signal Server. Describe both processes in detail and compare.

14 Integrated Encryption Tools

In addition to the regular functions, Spot-On Encryption Suite also has several tools that offer further useful features. These include, in particular, the functions of file encryption (File Encryptor), another tool for converting normal text and cipher text (Rosetta-CryptoPad), and the EPKS tool, with which the public keys for encryption are transmitted online in a secure channel to a friend or to a community. Furthermore, the pass-through functionality as well as the tools for statistics and analyzes should be mentioned.

14.1 Tool: Encryption of files with Spot-On FileEncryptor

Spot-On has additional encryption tools. In the main menu under tools the user finds the tool for encrypting files on the own hard disk ("File Encryption Tool").

Figure 81: File Encryptor - file encryption tool

This allows the user to specify a file from the hard drive, then specify the same path and choose any extension or change of file name - then enter password and pin (both of course again with at least 16 characters) and define with the radio select buttons, whether the file should be encrypted or decrypted.

Cipher and hash-type are also definable as well as that a signature in the encryption can optionally be installed to ensure that the encryption was made only by the defined user (and nobody else).

The file encryption tool is an offer to replace potentially insecure Truecrypt containers, or to encrypt or to back up individual files before the user transfers the files - whether as an e-mail in Spot-On, via StarBeam file transfer in Spot-On or over conventional, insecure ways - or simply to encrypt the files on the hard disk or when stored in online cloud stores like Dropbox or other.

14.2 Tool: The Rosetta CryptoPad for text conversion in Spot-On

The tool Rosetta CryptoPad takes its name from the "Stone of Rosette", which stands in the museum in London. It is considered a translation tool for Egyptian hieroglyphs in other languages.

The Rosetta CryptoPad included in Spot-On has its own key - as well as chat and e-mail and all other functions have their own keys like this.

The user also exchanges the Rosetta key with a friend, then enters text into the CryptoPad, selects the friend and, whether it is encryption or decryption, - and press the "Convert" button.

Then the bottom of the window of the output is displayed as cipher text. The user can easily copy it with the copy function and sends it via conventional online communication channels such as @-e-mail or another chat. Web boards or paste bins can also be used by the user as a place for encrypted communication.

It is, so to speak, "slow chat" by a manually clicked encryption of the chat text (although the encryption is faster than the copy/paste-process into other instances).

The Rosetta CryptoPad is an alternative to other solutions, as it is based on a-symmetric encryption (PKI).

Figure 82: Encryption of text with the Rosetta Crypto Pad

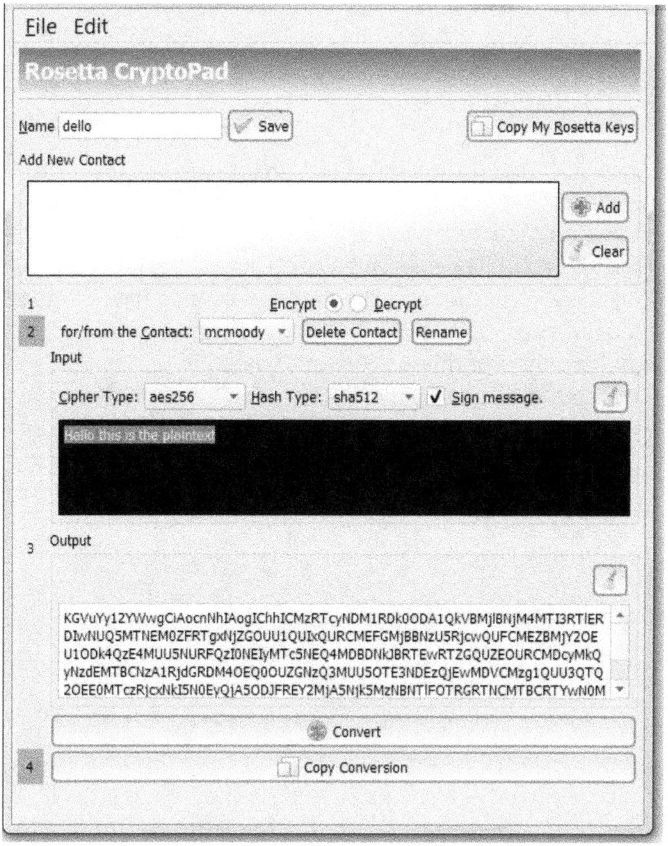

Rosetta CryptoPad
derives its name
from the "Stone of
Rosette" in the
Museum of London.

This method of slow chat also shows that applications that rely on encrypting each individual e-mail are an inconvenient method. Who wants to select the recipient for every e-mail and chat message, encrypt the message, decide whether the signature key should still be added or not before the message is sent?

Spot-On has the general advantage of exchanging the key just once with the friend during set up and then everything is encrypted at all times and the entire communication is transferred within the chosen encryption, with temporary keys and end-to-end passphrases can be renewed instantaneously at any time (e.g. with the Cryptographic Calling function).

14.3 Tool: Echo Public Key Share (EPKS) & AutoCrypt

When it comes to encryption, there is always the central question of how to safely transport the key to the friend.

Some architectures use key servers in which the user can store their public keys. This seems logical, after all it is a public key. Nevertheless, the key servers also have massive disadvantages, so we do not know if one has found the right key in it or if this is even up to date.

Instead, the Echo Public Key Share (EPKS) function makes it very easy to transfer keys in the Spot-On Encryption Suite.

Figure 83: EPKS - Echo Public Key Sharing

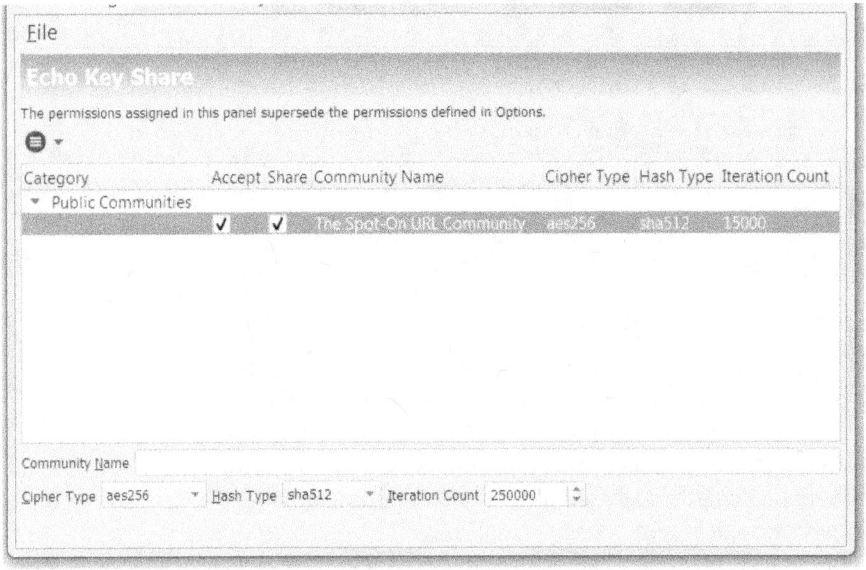

For this purpose, a symmetric key is defined with a community name in the p2p network of the Echo Protocol, through which all participants - who know the community name - can exchange the public keys.

The tool is linked via the main menu and opens a new pop-up window.

An example of a community is already there by default for the exchange of URL keys. The user sends the own URL key to this community and all other subscribers who are currently online in the p2p network receive this key.

It is a key exchange over a symmetric encrypted channel, where the password for end-to-end encryption is the name of the community. All users who know the name of the community will be able to receive and add the keys that users put into the secure channel to their Spot-On program.

14.4 Pass-Through functionality ("Patch-Points")

If two Spot-On clients have an existing connection over the Internet, this connection can be used as a tunnel to pass the data of another application through this tunnel. It has been mentioned a bit already above.

For this, a kind of proxy function of Spot-On is addressed with this pass-through functionality.

Patch Points describe a pass-through functionality.

This is an interesting feature to protect two clients of another program without encryption over the Internet with the encrypted connection via Spot-On.

Originally a pass-through was also named in the developer forum as a "Patch-Point".

Application => Spot-On => Spot-On-Server => Spot-On => Application

For another application, so to speak, a VPN tunnel is set up, which can even be equipped even with the McEliece algorithm or one of the other encryption algorithms. As long as no VPN provider offers McEliece encryption from start to end, the pass-through functionality is the right choice for a test. Spot-On represents here a kind of VPN tool. So far, no further tunnel software is known which applies McEliece.

The application to be connected should be tolerant to the order of the sent packets. It is an interesting research field that can be conducted with several possible applications and tests.

Figure 84: Spot-On as proxy: pass-through

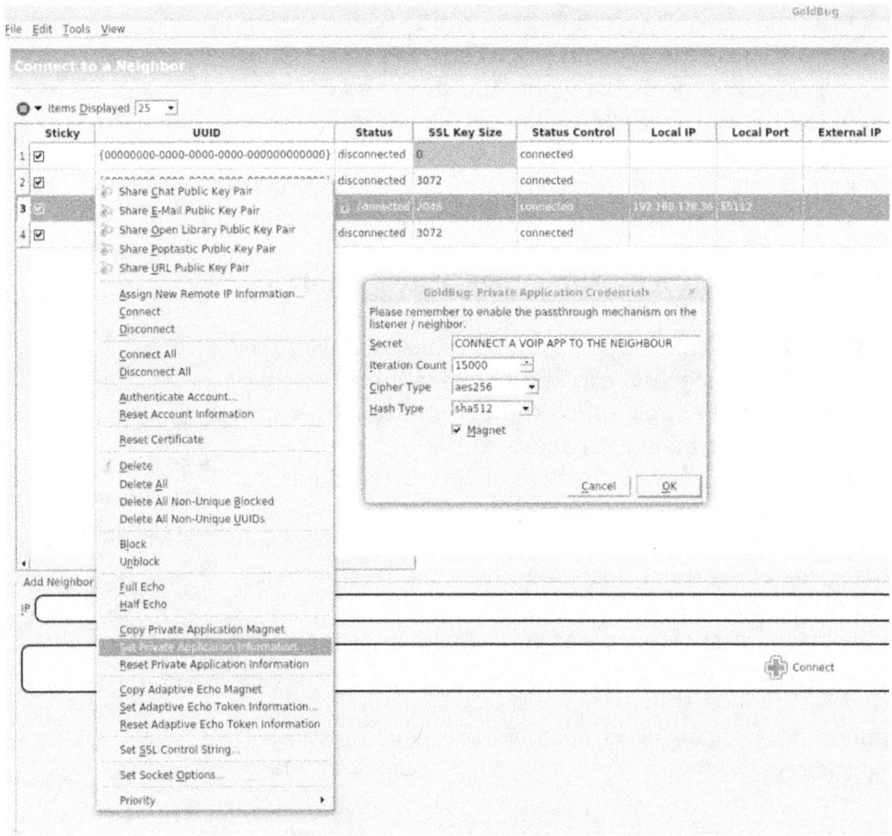

14.5 Statistics & Analyzing Tools

In addition to statistics overviews also analysis tools are included in Spot-On, such as the above-mentioned Star-Beam Analyzer. The listener and server tables also contain a lot of data information about sent packets, as well as statistics for the URL database.

Figure 85: Display of statistics

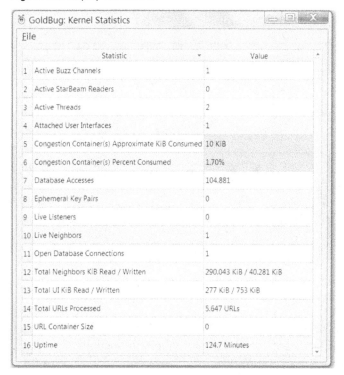

In addition to the usual user interface, Spot-On can also be installed in console form e.g. on a RasperryPi and retrieve the statistics overview with a corresponding command.

Figure 86: Statistics console on a Raspberry Pi

Raspberry PI - Statistics over Console

```
pi@snoopy:~ $ uname -a
Linux snoopy 4.1.13-v7+ #826 SMP PREEMPT Fri Nov 13 20:19:03 GMT 2015 armv7l GNU/Linux
pi@snoopy:~ $ sqlite3 spot-on/kernel.db
SQLite version 3.8.7.1 2014-10-29 13:59:56
Enter ".help" for usage hints.
sqlite> .d
PRAGMA foreign_keys=OFF;
BEGIN TRANSACTION;
CREATE TABLE kernel_gui_server (port INTEGER PRIMARY KEY NOT NULL CHECK (port >= 0 AND port <= 65535));
INSERT INTO "kernel_gui_server" VALUES(38328);
CREATE TABLE kernel_statistics (statistic TEXT PRIMARY KEY NOT NULL, value TEXT)
INSERT INTO "kernel_statistics" VALUES('Active Buzz Channels','0');
INSERT INTO "kernel_statistics" VALUES('Active StarBeam Readers','0');
INSERT INTO "kernel_statistics" VALUES('Active Threads','1');
INSERT INTO "kernel_statistics" VALUES('Attached User Interfaces','0');
INSERT INTO "kernel_statistics" VALUES('Congestion Container(s) Approximate MiB Consumed','2 MiB');
INSERT INTO "kernel_statistics" VALUES('Congestion Container(s) Percent Consumed','0.46%');
INSERT INTO "kernel_statistics" VALUES('Database Accesses','465,717');
INSERT INTO "kernel_statistics" VALUES('Ephemeral Key Pairs','0');
INSERT INTO "kernel_statistics" VALUES('Live Listeners','1');
INSERT INTO "kernel_statistics" VALUES('Live Neighbors','3');
INSERT INTO "kernel_statistics" VALUES('Open Database Connections','1');
INSERT INTO "kernel_statistics" VALUES('Total URLs Processed','0 URLs');
INSERT INTO "kernel_statistics" VALUES('URL Container Size','0');
INSERT INTO "kernel_statistics" VALUES('Uptime','875.2 Minutes');
CREATE TRIGGER kernel_gui_server_trigger BEFORE INSERT ON kernel_gui_server BEGIN DELETE FROM kernel_gui_server; END;
COMMIT;
```

The Pandamonium URL Web crawler also has corresponding statistics.

The Encryption Suite Spot-On is ideal for tests and learnings with this provided insight for different functions.

Questions and further Research & Development Fields

- Test the speed and measure the time to encrypt a movie file with FileEncryptor.
- Test the pass-through function with Gopher.
- Test a pass-through with any other network, e.g. Tor, I2P or Matrix.
- Test the pass-through function to send Echo packets through the Echo.
- Test the Rosetta CryptoPad for generating ciphertext.
- Define a Key Sharing Community in EPKS.

Figure 87: Pandamonium Web Crawler Stats

15 BIG SEVEN STUDY: Crypto-Messenger-Audit

The BIG SEVEN Study provides not only a security audit of the Spot-On Source code, but derives also 10 Trends in Cryptographic Messaging from several analyzed Messengers.

In the Study BIG SEVEN Crypto Messengers (2016) for Desktop Computers by David Adams and Ann-Kathrin Spot-On, respective the GoldBug Messenger GUI, was considered among seven open source Messengers. This international IT-audit-oriented evaluation regarded the software "more than audit-compliant" in more than 20 dimensions and "overall trustworthy". Also, the numerous code reviews gave hints in regard of an excellent programming.

The "10 Trends in Crypto-Messaging" have been identified by all seven messengers core competencies – and found all very elaborated within the research software of GoldBug and the underlaying Spot-On-Kernel architecture.

The following ten items to be considered in cryptographic programming have been pointed out:

1. Consolidation of chat and e-mail encryption: Messaging consolidates between chat and e-mail, the POP-TASTIC protocol is an ideal example, where e-mail servers are utilized for chat.
2. Storage of Data on the Hard Disc only encrypted: All data containers in the Spot-On architecture are fully encrypted as known from a truecrypt/veracrypt container.
3. SMP with zero-knowledge-proof processes for authentication: While the Socialist-Millionaire-Protocol is used to authenticate a friend, Secret Streams within the Spot-On architecture show how a bunch of ephemeral keys derived from the SMP process can secure end-to-end encryption without transferring the keys over the Internet.

4. Multi-Encryption: Several layers of encryption are provided e.g. with the Echo Protocol or with individual functions e.g. like a Nova-password on files.
5. Easy and decentral server setup: A listener for the Spot-On Server setup is created within a few clicks.
6. IPFS with Cryptographic Calling: Instant Perfect Forwarding Secrecy has been elaborated with several methods of Cryptographic Calling and even for Fiasco Forwarding a full bunch of keys will be transferred and tested.
7. Individual Crypto-DNA: Magnet-URI links contain many cryptographic values, which are bundled in the link of the Magnet-URI standard.
8. Manual definition of end-to-end encryption keys: #CSEK – Customer Supplied Encryption Keys – The user is requested to manually and individually define the passphrase for an end to end encryption key.
9. Avoiding of Metadata: With the graph theory within the Echo Network packets flood in every direction, so that meta data is hard to record.
10. Alternatives to RSA: e.g. McEliece Algorithm – As RSA is regarded officially as broken by NIST (2016) software needs to start to use alternative Algorithms, like NTRU or McEliece.

Spot-On covers these trends identified by the comparison of seven well known crypto messenger very elaborated. The procedures of the software are in each field still advanced of not leading. Research needs to (1) analyze further comparisons of applications and (2) implementations and standards, software development with cryptographic procedures needs to reach.

The ten fields with "Trends in Encrypting Processes" need to be further deepened also for other encrypting software besides messaging.

Figure 88: Big Seven Crypto Study: Trends in Crypto (2016)

Adams, D. / Maier, A.K. (2016)

Next to the auditing of the source code 2016, the architecture and processes of encryption as well as the functions in Spot-On, there are numerous other topics on which future research can orientate itself. As an example, the following questions should be mentioned for further evaluations and research needs, which may play a role in comparison with other processes and applications:

Criterion / Question	Spot-On	Lettera	Riot	Smoke	Signal	GoldBug	Retro-Share

- Is the application open source?
- Is it a tiered application: kernel and user interface processes?
- Are there proxy capabilities?
- Is it possible to send E-Mail messages to offline friends?
- Is it possible to send E-Mail with encrypted attachments?
- Are there different keys for different functions in place like Chat, E-Mail, CryptoPad, Filetransfer etc.?
- Is the key stuck to the IP Address of the user?
- How is mutual access authentication defined?
- Are there alternatives to RSA, like McEliece or NTRU? Can a NTRU-user chat to a RSA-user? With which library is McEliece implemented?
- Are there selectable SSL ciphers?
- Are there selectable hash algorithms?
- Is just connectivity needed, i.e. no key exchange is needed, are keys optional?
- Is trust needed, or can it be added as the user defines it?
- What about technical simplicity?
- Is it possible to determine, who is reading which message? Can a sent message be deleted?
- Local databases store all information in encrypted .db's?
- Is the authentication of messages optional?
- Can the user communicate without public keys, e.g. using Magnets?
- Support for TCP and UDP and SCTP communications?
- Support of multi-layers of encryption?
- Are multiple listeners possible?
- Is a multi-threaded kernel given?

- Are there IRC-like group chat channels?
- What about simple IP-based firewalls?
- Do scramblers send out fake messages?
- Is it possible to store messages in friends?
- Is there the option to use an individually defined and manually inserted end-to-end key for communication?
- Is there the option to renew the end-to-end key each time a user wants (not only session based)?
- Encrypted file transfer Protocol - Using a onetime Magnet (OTM) for a crypto channel?
- Having IPv6 support?
- Having Qt 5 and up deployed? Also a Java client in place?
- Sending a message to a friend to his dedicated connection and not to all or central connections?
- Hiding the key exchange online over encrypted solutions (e.g. REPLEO or EPKS channel)?
- Using different encryption keys for one file transfer?
- Adding a passphrase to a to be transferred file?

Questions and further Research & Development Fields

- Lookup the 20 audit criteria for the evaluation of IT Software according the Big 7 Study (2016).
- Go through the code of the latest Spot-On and note your findings.
- Choose one Trend-Dimension and analyze two applications in comparison in this regard.
- As it is not about the Application to compare, but the open source chat server to compare, please compare the two open source server applications for encrypted chat.
- Create a concept for a Crypto-Party evening to set up an own server. Note the questions of the guests and work out a procedure with recommendations for the server set up.

16 Outlook with Graph-Theory: Initial Welcome in the New Era of Exponential Encryption

The term "Era of Exponential Encryption" has been coined by Mele Gasakis and Max Schmidt in their book "Beyond Cryptographic Routing". Herein they describe the development within cryptography to multiply several methods, values and constants. Based on the therein provided analyzes and recent innovations in cryptography they provide a vision that can demonstrate an increasing multiplication of options for encryption and decryption processes: Also referred to their analysis of the Echo Protocol, especially if it is regarded in the context of Graph-Theory.

The Era of Exponential Encryption:

Beyond Cryptographic Routing.

Similar to a grain of rice that doubles exponentially in every field of a chessboard, more and more newer concepts and programming in the area of cryptography like the Echo Protocol increase these manifolds: both, encryption and decryption, require more session-related and multiple keys, so that numerous options exist for configuring encryption: with different keys and algorithms, symmetric and a-symmetrical methods, or even modern multiple encryption, with that cipher text is converted again and again to cipher text. It is also analyzed how a handful of newer applications and open source software programming implements these encryption mechanisms.

16.1 Multiplication towards Exponential

Next to hybrid-encryption, which means to apply both, symmetric and a-symmetric encryption or vice versa, also multi-encryption is mentioned, in which a cipher text is encrypted to cipher text and, again, several times to cipher text - possibly and intended with different methods or algorithms. Further is mentioned the turn back from session keys, so called ephemeral keys, towards a renewal of the session key by instant options for the user: to renew the key several times within the dedicated session. That has forwarded the term of "Perfect Forward Secrecy" to "Instant Perfect Forward Secrecy" (IPFS) – as we already know by end of this Handbook and User Manual.

But even more, if in advance a bunch of keys is sent, a decoding of a message has to consider not only one present session key, but also over dozens of keys sent prior before the message arrives. The new paradigm of IPFS has already turned into the newer concept of these Fiasco Keys. Fiasco Keys are keys, which provide over a dozen possible ephemeral keys within one session and define Fiasco Forwarding, the approach, which complements and follows IPFS.

Fiasco Keys have been coded into several applications like Smoke (Client) and SmokeStack (Chatserver). They provide in contrast to other more static and schematic Protocols like the Signal Protocol a vision into a more volatile world of encryption.

The Echo Protocol is Beyond Cryptographic Routing.

And further, adding routing- and graph theory to the encryption process, which is a constant part of the also in this Handbook in detail described Echo Protocol, an encrypted packet might take different graphs and routes within the network. This and the sum off all the mentioned innovations and development features described within the book "Beyond Cryptographic Routing" multiply also the options an invader against a defined encryption has to consider - and shifts the current status to a new age: The Era of Exponential Encryption, so the vision and description of the authors.

That means: If cipher text is now sent over the Internet, there exist also the manifold options in the networks of the analyzed applications that messages take undefined routes or even routes defined with cryptographic tokens. If the routing- and graph-theory is paired with encryption, the network theory of computer science gets quite new dimensions:

Based on the development of various proxy- or mix-networks, such as the well-known Tor-network (and further analyzed in their book), a development from so-called "Onion Routing" to "Echo Discovery" is described: That means the route of a packet to be sent can no longer be defined, as each node in the network independently decides the next hop.

Spot-On as Initial Welcome in the Era of Exponential Encryption (EEE)

On the other hand: The special case of a "sprinkling network" describes the learning of servers and nodes based on these cryptographic tokens. This Adaptive Echo offers advantages and disadvantages compared to the previous mix networks.

It is therefore not spoken in these flooding networks from the concept of "routing", as we know it from the well-known TCP Protocol, but of "discovery": If the cryptographic token is matching, the message belongs to me. The Echo Protocol is an example of the change from Onion Routing to Cryptographic Discovery.

Will servers within a network learn soon by cryptographic tokens?

Is it also a new option for new, better encryption in the network? If routing does not require destination information but is replaced by cryptographic insights, then it is "beyond cryptographic routing". Will servers within the network learn in the future through cryptographic tokens, which route a packet takes within the Internet and to which recipient it should be delivered and which recipient it should not be forwarded to? Well-known alternatives to popular messengers have announced that they will replace the sender with a cryptographic token, and thereby approach this property of the Echo that has existed for many years. Servers will learn now based on Cryptographic Discovery: The Artificial Intelligence – the learning of computers – will be steered in the future by Cryptographic Discovery? It can be spoken of Cryptographic Artificial Intelligence, in short: CAI.

The SECRED Protocol of the Sprinkling Effect is one element of Cryptographic Discovery.

At the same time, some are also analyzing and realizing a new way of thinking and working in the time after the Snowden Papers, - especially within the open source community - which differs from industrial development work for encryption programs to community-oriented open

Cryptographic Artificial Intelligence (CAI) is defined by Cryptographic Discovery and Machine Learning.

source developments. These in particular have, can and will arise innovations in cryptography (probably detached from the known insider circles of experts).

A prominent example of such an innovation is such of Cryptographic Calling: In this process, numerous keys for end-to-end encryption are promptly and several times within one push of a button individually defined and renewed after a user request. Only a few programs can do this so far.

The Echo Protocol, which is applied in a handful of software applications, is in this regard an initial welcome within the Era of Exponential Encryption. Encryption and Graph-Theory have been brought together. According to this, every message is encrypted several times and each network node sends a packet to all known neighbors. This compares and transforms classic mix networks like Tor or I2P and other to a new kind of flooding networks. A complex chaos is coming.

16.2 Four Arms within the Era of Exponential Encryption

Four Arms:
- *Multi-Encryption*
- *Avoiding Meta-Data*
- *Value-Diversification*
- *New Algorithms*

There are four arms to be identified within the "Era of Exponential Encryption", which refer to (1) multi-encryption: the conversion from cipher text to cipher text to cipher text, (2) meta-data resistance, and (3) third, the increasing diversification of cryptographic parameters: Key variables or applied algorithms, as well as (4) the trend towards new algorithms such as NTRU and McEliece, which are so far considered to be particularly more secure against the attacks of the fast Quantum Computing:

- Multi-Encryption as a result of numerous disruptive innovations in cryptography: Multi-Encryption is the conversion of cipher text to cipher text, if both a-symmetric and symmetric methods are used, hybrid multi-encryption can be defined.
- Avoiding Meta-data & Resistance to Meta-data Analysis: Big user data has become a gray fog or noise fac-

tor, which makes it difficult to decipher and in which a user may also hide with secret messages.

- Diversification of the user-defined cryptographic parameters: Users can use numerous algorithms, the individual cryptographic-DNA has been highly individualized.
- Switching from RSA Algorithm to NTRU and McEliece as a strengthening of Resistance to Quantum Computing: Since 2016, RSA has been officially insecure. Short, but fact. Switching to NTRU and McEliece plays a central role.

These research results and assumptions in the concept proposal of the NEW EEE-ERA is strengthening the ten crypto trends found proposed by Adams/Maier in 2016.

16.3 Implications

From these developments, social, legal, political and economic recommendations are derived, which are to be discussed more intensely, especially in educational processes: Our schools need more teaching and learning processes that understand and convey the beginning of the increasingly exponential cryptography.

Social, legal, political and economic implications.

Social implications:
"'The liberty of the other begins with the acceptance of his or her cipher text' - if the known quotation from Rosa Luxemburg (1918) may be applied to the next century in this wording. If it is difficult to accept the limits of the readable opinion of the other, how easily should one fall to accept the limits of the unreadable opinion of the other?", has to be asked. Combined with a suggestion, that multipliers within social groups help others to get a common understanding for cryptographic processes in society and for private people.

Legal implications:
The new status in the Era of Exponential Encryption shows that the legal requirements to judge cases are becoming

more complex: e.g. if non-license-free material is forwarded in an encrypted packet or if only "non-routed" communication content has to be decoded in a legal case – or if an Internet Service Provider should be able to decrypt at all? - The authors suggest to provide professional education already at high school for all law concerned professions.

Political implications:
Here the question is raised, how much competence development in a particular nation should this nation request? and how can political processes steer this? The authors suggest that encryption must be a well accepted science and practical process in politics and by politicians. A nation needs own research results in cryptography.

Economic implications:
Encryption is the basic process of the digital economy. The authors suggest that an initiative should equal the open source software with proprietary encryption solutions.

16.4 Outlook

A pleading for the compulsory subject computer-science already in school? - In any case, the so-called "digital immigrants" as well as members of the "Generation Y", who have grown up with the mobile phones, continue to develop the content of the cryptography in the curricula of schools and discuss the described innovations and questions towards the "Era of Exponential Encryption ".

It is necessary to develop teaching concepts that lead non-MIT and non-math students to cryptology & cryptography and, secondly, to address also the other group of non-students: technically interested people who have never seen a university from inside but are interested in technical development and its social discussion of the consequences of technology and/or not learning and applying of new technology.

Here, in the area of encryption, every reader and user is asked to consider how to learn, how to deepen the existing knowledge and to be learned content as well as practical application of the know-how of encryption.

The context content appeals to interested persons of computer science, math, and cryptography as well as to students who want to discuss new cryptographic innovations in tutorials and crypto-parties.

Questions and further Research & Development Fields

- Why are multi-encryption and individual Cryptographic DNA values influencing the multiplication of options?
- How is graph theory and networking within the Echo Protocol related to multiplied and exponential Encryption?
- What are the four arms of the New Era of Exponential Encryption?
- Which implications derive from the New Era of Exponential Encryption for the next Crypto-Party of students?
- Provide an action plan to update educational processes for one educational class curriculum, school or university based on 10 chapters of this handbook.
- Discuss Life-Cycle-Management for a RSA application and provide a start-up business-plan for a McEliece application. How has Chance Management to be steered of companies offering both software products?
- How can developers paid by government and working for public domain provide an open source alternative for WhatsApp based on open source chat server software everyone can install and use?

17 Digital Encryption of Private Communication in the Context of ...

This user manual is not only intended to technically describe the handling of encryption, its processes or the use of the individual tabs and buttons, but also to illustrate the meaning of the encryption as it stands in the light of various basic laws for the protection of private freedom and communication. The following basic laws should therefore be pointed out, which refer to them in their original texts.

17.1 Principles of the protection of private speech, communication and life: Universal Declaration of Human Rights, 1948 (Art. 12)

No one shall be subjected to arbitrary interference with his privacy, family, home or correspondence, nor to attacks upon his honor and reputation. Everyone has the right to the protection of the law against such interference or attacks.
http://www.un.org/en/documents/udhr/index.shtml#a12
Universal Declaration of Human Rights.

17.2 International Covenant on Civil & Political Rights, 1966 (Art. 17)

1. No one shall be subjected to arbitrary or unlawful interference with his privacy, family, home or correspondence, nor to unlawful attacks on his honour and reputation.
2. Everyone has the right to the protection of the law against such interference or attacks.

http://www.ohchr.org/EN/ProfessionalInterest/Pages/ CCPR.aspx International Covenant on Civil and Political Rights.

17.3 European Convention on Human Rights, 1950 (Art. 8)

1. Everyone has the right to respect for his private and family life, his home and his correspondence.
2. There shall be no interference by a public authority with the exercise of this right except such as is in accordance with the law and is necessary in a democratic society in the interests of national security, public safety or the economic well-being of the country, for the prevention of disorder or crime, for the protection of health or morals, or for the protection of the rights and freedoms of others.

http://conventions.coe.int/treaty/en/Treaties/Html/005.htm / European Convention on Human Rights.

17.4 Charter of Fundamental Rights of the European Union, 2000 (Art. 7, 8)

Article 7 - Respect for private and family life: Everyone has the right to respect for his or her private and family life, home and communications.

Article 8. Protection of personal data: 1. Everyone has the right to the protection of personal data concerning him or her. 2. Such data must be processed fairly for specified purposes and on the basis of the consent of the person concerned or some other legitimate basis laid down by law. Everyone has the right of access to data which has been collected concerning him or her, and the right to have it rectified. 3. Compliance with these rules shall be subject to control by an independent authority. Charter of Fundamental Rights of the European Union - Charter of Fundamental Rights of the European Union (Wikisource) Charter of Fundamental Rights of the European Union.

17.5 Basic Law e.g. for the Federal Republic of Germany, 1949 (Art. 2 Abs. 1 i. V. m. Art. 1 Abs. 1)

Article 2 - Personal freedoms: (1) Every person shall have the right to free development of his personality insofar as he does not violate the rights of others or offend against the constitutional order or the moral law. Article 1 [Human dignity – Human rights – Legally binding force of basic rights] (1) Human dignity shall be inviolable. To respect and protect it shall be the duty of all state authority. https://www.btg-bestellservice.de/pdf/80201000.pdf Basic Law for the Federal Republic of Germany.

Further: Article 1 and Article 10:

Art. 1 Human dignity – Human rights: Legally binding force of basic rights (1) Human dignity shall be inviolable. To respect and protect it shall be the duty of all state authority. (2) The German people therefore acknowledge inviolable and inalienable human rights as the basis of every community, of peace and of justice in the world. (3) The following basic rights shall bind the legislature, the executive and the judiciary as directly applicable law

17.6 Privacy of correspondence, posts and telecommunications (Art. 10)

Secrecy of correspondence - Fernmeldegeheimnis (Art. 10 Abs. 1 Grundgesetz)

§ 88 Abs. 1 Fernmeldegeheimnis - Telekommunikationsgesetz: (1) Dem Fernmeldegeheimnis unterliegen der Inhalt der Telekommunikation und ihre näheren Umstände, insbesondere die Tatsache, ob jemand an einem Telekommunikationsvorgang beteiligt ist oder war. Das Fernmeldegeheimnis erstreckt sich auch auf die näheren Umstände erfolgloser Verbindungsversuche. (2) Zur Wahrung des Fernmeldegeheimnisses ist jeder Diensteanbieter verpflichtet. Die Pflicht zur Geheimhaltung besteht auch nach dem Ende der Tätigkeit fort, durch die sie begründet worden ist. (3) Den nach Absatz 2 Verpflichteten ist es untersagt, sich oder anderen über das für die geschäftsmäßige Erbringung der Telekommunikationsdienste einschließlich des Schutzes ihrer technischen Systeme erforderliche Maß hinaus Kenntnis vom Inhalt oder den näheren Umständen der Telekommunikation zu verschaffen. Sie dürfen Kenntnisse über Tatsachen, die dem Fernmeldegeheimnis unterliegen, nur für den in Satz 1 genannten Zweck verwenden. Eine Verwendung dieser Kenntnisse für andere Zwecke, insbesondere die Weitergabe an andere, ist nur zulässig, soweit dieses Gesetz oder eine andere gesetzliche Vorschrift dies vorsieht und sich dabei ausdrücklich auf Telekommunikationsvorgänge bezieht. Die Anzeigepflicht nach § 138 des Strafgesetzbuches hat Vorrang. (4) Befindet sich die Telekommunikationsanlage an Bord eines Wasser- oder Luftfahrzeugs, so besteht die Pflicht zur Wahrung des Geheimnisses nicht gegenüber der Person, die das Fahrzeug führt oder gegenüber ihrer Stellvertretung.

17.7 Verletzung des Post- oder Fernmeldegeheimnisses (§ 206)

(1) Wer unbefugt einer anderen Person eine Mitteilung über Tatsachen macht, die dem Post- oder Fernmeldegeheimnis unterliegen und die ihm als Inhaber oder Beschäftigtem eines Unternehmens bekanntgeworden sind, das geschäftsmäßig Post- oder Telekommunikationsdienste erbringt, wird mit Freiheitsstrafe bis zu fünf Jahren oder mit Geldstrafe bestraft. (2) Ebenso wird bestraft, wer als Inhaber oder Beschäftigter eines in Absatz 1 bezeichneten Unternehmens unbefugt 1. eine Sendung, die einem solchen Unternehmen zur Übermittlung anvertraut worden und verschlossen ist, öffnet oder sich von ihrem Inhalt ohne Öffnung des Verschlusses unter Anwendung technischer Mittel Kenntnis verschafft, 2. eine einem solchen Unternehmen zur Übermittlung anvertraute Sendung unterdrückt oder 3. eine der in Absatz 1 oder in Nummer 1 oder 2 bezeichneten Handlungen gestattet oder fördert. (3) Die Absätze 1 und 2 gelten auch für Personen, die 1. Aufgaben der Aufsicht über ein in Absatz 1 bezeichnetes Unterneh-

men wahrnehmen, 2. von einem solchen Unternehmen oder mit dessen Ermächtigung mit dem Erbringen von Post- oder Telekommunikationsdiensten betraut sind oder 3. mit der Herstellung einer dem Betrieb eines solchen Unternehmens dienenden Anlage oder mit Arbeiten daran betraut sind. (4) Wer unbefugt einer anderen Person eine Mitteilung über Tatsachen macht, die ihm als außerhalb des Post- oder Telekommunikationsbereichs tätigem Amtsträger auf Grund eines befugten oder unbefugten Eingriffs in das Post- oder Fernmeldegeheimnis bekanntgeworden sind, wird mit Freiheitsstrafe bis zu zwei Jahren oder mit Geldstrafe bestraft. (5) Dem Postgeheimnis unterliegen die näheren Umstände des Postverkehrs bestimmter Personen sowie der Inhalt von Postsendungen. Dem Fernmeldegeheimnis unterliegen der Inhalt der Telekommunikation und ihre näheren Umstände, insbesondere die Tatsache, ob jemand an einem Telekommunikationsvorgang beteiligt ist oder war. Das Fernmeldegeheimnis erstreckt sich auch auf die näheren Umstände erfolgloser Verbindungsversuche. http://www.gesetze-im-internet.de/gg/art_10.html Secrecy of correspondence – Briefgeheimnis - (Fernmeldegeheimnis) - Postgeheimnis http://www.gesetze-im-internet.de/tkg_2004/__88.html http://www.gesetze-im-internet.de/stgb/__206.html

17.8 United States Constitution: Search and Seizure (Expectation of Privacy, US Supreme Court)

The right of the people to be secure in their persons, houses, papers, and effects, against unreasonable searches and seizures, shall not be violated, and no Warrants shall issue, but upon probable cause, supported by Oath or affirmation, and particularly describing the place to be searched, and the persons or things to be seized. http://www.usconstitution.net/const.html

18 History of Program Publications

The list of publications shows continuous updates and releases of the application over several years. The first publication dates back to 2013, and before that, another project also involved several years of research work. The release dates of the versions show on average almost monthly or at least quarterly a release. The notes makes it clear which feature has been added, improved, or published.

The history of the publications since 2013 and earlier can be found with approx. 40 Program releases in the wiki of the project page of the GoldBug release history, for Spot-On the release history is to be analysed in detail by the release notes, which moved from Sourceforge to Github and have been arrived there too:

- https://github.com/textbrowser/spot-on/tree/master/branches/Documentation
- https://sourceforge.net/p/goldbug/wiki/release-history/

19 Website

Further information can be found on the website:

- http://spot-on.sf.net
- https://textbrowser.github.io/spot-on/

20 Open source code & Compilation

The open source code and further compile information can be found at the repository at Github:
- https://github.com/textbrowser/spot-on
- The GoldBug GUI source code is also to be found in the Spot-On repository at Github.

20.1 Compile Information

Anyone who looks on the website of Spot-On, finds here the current release, especially for Windows. If the user has advanced computer skills, would like to compile the program from the source code or wants to learn from this example, this developer will find here more hints on how to proceed for the operating systems, e.g. Windows.

The compilation from the source code allows the developer to see how the source code forms into a binary file (.exe) and which program libraries are to be supplemented so that the executable file can run.

First, it is to download the Qt tool kit. Choose the offline (or online) installation of Qt with MingGW: e.g. Qt 5.X for Windows 32-bit (MinGW 4.9.2, 1.0 GB) at the URL: http://www.qt.io/download- open-source / # section-2

Then the source code has to be downloaded. For Windows all required dependencies and libraries are already integrated in the path of the source text. The Spot-On GUI and the Spot-On Kernel can be found at GitHub at the mentioned URL above: https://github.com/textbrowser/spot-on To download the source code, the developer can download the master tree on the website as a zip in the browser or use a GIT client.

For Linux, all these libraries should be installed:
- Qt 5.1.x or higher,

- libGeoIP 1.5.1,
- libcrypto 0.9.8 or later,
- libgcrypt 1.5.x, and
- libssl 0.9.8 or later.
- libsqlite3-dev
- libgcrypt11-dev
- libssl-dev
- libgeoip-dev
- libpq-dev,
- libeay,
- libgpg-error,
- libsshgcrypt-dev,
- libssh-gcrypt-dev,
- libgcrypt-dev,
- libgcrypt11-dev,
- libgl1-mesa-dev,
- libcurlpp-dev,
- libcurl4openssl-dev,
- libsctp-dev,
- libtool,
- libtool-dev,
- libntl.

The libGeoIP program library is optional and can be by-passed if the selected Qt-PRO project file is configured accordingly. It has to be checked, whether for Linux all mentioned, or more recent versions of these program libraries are installed on the machine. For Windows, the necessary program libraries are already attached to the source code (DLL files, even if not customary). Further compiling information can be found within the source code itself.

After the developer has installed Qt, the user starts the program Qt-Creator from the Qt directory.

Then the developer selects the relevant .pro file from the unpacked source code path and compiles the GUI and the kernel with Qt Creator. For the compilation of Spot-On the user installs Qt5 and then select the .pro file "Spot-On.Qt5.win.pro". This file opens both, kernel and GUI sub-pro files.

Then in QT-Creator the developer simply clicks on the green forward arrow and starts the compiling. At the end of the compilation process from the Qt Creator Spot-On.exe should then be bootable. If the developer wants to put the exe.file in a separate path on the own hard-disk, the developer has to add all needed DLL files (from the selected Qt version and from all current libraries) as well as the sub-paths e.g. for the sound or Qt files, as they already exist in the default installation zip for Spot-On Windows. The library DLL files for Window are also stored in the source code of the respective library paths for convenient and easy use.

The developer can of course compile with the Qt terminal window Spot-On also with manual DOS commands, without using Qt-Creator.

COMPILING PROCESS with C ++ / Qt:
- Windows: qmake -o Makefile Spot-On.win.qt5.pro
- make or mingw32-make
- or choose in Qt-Creator: Spot-On.win.qt5.pro

Spot-On does not provide checksums for the binary downloads as the source is given for those who want to build on their own. Please notice: Spot-On has a build date in the GUI so the sums might differ for each compile!

FURTHER INFO for other .pro files:
If header (h) or interface (ui) files have changed, please perform a distclean before building the application.
- Absolute cleaning: make distclean or mingw32-make distclean
- FreeBSD: qmake -o Makefile spot-on.freebsd.pro make
- Linux: qmake -o Makefile spot-on.pro make
- OS X: qmake -spec macx-g++ -o Makefile spot-on.osx.pro make

- Windows: qmake -o Makefile spot-on.win.pro
  make or mingw32-make

21 Bibliography

Adams, David / Maier, Ann-Kathrin: BIG SEVEN Study, open source crypto-messengers to be compared - or: Comprehensive Confidentiality Review & Audit of GoldBug, Encrypting E-Mail-Client & Secure Instant Messenger, Descriptions, tests and analysis reviews of 20 functions of the application GoldBug based on the essential fields and methods of evaluation of the 8 major international audit manuals for IT security investigations including 38 figures and 87 tables., URL: https://sf.net/projects/goldbug/files/bigseven-crypto-audit.pdf - English / German Language, Version 1.1, 305 pages, June 2016.

Akhoondi, Masoud; Yu, Curtis; Madhyastha, Harsha V. (May 2012). LASTor: A Low-Latency AS-Aware Tor Client (PDF). IEEE Symposium on Security and Privacy. Oakland, USA. Retrieved 28 April 2014.

Anand, M. Vijay / Jayakumar C.: Secured Routing Using Quantum Cryptography, in: Krishna, P. Venkata / Babu, M. Rajasekhara / Ariwa, Ezendu (Ed.): Global Trends in Computing and Communication Systems, Volume 269 of the series Communications in Computer and Information Science, pp. 714-725, Vellore, TN, India, 2011.

Arbeitskreis Vorratsdatenspeicherung (AKV), Bündnis gegen Überwachung et al.: List of Secure Instant Messengers, URL: http://wiki.vorratsdatenspeicherung.de/List_of_Secure_Instant_Messengers, Mai 2014.

Banerjee, Sanchari: EFYTIMES News Network: 25 Best Open Source Projects Of 2014: EFYTIMES ranked GoldBug Messenger # 4 on the overall Top 25 Best Open Source Projects Of 2014, URL: http://www.efytimes.com/e1/fullnews.asp?edid=148831, 2014.

Bangeman, Eric: "Security researcher Dan Egerstad stumbles across embassy E-Mail log-ins, Arstechnica.com, 2007.

Baran, Paul: Digital Simulation of Hot-Potato Routing in a Broadband Distributed Communications Network, URL: http://www.rand.org/about/history/baran.list.html, 1964.

Baran, Paul: On Distributed Communications Networks, RAND Corporation papers, document P-2626, URL: https://www.rand.org/pubs/papers/P2626.html, 1962.

Baran, Paul: Reliable Digital Communications Systems Using Unreliable Network Repeater Nodes, RAND Corporation papers, document P-1995, URL: https://www.rand.org/content/dam/rand/pubs/papers/2008/P1995.pdf, 1960.

Black, Michael: When I first heard of GoldBug - Review of GoldBug Secure Instant Messenger, URL: http://www.lancedoma.ru/, 29 Oct 2013

Bloomberg: The Big Hack: How China Used a Tiny Chip to Infiltrate U.S. Companies, https://www.bloomberg.com/news/features/2018-10-04/the-big-hack-how-china-used-a-tiny-chip-to-infiltrate-america-s-top-companies, 2018.

BMWI / BMI / BMVI DIGITALE AGENDA – Entwurf – Wir wollen Verschlüsselungs-Standort Nr. 1 auf der Welt werden, Stand: 09. Juli 2014:URL: https://netzpolitik.org/2014/wir-praesentieren-den-entwurf-der-digitalen-agenda/, 2016

Boie, Johannes: Zensur in sozialen Medien - Wie Facebook Menschen zum Schweigen bringt, URL: http://www.sueddeutsche.de/digital/zensur-in-sozialen-medien-wie-facebook-menschen-zum-schweigen-bringt-1.3130204, 22. August 2016.

Bolluyt, Jess: Does WhatsApp's Encryption Really Protect You?, URL: http://www.cheatsheet.com/gear-style/does-whatsapps-encryption-really-protect-you.html/?a=viewall, June 03, 2016.

Bonchev, Daniel / Rouvray, D. H.: Chemical Graph Theory: Introduction and Fundamentals, New York, 1991.

Brynjolfsson, Erik / McAfee, Andrew: The Second Machine Age: Work, Progress, and Prosperity in a Time of Brilliant Technologies, Norton 2014.

Cakra, Deden: Review of GoldBug Instant Messenger, Blogspot, URL http://bengkelcakra.blogspot.de/ 2014/12/free-download-goldbug-instant-messenger.html, 13. December 2014.

Cayley, Arthur: Chemical Graphs, in: Philosophical Magazine, Band 47, pp. 444–446, 1874.

Chang, Ernest J. H.: Echo Algorithms: Depth Parallel Operations on General Graphs, URL: http://ieeexplore.ieee.org/iel5/32/35929/01702961.pdf?arnu mber=1702961, 1982.

Chaum David: The dining cryptographers problem: unconditional sender and recipient untraceability. Journal of Cryptology, 1 (1):65–75, 1988.

Chaum, David / Das, Debajyoti / Kate, Aniket / Javani, Farid / Sherman, Alan T. / KrasNOVA, Anna / de Ruiter, Joeri: cMix: Anonymization by High-Performance Scalable Mixing, URL: https://eprint.iacr.org/2016/008.pdf, May 30, 2016.

Chaum, David: Untraceable electronic mail, return addresses, and digital pseudonyms. Communications of the ACM, 24(2), Feb. 1981.

Chen, Lily / Jordan, Stephen / Liu, Yi-Kai / Moody, Dustin / Peralta, Rene / Perlner, Ray / Smith-Tone, Daniel / NIST: NISTIR 8105, DRAFT, Report on Post-Quantum Cryptography, URL: http://csrc.nist.gov/publications/drafts/nistir-8105/nistir_8105_draft.pdf, National Institute of Standards and Technology. February 2016.

Christensen, Cayton M. / Raynor, Michael E. / McDonald, Rory: What Is Disruptive Innovation?, Harvard Business Review, URL: https://hbr.org/2015/12/what-is-disruptive-innovation, December 2015.

Christensen, Clayton M.: The innovator's dilemma: when new technologies cause great firms to fail, Harvard Business School Press, Boston, Massachusetts, ISBN 978-0-87584-585-2, 1997.

Cimpanu, Catalin: Tor Users Can Be Tracked Based on Their Mouse Movements, Softpedia& Slashdot, 2016.

Clarke, Ian / Sandberg, Oskar / Wiley, Brandon / Hong, Theodore W.: Freenet: A Distributed Anonymous Information Storage and Retrieval System". Designing Privacy Enhancing Technologies. Lecture Notes in Computer Science. 2001:46–66.

Constantinos / OsArena: GOLDBUG: ΜΙΑ ΣΟΥΙΤΑ ΓΙΑ CHATING ΜΕ ΠΟΛΛΑΠΛΗ ΚΡΥΠΤΟΓΡΑΦΗΣΗ, Latest Articles, URL: http://osarena.net/logismiko/applications /goldbug-miasouita-gia-chating-me-pollapli-kriptografisi.html, 25 March 2014.

Cordasco, Jared / Wetzel, Susanne: Cryptographic vs. Trust-based Methods for MANET Routing Security, URL: www.coglib.com/~jcordasC/Onsite/ cordasco_cryptographic_07.pdf, STM 2007.

Corrigan-Gibbs, H./ Boneh, D. / Mazieres, D.: Riposte: An Anonymous Messaging System Handling Millions of Users. ArXiv e-prints, Mar. 2015, https://www.youtube.com/watch?v=hL3AnIOfu4Y.

Corrigan-Gibbs, Henry / Ford, Bryan: Dissent: Accountable Group Anonymity, URL: http://dedis.cs.yale.edu/dissent/papers/ccs10/dissent.pdf, CCS 2010.

Cox, Joseph: The FBI Hacked Over 8,000 Computers In 120 Countries Based on One Warrant, URL: https://motherboard.vice.com/read/fbi-hacked-over-8000-computers-in-120-countries-based-on-one-warrant, November 22, 2016.

Crope, Frosanta / Sharma, Ashwani / Singh, Ajit / Pahwa, Nikhil: An efficient cryptographic approach for secure policy-based routing: (TACIT Encryption Technique), Electronics Computer Technology (ICECT), 2011 3rd International Conference on (Volume:5), India 2011.

Davies, Donald Watts / Barber, Derek L. A.: Communication networks for computers, Computing and Information Processing, John Wiley & Sons, 1973.

Demir, Yigit Ekim: Güvenli ve Hizli Anlik Mesajlasma Programi: Gold-Bug Instant Messenger programi, bu sorunun üstesinden gelmek isteyen kullanicilar için en iyi çözümlerden birisi haline geliyor ve en güvenli sekilde anlik mesajlar gönderebilmenize imkan taniyor (Translated: "Goldbug Instant Messenger Application is a best solution for users, who want to use one of the most secure ways to send instant messages"), News Portal Tamindir, URL: http://www.tamindir.com/goldbug-instant-messenger/, 2014.

Dijkstra, Edsger W.: A note on two problems in connexion with graphs, in: Numerische Mathematik, 1, URL: http://www-m3.ma.tum.de/twiki/pub/MN0506/WebHome/dijkstra.pdf, pp. 269–271, 1959.

Dingledine, Roger / Mathewson, Nick / Syverson, Paul: Tor - The Second-Generation Onion Router, in the Proceedings of the 13th USENIX Security Symposium, August 2004.

Dingledine, Roger: One cell is enough to break Tor's anonymity, Tor Project. 18 February 2009.

Dingledine, Roger: Pre-alpha: run an onion proxy now!, or-dev (Mailing list). 20 September 2002.

Dolev, Danny / Dwork, Cynthia / Naor, Moni: Nonmalleable Cryptography, SIAM Journal on Computing 30 (2), 391–437, URL: https://dx.doi.org/10.1137%2FS0097539795291562, 2000.

Dooble: Dooble Web Browser, URL: http://dooble.sourceforge.net.

Dragomir, Mircea: GoldBug Instant Messenger - Softpedia Review: This is a secure p2p Instant Messenger that ensures private communication based on a multi encryption technology constituted of several security layers, URL: http://www.softpedia.com/get/Internet/Chat/Instant-Messaging/GoldBug-Instant-Messenger.shtml, Softpedia Review, January 31st, 2016.

ECRYPT-CSA: Post-Snowden Cryptography, URL: https://hyperelliptic.org/PSC/, Brussels, December 9 & 10, 2015.

Fadilpašić, Sead: WhatsApp encryption pointless, researchers claim, URL: http://www.itproportal.com/2016/05/09/whatsapp-encryption-pointless-researchers-say/, May 2016.

Fagoyinbo, Joseph Babatunde: The Armed Forces: Instrument of Peace, Strength, Development and Prosperity, AuthorHouse, 2013.

Filecluster: GoldBug Instant Messenger - Un programme très pratique et fiable, conçu pour créer un pont de communication sécurisé entre deux ou plusieurs utilisateurs, URL: https://www.filecluster.fr/logiciel/GoldBug-Instant-Messenger-174185.html.

Fousoft: GoldBug Instant Messenger, URL: https://www.fousoft.com/goldbug-instant-messenger.html, March 16, 2017.

Galloway, Scott: Gang of Four Horsemen of the Apocalypse: Amazon/Apple/Facebook & Google - Who Wins/Loses, DLDconference, URL:

https://www.youtube.com/watch?v=XCvwCcEP74Q, Youtube 20.01.2015.

Gans, Joshua: Keep Calm and Manage Disruption, MIT Sloan Management Review, February 22, 2016.

Garanich, Gleb: Click bait: Tor users can be tracked by mouse movements, Reuters, 2016.

Gasakis, Mele / Schmidt, Max: Beyond Cryptographic Routing: The Echo Protocol in the new Era of Exponential Encryption (EEE) - A comprehensive essay about the Sprinkling Effect of Cryptographic Echo Discovery (SECRED) and further innovations in cryptography around the Echo Applications Smoke, Smoke-Stack, Spot-On, Lettera and GoldBug Crypto Chat Messenger addressing Encryption, Graph-Theory, Routing and the change from Mix-Networks like Tor or I2P to Peer-to-Peer-Flooding-Networks like the Echo respective to Friend-to-Friend Trust-Networks like they are built over the POPTASTIC protocol, BoD, ISBN 978-3-7481-5198-2, Norderstedt Hardcover & eBook 2018, Paperback 2019.

Generation NT: Sécuriser ses échanges par messagerie: Apportez encore plus de la confidentialité dans votre messagerie, URL: https://www.generation-nt.com/goldbug-messenger-securiser-echanger-communiquer-discuter-messagerie-securite-echange-communication-telecharger-telechargement-1907585.html.

Goel, S. / Robson, M. / Polte, M. / Sirer, E.G.: Herbivore - A Scalable and Efficient Protocol for Anonymous Communication, Technical Report 2003-1890, Cornell University, Ithaca, NY, February 2003.

Goldberg, Ian / Stedman, Ryan / Yoshida. Kayo: A User Study of Off-the-Record Messaging, University of Waterloo, Symposium On Usable Privacy and Security (SOUPS) 2008, July 23–25, Pittsburgh, PA, USA, URL: http://www.cypherpunks.ca/~iang/pubs/otr_userstudy.pdf, & URL: https://otr.cypherpunks.ca/Protocol-v3-4.0.0.html, 2008.

GoldBug-manual – German Manual of the GoldBug Crypto Messenger https://compendio.github.io/goldbug-manual-de/, (2014, Review at Github 2018).

Golle, Philippe / Juels, Ari: Dining Cryptographers Revisited, URL: https://www.gnunet.org/sites/default/files/golle-eurocrypt2004.pdf, 2004.

Gray, Patrick: The hack of the year, Sydney Morning Herald, 13 November 2007.

Grothoff, Christian / Patrascu, Ioana / Bennett, Krista / Stef, Tiberiu / Horozov, Tzvetan: The GNet whitepaper (Technical report). Purdue University, 2002.

Hacker News: Tor anonymizing network compromised by French researchers, The Hacker News, 24 October 2011.

Halabi, Sam: Internet Routing Architectures, Cisco Press, 2000.

Hartshorn, Sarah: GoldBug Messenger among: 3 New Open Source Secure Communication Projects, URL: http://blog.vuze.com/2015/05/28/3-new-open-source-secure-communication-projects/, May 28, 2015.

Harvey, Cynthia / Datamation: 50 Noteworthy Open Source Projects – Chapter Secure Communication: GoldBug Messenger ranked on first # 1 position, URL: http://www.datamation.com/open-source/50-noteworthy-new-open-source-projects-3.html, posted September 19, 2014.

Hayden, M.: The price of privacy: Re-evaluating the NSA. Johns Hopkins Foreign Affairs Symposium, Apr. 2014. https://www.youtube.com/watch?v=kV2HDM86XgI&t=17m50s

Hazewinkel, Michiel (Ed.): "Isomorphism", Encyclopedia of Mathematics, Springer 2001.

Heise: GoldBug kann Schlüssel selbst encodiert versenden, URL: http://www.heise.de/download/goldbug-1192605.html.

Herrmann, Michael: „Auswirkung auf die Anonymität von performanzbasierter Peer-Auswahl bei Onion-Routern: Eine Fallstudie mit I2P", Masterarbeit in Informatik, durchgeführt am Lehrstuhl für Netzarchitekturen und Netzdienste Fakultät für Informatik Technische Universität München, https://gnunet.org/sites/default/files/herrmann2011mt.pdf, 2011.

Huitema, Christian: Routing in the Internet, Second Ed. Prentice-Hall, 2000.

Informationweek: Google's Cloud Lets You Bring customer-supplied encryption keys (CSEK), URL:

http://www.informationweek.com/cloud/infrastructure-as-a-service/googles-cloud-lets-you-bring-your-own-encryption-keys/d/d-id/1326482, 2016.

Isaacson, Walter: The Innovators - How a Group of Hackers, Geniuses, and Geeks Created the Digital Revolution, 2015.

Jackson, Patrick Thaddeus / Nexon, Daniel H.: Representation is Futile?: American Anti-Collectivism and the Borg, in Jutta Weldes, ed., To Seek Out New Worlds: Science Fiction and World Politics. 2003:143–167.

Jansen, Rob / Tschorsch, Florian / Johnson, Aaron; Scheuermann, Björn: The Sniper Attack: Anonymously Deanonymizing and Disabling the Tor Network. 21st Annual Network & Distributed System Security Symposium, April 2014.

Johnston, Erik: Matrix - An open standard for decentralised persistent communication, URL: http://matrix.org/ & https://github.com/matrix-org/synapse/commit/ 4f475c76977 22e946e39e 42f38f3dd03a95d8765, fist Commit on Aug 12, 2014.

Joos, Thomas: Sicheres Messaging im Web, URL: http://www.pcwelt.de/ratgeber/ Tor__l2p__Gnunet__RetroShare__Freenet__GoldBug__Spurl os_im_Web-Anonymisierungsnetzwerke-8921663.html, PCWelt Magazin, 01. Oktober 2014.

Joseph L. Bower, Clayton M. Christensen: Disruptive Technologies, Catching the Wave, in: Harvard Business Review, ISSN 0007-6805, Bd. 69 pp. 19–45, 1995.

Karinthy, Frigyes: Láncszemek, 1929.

Kišasondi, Tonimir / Hutinski, Željko: Cryptographic routing protocol for secure distribution and multiparty negotiatiated access control, URL: http://www.ceciis.foi.hr/app/index.php/ceciis/2009/paper/do wnload/219/209, Varazdin, Croatia 2009.

Koch, Werner: OpenPGP Web Key Service draft-koch-openpgp-webkey-service-00, URL: https://tools.ietf.org/html/draft-koch-openpgp-webkey-service-00, May 2016.

Kőnig, Dénes: Theorie der Endlichen und Unendlichen Graphen: Kombinatorische Topologie der Streckenkomplexe, Akademische Verlagsgesellschaft, Leipzig 1936.

Kwon, Albert / Lazar, David / Devadas, Srinivas / Ford, Bryan: Riffle - An Efficient Communication System With Strong Anonymity, URL: https://people.csail.mit.edu/devadas/pubs/riffle.pdf, in: Proceedings on Privacy Enhancing Technologies, 1–20, 2016.

Le Blond, Stevens / Manils, Pere / Chaabane, Abdelberi / Ali Kaafar Mohamed / Castelluccia, Claude / Legout, Arnaud / Dabbous, Walid: One Bad Apple Spoils the Bunch: Exploiting p2p Applications to Trace and Profile Tor Users, 4th USENIX Workshop on Large-Scale Exploits and Emergent Threats (LEET '11), National Institute for Research in Computer Science and Control, March 2011.

Leigh, David / Harding, Luke: WikiLeaks: Inside Julian Assange's War on Secrecy, PublicAffairs, 2011.

Lemos, Robert: Tor hack proposed to catch criminals, SecurityFocus, 8 March 2007.

Levine, Yasha: Almost everyone involved in developing Tor was (or is) funded by the US government, URL: http://pando.com/2014/07/16/tor-spooks, Pando Daily, 16 July 2014.

Levine, Yasha: How leading Tor developers and advocates tried to smear me after I reported their US Government ties, URL: https://pando.com/2014/11/14/tor-smear/ , written on November 14, 2014.

Lewis, E. St. Elmo: Catch-Line and Argument. In: The Book-Keeper, Vol. 15, p. 124, Februar 1903.

Lindner, Mirko: POPTASTIC: Verschlüsselter Chat über POP3 mit dem GoldBug Messenger, Pro-Linux, URL: http://www.pro-linux.de/news/1/21822/poptastic-verschluesselter-chat-ueber-pop3.html, 9. Dezember 2014.

Lindsay, G.: The government is reading your E-Mail. TIME DIGITAL DAILY, June 1999.

Luxemburg, Rosa: Die russische Revolution, 1918.

Marconi, Guglielmo: Nobel Lecture, Wireless telegraphic communication, 1909

Majorgeeks: GoldBug Secure Email Client & Instant Messenger, URL:http://www.majorgeeks.com/files/details/goldbug_secur e_email_Client_instant_messenger.html.

Malhotra, Ravi: IP Routing, O'Reilly Media, 1st edition, 2002.

Manils, Pere / Abdelberri, Chaabane / Le Blond, Stevens / Kaafar, Mohamed Ali / Castelluccia, Claude / Legout, Arnaud / Dabbous, Walid: Compromising Tor Anonymity Exploiting p2p Information Leakage. 7th USENIX Symposium on Network Design and Implementation. 2008.

Manral, V. / Bhatia, M. / Jaeggli, J. / White, R.: Issues with Existing Cryptographic Protection Methods for Routing Protocols, URL: http://info.internet.isi.edu/in-notes/pdfrfc/rfc6039.txt.pdf, 2010.

Matejka, Petr: Security in Peer-to-Peer Networks, Charles University, Prague 2004, URL: http://turtle-p2p.sourceforge.net/thesis2.pdf

Mazur, Barry: When is one thing equal to some other thing? URL http://www.math.harvard.edu/~mazur/preprints/when_is_o ne.pdf, June 2007.

McCoy, Damon / Bauer, Kevin / Grunwald, Dirk / Kohno, Tadayoshi / Sicker, Douglas: Shining Light in Dark Places: Understanding the Tor Network, Proceedings of the 8th International Symposium on Privacy Enhancing Technologies. 8th International Symposium on Privacy Enhancing Technologies. Berlin, Germany: Springer-Verlag, p. 63–76, 2008.

McDonald, Duff: The Firm: The Story of McKinsey and Its Secret Influence on American Business, p. 57-58, 2013.

McEliece, Robert J.: A Public-Key Cryptosystem Based on Algebraic Coding Theory. In: Deep Space Network Progress Report. Band 42, Nr. 44, 1978, S. 114–116, URL: http://ipnpr.jpl.nasa.gov/progress_report2/42-44/44N.PDF

McEliece, Robert J.: The theory of information and coding, Cambridge University Press, Cambridge 2002

McNoodle Library: Implementation of the McEliece Algorithm in C++, Github, 2016.

Medhi, Deepankar / Ramasamy, Karthikeyan: Network Routing: Algorithms, Protocols, and Architectures, Morgan Kaufmann, 2007.

Menezes, Alfred J. / van Oorschot, Paul C. / Vanstone, Scott A.: Handbook of Applied Cryptography. CRC Press, URL: http://cacr.uwaterloo.ca/hac/about/chap12.pdf, Definition Forward Secrecy, 12.16, p. 496, 1996.

Mennink, B. / Preneel, B.: Triple and Quadruple Encryption: Bridging the Gaps - IACR Cryptology ePrint Archive, eprint.iacr.org, URL: http://eprint.iacr.org/2014/016.pdf, 2014.

Milgram, Stanley: "The Small World Problem". Psychology Today. Ziff-Davis Publishing Company. May 1967.

Michael Christen: YaCy - Peer-to-Peer Web-Suchmaschine in Die Datenschleuder, #86, p.54-57, 2005.

MOMEDO: Open Source Mobiler Messenger für kommunale und schulische Zwecke mit Verschlüsselung, Github, URL: https://momedo.github.io/momedo/   & https://github.com/momedo/momedo/blob/master/README.md , 2018.

Murdoch, Steven J. / Danezis, George: Low-Cost Traffic Analysis of Tor, 19. January 2006.

Nogami, Glenda Y., Julle Colestock and Terry A. Phoenix: U.S. Army War College Alumni Survey. Graduates from 1983-1989 (Carlisle Barracks, PA: U.S. Army War College, 1989.

NOVAk, Matt: Edward Snowden Isn't Right About Everything, URL: http://www.gizmodo.co.uk/2016/11/edward-snowden-isnt-right-about-everything/, 18 Nov 2016.

Pandamonium   Web   Crawler: Github https://github.com/textbrowser/pandamonium and Binary at the   GoldBug-Project https://sourceforge.net/projects/goldbug/files/pandamonium-webcrawler/, 2015.

Perrig, Adrian: Cryptographic Approaches for Securing Routing Protocols   URL: dimacs.rutgers.edu/Workshops/Practice/slides/perrig.pdf, 2004.

Perrin,   Trevor: The   Noise   Protocol   Framework,   URL: http://noiseprotocol.org/noise.pdf   & https://github.com/noiseprotocol/noise_spec/commit/c627f8 056ffb9c7695d3bc7bafea8616749b073f, Revision 30, 2016-07-14   respective: first   commit c627f8056ffb9c7695d3bc7bafea8616749b073f   committed Aug 4, 2014.

Popescu, Bogdan C. / Crispo, Bruno / Tanenbaum, Andrew S.: Safe and Private Data Sharing with Turtle: Friends Team-Up and

Beat the System, URL: http://turtle-p2p.sourceforge.net/turtleinitial.pdf, 2004.

Por, Julianna Isabele: Segurança em primeiro lugar, URL: https://www.baixaki.com.br/download/goldbug.htm

Positive Technologies: Whatsapp encryption rendered ineffective by SS7 Vulnerabilities, URL:https://www.ptsecurity.com/wwa/news/57894/, May 06 2016.

PRISM Programm: URL: https://de.wikipedia.org/wiki/PRISM, 2016.

Qt Digia: Qt Digia has awarded GoldBug IM as reference project for Qt implementation in the official Qt-Showroom of Digia: show-room.qt-project.org/goldbug/, 2015.

Rasmussen, Rod: The Pros and Cons of DNS Encryption, URL: http://www.infosecurity-magazine.com/opinions/the-pros-and-cons-of-dns-encryption/, 14 Sep 2016.

Raymond, Eric S.:The Cathedral & the Bazaar. Musings on Linux and Open Source by an Accidental Revolutionary. O'Reilly & Asso-ciates.2000.

Reed, Michael G. / Sylverson, Paul F. / Goldschlag David M.: Anony-mous connections and onion routing, US patent 6266704, IEEE Journal on Selected Areas in Communications, 16(4), pp.482-494, 1998.

Reuter, Markus: Sommer der inneren Sicherheit: Was die Innenminis-ter von Frankreich und Deutschland wirklich fordern, URL: https://netzpolitik.org/2016/sommer-der-inneren-sicherheit-was-die-innenminister-von-frankreich-und-deutschland-wirklich-fordern/, 24. August 2016,

Sabtu: Free GoldBug Instant Messenger 1.7, URL: http://bengkelcakra.blogspot.de/2014/12/free-download-goldbug-instant-messenger.html, 13 December 2014.

Sanatinia, Amirali / Noubir, Guevara: HOnions: Towards Detection and Identification of Misbehaving Tor-HSDirs, URL: https://www.securityweek2016.tu-darm-stadt.de/fileadmin/user_upload/Group_securityweek2016/pe ts2016/10_honions-sanatinia.pdf, Northeastern University 2016.

Scherschel, Fabian A.: Keeping Tabs on WhatsApp's Encryption, URL: http://www.heise.de/ct/artikel/Keeping-Tabs-on-WhatsApp-s-Encryption-2630361.html, Heise 30.04.2015.

Scherschel, Fabian: Test: Hinter den Kulissen der WhatsApp-Verschlüsselung, http://www.heise.de/security/artikel/Test-Hinter-den-Kulissen-der-WhatsApp-Verschluesselung-3165567.html, 08.04.2016.

Schneier, Bruce / Seidel, Kathleen / Vijayakumar, Saranya: A World-wide Survey of Encryption Products, February 11, 2016 Version 1.0., zit. nach Adams, David / Maier, Ann-Kathrin (2016): BIG SEVEN Study, open source crypto-messengers to be compared - or: Comprehensive Confidentiality Review & Audit of GoldBug, Encrypting E-Mail-Client & Secure Instant Messenger, Descriptions, tests and analysis reviews of 20 functions of the application based on the essential fields and methods of evaluation of the 8 major international audit manuals for IT security investigations including 38 figures and 87 tables, URL: https://sf.net/projects/goldbug/files/bigseven-crypto-audit.pdf - English / German Language, Version 1.1, 305 pages, June 2016.

Schulte, Wolfgang: Handbuch der Routing-Protokolle: Eine Einführung in RIP, IGRP, EIGRP, HSRP, VRRP, OSPF, IS-IS und BGP, VDE VERLAG, 2016.

Seba, Tony: Clean Disruption - Clean Disruption of Energy and Transportation: How Silicon Valley Will Make Oil, Nuclear, Natural Gas, Coal, Electric Utilities and Conventional Cars Obsolete by 2030, Beta edition, May 20, 2014.

Seba, Tony: Winners Take All - The 9 Fundamental Rules of High Tech Strategy, Lulu, September 28, 2007.

Security Blog: Secure chat communications suite GoldBug. Security Blog, 25. März 2014, http://www.hacker10.com/other-computing/secure-chat-communications-suite-GoldBug/.

SINA: Sichere Inter-Netzwerk Architektur, URL: https://de.wikipedia.org/wiki/Sichere_Inter-Netzwerk_Architektur, Ederung 29.08.2016.

Slashdot: Gnutella: https://en.wikipedia.org/wiki/Gnutella, & https://slashdot.org/story/00/03/14/0949234/open-source-napster-gnutella, 2000.

Smoke: Documentation of the Android Messenger Application Smoke with Encryption, URL:https://github.com/textbrowser/smoke/raw/master/Documentation/Smoke.pdf , 2017.

Spot-On (2011): Documentation of the Spot-On-Application, URL: https://sourceforge.net/p/spot-on/code/HEAD/tree/, under this URL since 06/2013, Sourceforge, including the Spot-On: Documentation of the project draft paper of the pre-research project since 2010, Project Ne.R.D.D., Registered 2010-06-27, URL: https://sourceforge.net/projects/nerdd/ has evolved into Spot-On. Please see http://spot-on.sf.net and URL: https://github.com/textbrowser/spot-on/blob/master/branches/Documentation/RELEASE-NOTES.archived, 08.08.2011.

Spot-On (2013): Documentation of the Spot-On-Application, URL: https://github.com/textbrowser/spot-on/tree/master/branches/trunk/Documentation, Github 2013.

Spot-On (2014): Documentation of the Spot-On-Application, URL: https://github.com/textbrowser/spot-on/tree/master/branches/trunk/Documentation, Github 2014.

Spot-On (2018): Documentation of the Spot-On-Application, URL: https://github.com/textbrowser/spot-on/tree/master/branches/trunk/Documentation, Github 2018.

Stanley Milgram: The Small World Problem. In: Psychology Today, URL: http://measure.igpp.ucla.edu/GK12-SEE-LA/Lesson_Files_09/Tina_Wey/TW_social_networks_Milgram_1967_small_world_problem.pdf, ISSN 0033-3107, pp. 60–67, Mai 1967.

Stiftung Zukunft: Antrag auf Förderung des Projektes " Web-Suche in einem Netzwerk dezentraler URL-Datenbanken" mit 30 zu fördernden Abschlussarbeiten an Hochschulen und Einbezug von 30 Auszubildenden aus Mitgliedsorganisationen durch die Stiftung Zukunft, Nürnberg, 29.06.2015.

Studie Users Get Routed: Traffic Correlation on Tor by Realistic Adversaries, URL: http://www.ohmygodel.com/publications/usersrouted-ccs13.pdf.

Theisen, Michaela: GoldBug Instant Messenger - Beliebte Software, Sicherer Instant Messenger, URL: https://www.freeware-

base.de/freeware-zeige-details-28142-
GoldBug_Instant_Messenger.html, 2015.

Tummarello, Kate: Give Congress Time to Debate New Government
Hacking Rule, URL:
https://www.eff.org/deeplinks/2016/11/give-congress-time-
debate-new-government-hacking-rule, November 17, 2016.

Tur, Henryk / Computerworld: GoldBug Secure Email Client & Instant
Messenger, https://www.computerworld.pl/ftp/goldbug-
secure-email-Client-instant-messenger.html, 11.01.2018.

Van den Hooff, Jelle / Lazar, David / Zaharia, Matei / Zeldovich,
Nickolai: Vuvuzela: Scalable Private Messaging Resistant to
Traffic Analysis, ULR:
https://davidlazar.org/papers/vuvuzela.pdf, 08.09.2015.

Vaughan-Nichols, Steven J.: How to recover from Heartbleed, ZDNet,
April 9, 2014, http://www.zdnet.com/how-to-recover-from-
heartbleed-7000028253.

Vinberg, Ėrnest Borisovich: A Course in Algebra, American Mathematical Society, p. 3., 2003.

Weller, Jan: Testbericht zu GoldBug für Freeware, Freeware-Blog, URL:
https://www.freeware.de/download/goldbug/, 2013.

Wolinsky, D. I. / Corrigan-Gibbs, H. / Ford, B / Johnson, A: Dissent in
numbers - Making strong anonymity scale. In Proceedings of
the 10th Symposium on Operating Systems Design and Implementation (OSDI), Hollywood, CA, Oct. 2012.

Wouters, P.: RFC 7929 - DNS-Based Authentication of Named Entities
(DANE) Bindings for OpenPGP URL:
https://datatracker.ietf.org/doc/rfc7929/, August 2016.

Zantour, Bassam / Haraty, Ramzi A.: I2P Data Communication System,
Proceedings of ICN 2011: The Tenth International Conference
on Networks (IARIA): 401–409, 2011.

Zetter, Kim: Rogue Nodes Turn Tor Anonymizer Into Eavesdropper's
Paradise, Wired, 16 September 2007.

22 Index of Figures

23 Glossary

- **2WIPFS:** See: Two-way instant perfect forward secrecy.
- **4710**: Port for the applications Spot-On and other Echo clients.
- **Access Controls:** means to ensure that access to assets is authorized and restricted based on business and security requirements. Related to authorization of users, and assessment of rights.
- **Adaptive Echo (AE):** The Adaptive Echo does not send in terms of the normal Echo a message-packet to each connected node, instead, for the over giving of a message a cryptographic token is needed. The Echo-Protocol is equipped for the Adaptive Echo Modus with a routing information. Only nodes, which have a certain cryptographic token available, get the message forwarded.
- **AES:** The Advanced Encryption Standard (AES), also known as Rijndael (its original name), is a specification for the encryption of electronic data established by the U.S. National Institute of Standards and Technology (NIST) in 2001. AES is based on the Rijndael cipher developed by two Belgian cryptographers, Joan Daemen and Vincent Rijmen, who submitted a proposal to NIST during the AES selection process.
- **AE-Token:** The AE-Token is a cryptographic token used to deploy the Adaptive Echo (AE) modus. It is a kind of password or string, which is entered the node, to avoid messages to be sent to nodes, without the AE-Token. AE-Tokens can help to create a self-learning, adaptive network. The token must contain at least thirty-six characters.
- **Algorithm:** In mathematics and computer science, an algorithm is a self-contained step-by-step set of operations to be performed. Algorithms exist that perform calculation, data processing, and automated reasoning.

- **Android:** Android is a mobile operating system which allows to deploy mobile devices similar as an Raspberry Pi with server software, e.g. like the encrypting chat server SmokeStack for Android.

- **Answer Method:** The Answer Method is a procedure for the login into an application. It is applied in the software Spot-On and GoldBug. Here the login into the application can be done over a password, or, the password is replaced by two entry text fields. One string covers the question, and the other string covers the referring answer to the question. Both values are hashed and processes in a cryptographic way. The right answers are not stored on the hard disk in plain text, so that the process provides a different method and offers more security. An attacker does not know, if a user has used the password or the question/answer login method.

- **Asymmetric Calling:** Cryptographic Calling is the immediate transfer of end-to-end encrypting encryption credentials to secure a communication channel. Cryptographic calling has been invented by the Software Project Spot-On. Asymmetric Calling is some modus for Cryptographic Calling, which sends temporary asymmetric keys for end-to-end encryption. It refers to send one asymmetric key (pair) through one secured channel. The Call with asymmetric credentials refers to ephemeral asymmetric keys, which are used for the time of the call. This could be one session or even a shorter part of time of the session. It depends whenever a communication partner starts to initiate a call. The asymmetric ephemeral credentials for the call should be transferred over a secure connection, which is either a symmetric key, over a a-symmetric key (PKI) or over an already existent call-connection, in this case an ephemeral asymmetric temp-key.

- **Asymmetric Encryption:** In cryptography, encryption is the process of encoding messages or information in such a way that only authorized parties can read it. In public-key encryption schemes, the encryption key is published for anyone to use and encrypt messages. However, only the receiving party has access to the decryption key that enables messages to be read. Public-key encryption was first described in a secret document in 1973; before then all encryption schemes were symmetric-key (also called private-key).

- **Attack:** attempt to destroy, expose, alter, disable, steal or gain unauthorized access to or make unauthorized use of an asset.

- **Audit:** systematic, independent and documented process for obtaining audit evidence and evaluating it objectively to determine the extent to which the audit criteria are fulfilled. An audit can be an internal audit (first party) or an external audit (second party or third party), and it can be a combined audit (combining two or more disciplines).

- **Auditing and Logging:** Related to auditing of actions, or logging of problems.

- **Authentication:** provision of assurance that a claimed characteristic of an entity is correct. Related to the identification of users.

- **Autocrypt:** AutoCrypt is an automatic key exchange. This has originally been invented by the Spot-on Project and refers to the protocol definitions of a REPLEO and the EPKS protocol. A REPLEO is the method to encrypt the own Public Key with the received Public Key of a friend. That hides the own public key from public by using encryption method. The EPKS Protocol is the Echo Public Key Sharing Protocol, which allows to send the own key over an existing encrypted connection to one or several friends. The EPKS protocol has been invented in the Spot-On project and GoldBug Project and has been overtaken by other projects in an automated way for an e-mail reply. That means two users of the same e-Mail client exchange the public encryption key and are from that point of time secured for all further communication. The EPKS Protocol provides this many years before the Term AutoCrypt went public. Other project also copied this invention under the Name KeySync. The new process is, that the key is not stored and searched on a Key server, but sent from node to node in a secure channel, either by manual sent-out or an automated ex-change of two nodes, e.g. e-mail-clients or Spot-On Clients over the EPKS protocol.

- **Availability:** property of being accessible and usable upon demand by an authorized entity.

- **Bluetooth:** Bluetooth is a wireless technology standard for exchanging data over short distances (using short-wavelength UHF radio waves in the ISM band from 2.4 to 2.485 GHz) from fixed and mobile devices and building personal area networks (PANs).

- **Broadcast:** Broadcast is as term widely known. In Cryptog-raphy it is known from the Spot-On application to send the public encryption key over an IP-network connection, so that all connected nodes can pick-up the sent key. A cryp-tographic Broadcast is a wider form of AutoCrypt and in-cludes as well the EPKS channel. It is also possible to send the Cryptographic Broadcast over a not encrypted connec-tion, while a broadcast over the Echo Network or the Echo Public Key Sharing function of the Spot-On Client would provide always an encrypted connection, e.g. based on the symmetric key, which allows only people who know the key to have access.

- **Button:** A button is the most discussed element in an ap-plication, respective GUI development.

- **Buzz:** Buzz is the name of the libspoton to provide Echoed IRC(e*IRC). So Buzz is another word for IRC, respective e*IRC, used by the library.

- **C/O (Care-of)-Function:** "Care of", used to address a letter when the letter must pass through an intermediary (also written C/O). Neighbors are often asked to care of your postal letters, in case you live with them in one house or have a relationship to them. As well parcel stations, letter boxes or just persons e.g. at your home or in the neighbor-hood provide a local delay of your envelopes and parcels, in case you are at work and want to receive the parcel or letter in the evening. The included Email Function of Spot-On provides such a feature.

- **Calling:** A "Call" transfers over a public/private key encrypted environment a symmetric key (e.g. AES). It is a password for the session talk, only the two participants know. With one click you can instantly renew the end-to-end encryption password for your talk. It is also possible to manually define the end-to-end encrypted password (manually defined Calling). There are five further different ways to call: Asymmetric Calling, Forward Secrecy Calling, Symmetric Calling, SMP-Calling and 2-Way-Calling. The term of a "Call" in Cryptography has been introduced by Spot-on, the integrated library and kernel of the Spot-On Application, and refers to sending a new end-to-end encryption password to the other participant.

- **CBC:** Cipher Block Chaining – Ehrsam, Meyer, Smith and Tuchman invented the Cipher Block Chaining (CBC) mode of operation in 1976. In CBC mode, each block of plaintext is XORed with the previous ciphertext block before being encrypted. This way, each ciphertext block depends on all plaintext blocks processed up to that point.

- **Cipher text:** Cipher text is the result of encryption performed on plaintext using an algorithm, called a cipher. Cipher text is also known as encrypted or encoded information because it contains a form of the original plain text that is unreadable by a human or computer without the proper cipher to decrypt it. Decryption, the inverse of encryption, is the process of turning ciphertext into readable plaintext. Cipher text is not to be confused with code-text because the latter is a result of a code, not a cipher.

- **Cipher:** In cryptography, a cipher is an algorithm for performing encryption or decryption—a series of well-defined steps that can be followed as a procedure. An alternative, less common term is encipherment. To encipher or encode is to convert information into cipher or code. In common parlance, 'cipher' is synonymous with 'code'. Codes generally substitute different length strings of characters in the output, while ciphers generally substitute the same number of characters as are input.

- **Clientside Encryption:** Client-side encryption is the cryptographic technique of encrypting data before it is transmitted to a server in a computer network. Usually, encryption is performed with a key that is not known to the server. Consequently, the service provider is unable to decrypt the hosted data. In order to access the data, it must always be decrypted by the client. Client-side encryption allows for the creation of zero knowledge applications whose providers cannot access the data its users have stored, thus offering a high level of privacy.

- **C-mail:** C-mail as a term describing e-mail, that is encrypted. This term was introduced due to the awareness, that each e-mail is distributed over Internet servers readable like a postcard to any admin.

- **Confidentiality:** property that information is not made available or disclosed to unauthorized individuals, entities, or processes.

- **Configuration:** Related to security configurations of servers, devices, or software.

- **Congestion Control:** Congestion control concerns controlling traffic entry into a telecommunications network, so as to avoid congestive collapse by attempting to avoid oversubscription of any of the processing or link capabilities of the intermediate nodes and networks and taking resource reducing steps, such as reducing the rate of sending packets.

- **Continuous improvement:** recurring activity to enhance performance.

- **Corrective action:** action to eliminate the cause of a nonconformity and to prevent recurrence.

- **Crawler:** A Web crawler, sometimes called a spider or spiderbot and often shortened to crawler, is an Internet bot that systematically browses the World Wide Web, typically for the purpose of Web indexing (web spidering). Web search engines and some other sites use Web crawling or spidering software to update their web content or indices of others sites' web content. Web crawlers copy pages for processing by a search engine which indexes the down-loaded pages so users can search more efficiently.

- **Cryptogramm:** Verbal arithmetic, also known as alphamet-ics, cryptarithmetic, crypt-arithmetic, cryptarithm, mprovemen or word addition, is a type of mathematical game consisting of a mathematical equation among un-known numbers, whose digits are represented by letters. The goal is to identify the value of each letter. The name can be extended to puzzles that use non-alphabetic sym-bols instead of letters.

- **Cryptographic Calling:** Cryptographic Calling is a way to provide end-to-end credentials over a secure connection. The temporary key can be a-symmetric (PKI) or symmetric (a password string also known as a passphrase). The idea is to make end-to-end encryption as easy as calling a partner over a phone, just taking the phone, call, and if the session has to end, to change the temporary keys again and quit the call.

- **Cryptographic Discovery:** Cryptographic Discovery de-scribes the method of an Echo-ing Protocol to find nodes in an Echo Network. Peers are aware of other peers and their cryptographic identities based on a cryptographic discovery within the network. Nodes inform other nodes about their neighbors, so that they can be addressed.

- **Cryptographic Routing:** Cryptographic Routing is a term, which has been used as an antagonism for describing the Echo Protocol, as this is beyond Routing. Echo means for-warding a message, which is address-less. So no routing is given within Echo. A Cryptographic Routing would be giv-en, if a node would have a certain cryptographic token as identifier. This is the case within Adaptive Echo (AE). Here in partial one can speak of cryptographic routing, as a tar-get address might be given.

- **Cryptographic Torrents:** Cryptographic Torrents are defined by a bunch of cryptographic values, listed in a link to gen-erate a download of a file. Similar to Torrent Links the download is started packet by packet, just with the difference that all packets are encrypted, and the link contains an assortment of cryptographic values.

- **Cryptographic-DNA:** Cryptographic DNA is derived as term – in allusion to the DNA term taken from biology - from Magnet-URI-Links containing an assortment of specific cryptographic values. These values describe key size, algorithm, hash, iteration count etc. As each link can be different, the term DNA describes the specific uniqueness or footprint of such a bundle.

- **Cryptography:** Related to mathematical protections for data.

- **CryptoPad:** A Cryptopad is a tool, to convert plain text to cipher text. A first suite integrated pad has been developed by the Spot-On application under the name Rosetta Crypto Pad. The name derives from the Stone of Rosette in the Museum of London, which is an index to read hieroglyphs. The Rosetta CryptoPad uses asymmetric keys, so it is based on PKI and both participants need to share (and enter) the public key. It is not based on symmetric key, so that the other user just has to enter a passphrase-string like some PDF files are often encrypted.

- **Crypto-Parties:** A Crypto-Party is a grassroots global endeavour to introduce the basics of practical cryptography such as the Tor anonymity network, key signing parties, disk encryption and virtual private networks to the general public. The project primarily consists of a series of free public workshops. Marcin de Kaminski, founding member of Piratbyrån which in turn founded The Pirate Bay, regards CryptoParty as the most important civic project in cryptography today, and Cory Doctorow has characterized a CryptoParty as being "like a Tupperware party for learning crypto." Der Spiegel in December 2014 mentioned "crypto parties" in the wake of the Edward Snowden leaks in an article about the NSA.

- **CSEK:** CSEK is the short abbreviation of Customer Supplied Encryption Keys. This refers to services, Internet offers and software architecture, which provides the option, that the user brings in his own keys, either symmetric or asymmetric. This is especially important for applications providing end to end encryption that users can insert or define their own password and use other channels to exchange the password.

- **Customer Supplied Encryption Keys (#CECS):** Customer Supplied Encryption Keys have been introduced as term by google to provide customers to use own keys for the encryption of data within the google cloud.

- **Data Exposure:** Related to unintended exposure of sensitive information.

- **Data Validation:** Related to improper reliance on the structure or values of data.

- **Decentralized computing:** Decentralized computing is the allocation of resources, both hardware and software, to each individual workstation, or office location. Decentral means, there is no central server nor a web-interface, you can lof into a service. A client needs to be installed and adjusted locally on your device. Another term is: Distributed computing. Distributed computing is a field of computer science that studies distributed systems. A distributed system is a software system in which components located on networked computers communicate and coordinate their actions by passing messages. Based on a "grid model" a peer-to-peer system, or P2P system, is a collection of applications run on several local computers, which connect remotely to each other to complete a function or a task. There is no main operating system to which satellite systems are subordinate. This approach to software development (and distribution) affords developers great savings, as they don't have to create a central control point. An example application is LAN messaging which allows users to communicate without a central server.

- **Distributed Hash Table:** A Distributed Hash Table (DHT) is a class of a decentralized distributed system that provides a lookup service similar to a hash table: (key, value) pairs are stored in a DHT, and any participating node can efficiently retrieve the value associated with a given key. Keys are unique identifiers which map to particular values, which in turn can be anything from addresses, to documents, to arbitrary data.

- **DNS:** The Domain Name System (DNS) is a hierarchical and decentralized naming system for computers, services, or other resources connected to the Internet or a private network. It associates various information with domain names assigned to each of the participating entities. Most prominently, it translates more readily memorized domain names to the numerical IP addresses needed for locating and identifying computer services and devices with the underlying network protocols. By providing a worldwide, distributed directory service, the Domain Name System has been an essential component of the functionality of the Internet since 1985.

- **Documented information:** information required to be controlled and maintained by an organization and the medium on which it is contained. Note: Documented information can be in any format and media and from any source.

- **Dooble:** Dooble is a free and open source Web browser. Dooble was created to improve privacy. Currently, Dooble is available for FreeBSD, Linux, OS X, OS/2, and Windows. Dooble uses Qt for its user interface and abstraction from the operating system and processor architecture. As a result, Dooble should be portable to any system that supports OpenSSL, POSIX threads, Qt, SQLite, and other libraries.

- **DTLS:** Datagram Transport Layer Security (DTLS) is a communications protocol that provides security for datagram-based applications by allowing them to communicate in a way that is designed to prevent eavesdropping, tampering, or message forgery. The DTLS protocol is based on the stream-oriented Transport Layer Security (TLS) protocol and is intended to provide similar security guarantees. The DTLS protocol datagram preserves the semantics of the underlying transport—the application does not suffer from the delays associated with stream protocols, but because it uses UDP, the application has to deal with packet reordering, loss of datagram and data larger than the size of a datagram network packet. Because DTLS uses UDP rather than TCP, it avoids the "TCP meltdown problem", when being used to create a VPN tunnel.

- **Echo Accounts:** Echo Accounts define an authorization scheme for the access to neighbour-nodes respective to the listener of a server. At the same time, they can form a Web-of-Trust. One-Time-Accounts regulate the assignment of an access, which can be used on time.

- **Echo Match:** The Echo Match is a specific cryptographic process to check the provided hash of the original plain text message with the hash of the conversion of the ciphertext with a specific key. If both hashes are the same, the right key has been chosen. Because the hash function cannot be inverted, the provided hash of the original plain text message does not provide any information about this message. Only if both hashes are the same, the conversion from cipher text to plain text has been successful and the right user with the right key can read the message. This requires that each given key must be tried out and if the message cannot be converted successfully, that the message has to be provided to all known network connections and nodes to be tried out there: the message cannot be read by this node with given keys.

- **Echo Network:** The Echo Network is a network based on Echo Nodes communicating over the Echo Protocol (and HTTPS). Often the letters E_C_H_O are used to provide a template for such a network within graph theory. The Echo network consists of servers and clients, within the Spot-On clients the server software is already included, so that nodes can be in a hybrid position, to be a server connected to a server, a server connected to a node or a node connected to a server. The Echo Network is speaking of Neighbors for another node.

- **Echo:** Spot-On introduced the Echo. The Echo is a malleable concept. That is, an implementation does not require rigid details. Each model may adhere to their own peculiar obligations. The Echo functions on the elementary persuasion that information is dispersed over multiple or singular passages and channel endpoints evaluate the suitability of the received data. Because data may become intolerable, Spot-On implements its own congestion control algorithm. Received messages that meet some basic criteria are labeled and duplicates are discarded. Advanced models may define more sophisticated congestion-avoidance algorithms based upon their interpretations of the Echo. The Echo combines encryption and graph theory: With the Echo Protocol is meant - simply put – that first, every message transmission is encrypted and second, in the Echo Network, each connection node sends each message to each connected neighbor. As third criterion for the Echo Protocol can be added, that there is a special feature when unpacking the encrypted capsule: The capsules have neither a receiver nor sender information included - and here they are different from TCP packets. The message is identified by the hash of the unencrypted message (compared to the conversion text of all known keys in the node) as to whether the message should be displayed and readable to the recipient in the user interface or not. For this so-called "Echo Match" see even more detailed at referring keyword. Spot-On provides two modes of operation for the general Echo, Full Echo and Half Echo. The Full Echo permits absolute data flow. The Half Echo defines an agreement between two endpoints. Within this agreement, information from other endpoints is prohibited from traveling along the private channel.

- **Echo-Grid:** The Echo-Grid is a graphical representation of a template for the Echo-protocol, do be able to illustrate different nodes and communicational relations in a graphic and within graph-theory. For that the letters for the word ECHO, respective the both characters AE are drawn and connected on a base-line. All angle corners of each letter further represent potential nodes in communicational networks, which can be per letter be consecutively numbered, example: E1 ... E1 for the six nodes of the letter E. Then it is possible to talk about the communicational paths of drawn users from E to O.

- **Echo-Protocol:** The Echo protocol means from an operational view: you send only encrypted messages, but you send your to-be-send-message to all of your connected friends. They do the same. You maintain your own network, everyone has every message and you try to decrypt every message. In case you can read and unwrap it, it is a message for you. Otherwise you share the message with all your friends and the message remains encrypted. Echo is very simple, and the principle is over 30 years old – nothing new. As Echo uses HTTP as a protocol, there is no forwarding or routing of messages: no IPs are forwarded, e.g. like it is if you send your message e.g. from your home laptop to your webserver. The process starts at each destination new – as you define it. The Echo protocol provided by spot-on has nothing to do with RFC 862. A new Echo protocol RFC has to be written or re-newed and extended – with or without that RFC-Number it refers to a p2p network.

- **Edgar Allan Poe:** Edgar Allan Poe (1809 – 1849) was an American writer, editor, and literary critic. Poe is best known for his poetry and short stories, particularly his tales of mystery and the macabre. He is widely regarded as a central figure of Romanticism in the United States and of American literature as a whole, and he was one of the country's earliest practitioners of the short story. One very popular short story was the story of "GoldBug". Hence, the software application also named GoldBug as an alternative GUI for the Spot-On kernel is a reminiscence to this writer. Poe is generally considered the inventor of the detective fiction genre and is further credited with contributing to the emerging genre of science fiction. He was the first well-known American writer to earn a living through writing alone, resulting in a financially difficult life and career. Poe was born in Boston and his works influenced literature around the world, as well as specialized fields such as cosmology and cryptography. He was a popular writer of cryptograms and interested in bringing the knowledge of cryptographic thinking to the population.

- **ElGamal:** In cryptography, the ElGamal encryption system is an asymmetric key encryption algorithmfor public-key cryptography which is based on the Diffie–Hellman key exchange. It was described by Taher ElGamal in 1985. ElGamal encryption is used in the free GNU Privacy Guard software, recent versions of PGP, and other cryptosystems.

- **E-Mail Institution:** An E-Mail-institution describes an E-Mail-Postbox within the p2p network of the Echo protocol. Per definition of an address-like Description for the institution, E-Mails of users within the p2p network can temporarily be stored within one other node. As well it is possible, to send E-Mail to friends, which are currently offline. Institutions describe a standard, how to configure an E-Mail-Postbox within a p2p network – like today POP3 and IMAP allow to provide a Mailbox. The Mailbox of the E-Mail-Institution is inserted by a Magnet-URI-Link within the client, which want to use the Postbox. At the E-Mail-Institution only the public E-Mail-Encryption-Key of the postbox-users has to be entered.

- **Encapsulation:** The capsule (like a zip) within the Echo describes a bundle of message elements, like the cipher text of the original message, the hash for the plain text of the message and also further elements like signature keys etc. In case an Echo Match was not successful, the elements of the capsule are encapsulated again and sent to further neighbors.

- **Encrypt-then-MAC(ETM):** The plaintext is first encrypted, then a MAC is produced based on the resulting ciphertext. The ciphertext and its MAC are sent together. Used in, e.g., Ipsec. The standard method according to ISO/IEC 19772:2009. This is the only method which can reach the highest definition of security in authenticated encryption, but this can only be achieved when the MAC used is "Strongly Unforgeable". In November 2014, TLS and DTLS extension for EtM has been published as RFC 7366.

- **End-to-End:** The end-to-end principle is a classic design principle of computer networking, first explicitly articulated in a 1981 conference paper by Saltzer, Reed, and Clark. The end-to-end principle states that application-specific functions ought to reside in the end hosts of a network rather than in intermediary nodes – provided they can be implemented "completely and correctly" in the end hosts. In debates about network neutrality, a common interpretation of the end-to-end principle is that it implies a neutral or "dumb" network. End-to-end encryption (E2EE) is an uninterrupted protection of the confidentiality and integrity of transmitted data by encoding it at its starting point and decoding it at its destination. It involves encrypting clear (red) data at source with knowledge of the intended recipient, allowing the encrypted (black) data to travel safely through vulnerable channels (e.g. public networks) to its recipient where it can be decrypted (assuming the destination shares the necessary key-variables and algorithms). An end-to-end encryption is often reached by providing an encryption with the AES Passphrase.

- **Ephemeral Keys:** Ephemeral Keys are temporarily used keys for encryption, often used for end-to-end encryption and/or to provide Forward Secrecy: Temporary keys are more deniable than permanent keys.

- **EPKS (Echo Public Key Share):** Echo Public Key Share (EPKS) is a function implemented in Spot-On to share public encryption keys over the Echo Network. This allows a group to share keys over secure channels so that a classical key server it not needed. It is a way of key exchange to a group or one individual user. The key exchange (also known as "key establishment") is any method in cryptography by which cryptographic keys are exchanged between users, allowing use of a cryptographic algorithm. If sender and receiver wish to exchange encrypted messages, each must be equipped to encrypt messages to be sent and decrypt messages received. The nature of the equipping they require depends on the encryption technique they might use. If they use a code, both will require a copy of the same codebook. If they use a cipher, they will need appropriate keys. If the cipher is a symmetric key cipher, both will need a copy of the same key. If an asymmetric key cipher with the public/private key property, both will need the other's public key. The key exchange problem is how to exchange whatever keys or other information are needed so that no one else can obtain a copy. Historically, this required trusted couriers, diplomatic bags, or some other secure channel. With the advent of public key / private key cipher algorithms, the encrypting key (aka public key) could be made public, since (at least for high quality algorithms) no one without the decrypting key (aka, the private key) could decrypt the message. Diffie–Hellman key exchange: In 1976, Whitfield Diffie and Martin Hellman published a cryptographic protocol, (Diffie–Hellman key exchange), which allows users to establish 'secure channels' on which to exchange keys, even if an Opponent is monitoring that communication channel. However, D–H key exchange did not address the problem of being sure of the actual identity of the person (or 'entity').

- **Exponential Encryption:** Exponential Encryption is a term coined by the analysts and authors Meke Gasakis and Max Schmidt in their book about „The New Era of Exponential Encryption", in which they analyze based on the Echo Protocol the trends and their vision to provide exponential options for encryption and decryption processes in combination with graph-theory within Echo networks. Here each node sends each message to each known neighbor, which multiplicities the options like a rice corn – according to a popular story - doubling at each field of a chess board.

- **Fiasco Keys:** Fiasco Keys are temporary keys, which were first introduced within the Smoke Mobile Echo Client. These keys are a bunch of temporary keys provided in a cache for end to end encryption. Starting from the newest, all keys in that cache for Fiasco Forwarding have to be tried out. This is a more volatile construction than schematic key transmission known form other protocols.

- **File Encryption Tool:** The File Encryption Tool of Spot-On has the function to encrypt and decrypt files on the hard disk. Here as well many values for the encryption details can be set individually. The tool is useful, in case files have to be sent - either over encrypted or unencrypted connections. As well for the storage of files, either on your local hard disc or as well remote in the cloud, this tool is very helpful, to secure own data.

- **File-Encryptor:** File-Encryptor is a tool within the Spot-On Encryption Suite to encrypt files before they are sent out over encrypted or unencrypted connection or are stored within a cloud or foreign storage option.

- **File-Sharing:** File sharing is the practice of distributing or providing access to digital media, such as computer programs, multimedia (audio, images and video), documents or electronic books. File sharing may be achieved in a number of ways. Common methods of storage, transmission and dispersion include manual sharing utilizing removable media, (de-)centralized servers on computer networks, World Wide Web-based hyperlinked documents, and the use of (mobile) distributed peer-to-peer networking.

- **FireChat:** FireChat is an IRC-like group chat within the Smoke Mobile Echo Client and compatible to the BUZZ-Chat in the

- **Forward Secrecy (FS):** In cryptography, forward secrecy (FS; also known as perfect forward secrecy) is a property of secure communication protocols: a secure communication protocol is said to have forward secrecy if compromise of long-term keys does not compromise past session keys.[2] FS protects past sessions against future compromises of secret keys or passwords. If forward secrecy is utilized, encrypted communications recorded in the past cannot be retrieved and decrypted should long-term secret keys or passwords be compromised in the future.

- **Forward-Secrecy-Calling:** Forward-Secrecy-Calling is some modus for Cryptographic Calling, which sends temporary asymmetric keys for end-to-end encryption and is referred to asymmetric calling. It refers to send several asymmetric key (pairs) through one secured channel. The symmetric end-to-end encryption key is sent in the Forward Secrecy Calling (FSC) not over the permanent (a-symmetric) e.g.

chat key or over the channel of an existing (symmetric) end-to-end encryption key, but by the new ephemeral, temporary and a-symmetric (e.g. chat) key. While sending an end-to-end encryption key over an existing end-to-end symmetric encrypted channel defines a "symmetric" "instant perfect forward secrecy", sending an end-to-end encrypting key over the ephemeral keys of the initiated "forward secrecy" (in e.g. the chat function) may be considered an "a-symmetric" one of "Instant Perfect Forward Secrecy".

- **Forward Secrecy:** Forward Secrecy (FS), also known as perfect forward secrecy (PFS), is a feature of specific key agreement protocols that gives assurances your session keys will not be compromised even if the private key of the server is compromised. Forward secrecy protects past sessions against future compromises of secret keys or passwords. By generating a unique session key for every session a user initiates, even the compromise of a single session key will not affect any data other than that exchanged in the specific session protected by that particular key.

- **Friend-to-Friend (F2F):** A friend-to-friend (or F2F) computer network is a type of peer-to-peer network in which users only make direct connections with people they know. Passwords or digital signatures can be used for authentication. Unlike other kinds of private P2P, users in a friend-to-friend network cannot find out who else is participating beyond their own circle of friends, so F2F networks can grow in size without compromising their users' anonymity.

- **Full Echo:** See Echo.

- **Galois/Counter Mode (GCM)-Algorithm:** Galois/Counter Mode (GCM) is a mode of operation for symmetric key cryptographic block ciphers that has been widely adopted because of its efficiency and performance. GCM throughput rates for state of the art, high speed communication channels can be achieved with reasonable hardware resources.

- **Gemini:** The Gemini is a feature in Spot-On Secure Instant Messenger to add another security layer to the chatroom with an AES Key for end-to-end

- **GnuPG:** GNU Privacy Guard (GnuPG or GPG), a free-software replacement for Symantec's PGP cryptographic software suite, complies with RFC 4880, the IETF standards-track specification of OpenPGP. Modern versions of PGP are interoperable with GnuPG and other OpenPGP-compliant systems. GnuPG is a hybrid-encryption software program because it uses a combination of conventional symmetric-key cryptography for speed, and public-key cryptography for ease of secure key exchange, typically by using the recipient's public key to encrypt a session key which is only used once. GnuPG encrypts messages using asymmetric key pairs individually generated by GnuPG users. The resulting public keys may be exchanged with other users in a variety of ways. GnuPG also supports symmetric encryption algorithms. By default, GnuPG uses the CAST5 symmetrical algorithm.

- **Gnutella:** Gnutella is a large peer-to-peer network. It was the first decentralized peer-to-peer network of its kind, leading to other, later networks adopting the model.

- **GoldBug (Application):** The GoldBug Messenger and E-Mail-Client is a user interface, which offers for the kernel and the application Spot-On an alternative to the originally offered user interface of Spot-on, which contains many options. The GoldBug Graphical User Interface (GUI) therefore has the approach, to have a more simplified user interface designed, which is useable not only on the desktop, but also can be deployed for mobile devices.

- **GoldBug (E-Mail Password):** The GoldBug-feature is used in the integrated email client to add here as well an end-to-end AES Encryption layer – the GoldBug, or: just a password, both users use to encrypt their emails once more. So with the GoldBug, you need a kind of password (e.g. AES-string) to open the email of a friend or to be able to chat with him.

- **Graph-Theory:** In mathematics, and more specifically in graph theory, a graph is a representation of a set of objects where some pairs of objects are connected by links. The interconnected objects are represented by mathematical abstractions called vertices (also called nodes or points), and the links that connect some pairs of vertices are called edges (also called arcs or lines). Typically, a graph is depicted in diagrammatic form as a set of dots for the vertices, joined by lines or curves for the edges. Graphs are one of the objects of study in discrete mathematics.

- **Group chat:** The term group chat, or group chat room, is primarily used to describe any form of synchronous conferencing, occasionally even asynchronous conferencing. The term can thus mean any technology ranging from real-time online chat and online interaction with strangers (e.g., online rooms) to fully immersive graphical social environments. The primary use of a group chat room is to share information via text with a group of other users. Generally speaking, the ability to converse with multiple people in the same conversation differentiates group chat rooms from instant messaging programs, which are more typically designed for one-to-one communication - though two users also can define a group for private conversations.

- **GUI:** In computer science, a graphical user interface or GUI is a type of interface that allows users to interact with electronic devices through graphical icons and visual indicators such as secondary notation, as opposed to text-based interfaces, typed command labels or text navigation.

- **Half Echo:** Spot-On provides two modes of operation for the general Echo, Full Echo and Half Echo. The Full Echo permits absolute data flow. The Half Echo defines an agreement between two endpoints. Within this agreement, information from other endpoints is prohibited from traveling along the private channel. If you use the modus "half Echo", then your message is not shared with other, third participants (Model: A -> B -> C). Only direct connections are used (Model A -> B). It requires only one direct connection to one friend. With the modus "Full Echo" your message is forwarded from friend to friend and so on, until the recipient could decrypt the envelope and read the message.

- **Hash:** A hash function is any function that can be used to map data of arbitrary size to data of fixed size. The values returned by a hash function are called hash values, hash codes, hash sums, or simply hashes. A cryptographic hash function is a hash function which is considered practically impossible to invert, that is, to recreate the input data from its hash value alone. These one-way hash functions have been called "the workhorses of modern cryptography". The input data is often called the message, and the hash value is often called the message digest or simply the digest.

- **HMAC:** HMAC (sometimes expanded as either keyed-hash message authentication code or hash-based message authentication code) is a specific type of message authentication code (MAC) involving a cryptographic hash function and a secret cryptographic key. It may be used to simultaneously verify both the data integrity and the authentication of a message, as with any MAC. Any cryptographic hash function, such as SHA-256 or SHA-3, may be used in the calculation of an HMAC; the resulting MAC algorithm is termed HMAC-X, where X is the hash function used (e.g. HMAC-SHA256 or HMAC-SHA3). The cryptographic strength of the HMAC depends upon the cryptographic strength of the underlying hash function, the size of its hash output, and the size and quality of the key. HMAC uses two passes of hash computation. The secret key is first used to derive two keys – inner and outer. The first pass of the algorithm produces an internal hash derived from the message and the inner key. The second pass produces the final HMAC code derived from the inner hash result and the outer key. Thus, the algorithm provides better immunity against length extension attacks. An iterative hash function breaks up a message into blocks of a fixed size and iterates over them with a compression function. For example, SHA-256 operates on 512-bit blocks. The size of the output of HMAC is the same as that of the underlying hash function (e.g., 256 and 1600 bits in the case of SHA-256 and SHA-3, respectively), although it can be truncated if desired. HMAC does not encrypt the message. Instead, the message (encrypted or not) must be sent alongside the HMAC hash. Parties with the secret key will hash the message again themselves, and if it is authentic, the received and computed hashes will match. The definition and analysis of the HMAC construction was first published in 1996 in a paper by Mihir Bellare, Ran Canetti, and Hugo Krawczyk, and they also wrote RFC 2104 in 1997.

- **HTTPS:** HTTPS (also called HTTP over TLS, HTTP over SSL, and HTTP Secure) is a protocol for secure communication over a computer network which is widely used on the Internet. HTTPS consists of communication over Hypertext Transfer Protocol (HTTP) within a connection encrypted by Transport Layer Security or its predecessor, Secure Sockets Layer. The main motivation for HTTPS is authentication of the visited website and protection of the privacy and integrity of the exchanged data.

- **Human Rights:** Human rights are the basic rights and freedoms to which all humans are entitled". Examples of rights and freedoms which are often thought of as human rights include civil and political rights, such as the right to life, liberty, and property, freedom of expression, pursuit of happiness and equality before the law; and social, cultural and economic rights, including the right to participate in science and culture, the right to work, and the right to education and the right of privacy.

- **Hybrid Encryption:** See also Multi-Encryption. Hybrid Encryption points especially out that symmetric and asymmetric encryption has been applied either in one application or to a plain text.

- **IMAP:** In computing, the Internet Message Access Protocol (IMAP) is an Internet standard protocol used by e-mail clients to retrieve e-mail messages from a mail server over a TCP/IP connection. IMAP is defined by RFC 3501. IMAP was designed with the goal of permitting complete management of an email box by multiple email clients, Therefore, clients generally leave messages on the server.

- **Impersonator:** Impersonator is a function, which sends from the Spot-On Client a message from time to time into the network, which contains only random characters. With this method it is made more difficult for attackers to conduct time analysis of communications. Also, real cipher text messages should be harder to recognize and harder to differ from such messages with random characters.

- **Information security:** information security preservation of confidentiality, integrity and availability of information

- **Innovation:** Innovation in its modern meaning is a "new idea, creative thoughts, new imaginations in form of device or method". Innovation is often also viewed as the application of better solutions that meet new requirements, unarticulated needs, or existing market needs. Such innovation takes place through the provision of more-effective products, processes, services, technologies, or business models that are made available to markets, governments and society. An innovation is something original and more effective and, as a consequence, new, that "breaks into" the market or society. Innovation is related to, but not the same as, invention, as innovation is more apt to involve the practical implementation of an invention (i.e. new/improved ability) to make a meaningful impact in the market or society, and not all innovations require an invention.

- **Instant Perfect Forward Secrecy (IPFS):** While Perfect Forward Secrecy, often also called only Forward Secrecy, describes within many applications and as well from a conceptional approach the transmission of ephemeral– this means temporary - keys, it is implicit connected, that this is proceeded one time per online session. With Spot-On and the underlying architecture of the Spot-On Kernel a new paradigm has been implemented. Forward Secrecy or Perfect Forward Secrecy, has developed further to Instant Perfect Forward Secrecy (IPFS). While Forward Secrecy means to be able to neglect to have used a certain key in the past if one further key is compromised, this concept addresses to end-to-end encryption. With Instant Perfect Forward Secrecy the Cryptographic Calling comes into the frame: A user is able to renew the end-to-end encrypting credentials like in a call: Instantly and several times within a session the user should be able to renew temporary keys for end-to-end encryption. An even further development of this concept has been taken place by the development of Fiasco Forwarding, which sends a full bundle of keys within one session or with a(n automated) call action for future sessions.The end-to-end-encryption with temporary keys can be changed at any time, this means also per any second. This describes the term of Instant Perfect Forward Secrecy (IPFS). Via a so-called "Call" the end-to-end-encryption can be renewed. Instantly. Also, the term of a "call" for the transmission of a to-be-created or to-be-renewed end-to-end-encryption has been introduced by Spot-on into cryptography.

- **Institution:** An Institution in Cryptography is an e-mail postbox to save messages for offline participants within a peer-to-peer Echo Network. The institution is based on cryptographic credentials, so that in one node subscribed participant with their public encryption key can deposit, save and retrieve messages. The advantage despite other methods e.g. storing the data within a common friend) is that the providing node of an Institution need not to give out the own public encryption key.

- **Integer factorization:** In number theory, integer factorization is the decomposition of a composite number into a product of smaller integers. If these integers are further restricted to prime numbers, the process is called prime factorization. When the numbers are very large, no efficient, non-quantum integer factorization algorithm is known; an effort by several researchers concluded in 2009, factoring a 232-digit number (RSA-768), utilizing hundreds of machines took two years and the researchers estimated that a 1024-bit RSA modulus would take about a thousand times as long.

- **Integrity:** property of accuracy and completeness.

- **IPFS:** IPFS is the abbreviation of Instant Perfect Forward Secrecy.

- **IRC:** Internet Relay Chat (IRC) is an application layer protocol that facilitates communication in the form of text. The chat process works on a client/server networking model. IRC clients are computer programs that users can install on their system or web based applications running either locally in the browser or on 3rd party server. These clients communicate with chat servers to transfer messages to other clients. IRC is mainly designed for group communication in discussion forums, called channels, but also allows one-on-one communication via private messages as well as chat and data transfer, including file sharing.

- **Iteration Function:** In mathematics, an iterated function is a function X? X (that is, a function from some set X to itself) which is obtained by composing another function f : X ? X with itself a certain number of times. The process of repeatedly applying the same function is called iteration. Iterated functions are objects of study in computer science, fractals, dynamical systems, mathematics and renormalization group physics.

- **Java:** Java is a general-purpose computer-programming language that is concurrent, class-based, object-oriented, and specifically designed to have as few implementation dependencies as possible. It is intended to let application developers "write once, run anywhere" (WORA), meaning that compiled Java code can run on all platforms that support Java without the need for recompilation.

- **Kerckhoffs's principle:** Kerckhoffs's principle was stated by Netherlands born cryptographer Auguste Kerckhoffs in the 19th century: A cryptosystem should be secure even if everything about the system, except the key, is public knowledge. Kerckhoffs's principle was reformulated (or possibly independently formulated) by American mathematician Claude Shannon as "the enemy knows the system", i.e., "one ought to design systems under the assumption that the enemy will immediately gain full familiarity with them". In that form, it is called Shannon's maxim. Kerckhoffs's principle (Shannon's maxim) is widely embraced by cryptographers.

- **Kernel:** In computing, the kernel is a computer program that manages input/output requests from software and translates them into data processing instructions for the central processing unit and other electronic components of a computer. The kernel is a fundamental part of a modern computer's operating system or of applications.

- **Keyboard:** In computing, a computer keyboard is a type-writer-style device which uses an arrangement of buttons or keys to act as mechanical levers or electronic switches. Keyboard keys (buttons) typically have characters engraved or printed on them, and each press of a key typically corresponds to a single written symbol. Virtual keyboards in software with encryption prevent that key-loggers record the typing - as mouse clicks do not indicate, which symbol has been klicked.

- **Keyed-Hash Message Authentication Code (HMAC):** In cryptography, a keyed-hash message authentication code (HMAC) is a specific construction for calculating a message authentication code (MAC) involving a cryptographic hash function in combination with a secret cryptographic key. As with any MAC, it may be used to simultaneously verify both the data integrity and the authentication of a message. Any cryptographic hash function, such as MD5 or SHA-1, may be used in the calculation of an HMAC; the resulting MAC algorithm is termed HMAC-MD5 or HMAC-SHA1 accordingly. The cryptographic strength of the HMAC depends upon the cryptographic strength of the underlying hash function, the size of its hash output, and on the size and quality of the key.

- **KeySync:** KeySyc is a term deriving from the context of the term AutoCrypt, which are both a follow up of the idea of a REPLEO, respective a key exchange over the EPKS – Echo Public Key Sharing – Protocol. Here two participants share over a channel the public keys and integrate the received keys into the own nodes.

- **Libcurl:** cURL is a computer software project providing a library and command-line tool for transferring data using various protocols. The cURL project produces two products, libcurl and cURL. It was first released in 1997. The name originally stood for "see URL".

- **Listener:** A listener is a software design pattern in which an object maintains a list of its dependents and notifies them automatically of any state changes, usually by calling one of their methods. It is mainly used to implement distributed event handling systems. It is often used for creating or opening a port on which the service or chat-server then is "listening" for incoming data connections.

- **Login:** In computer security, logging in (or logging on or signing in or signing on) is the process by which an individual gains access to a computer system by identifying and authenticating themselves. The user credentials are typically some form of "username" and a matching "password", and these credentials themselves are sometimes referred to as a login, (or a logon or a sign-in or a sign-on).

- **MAC (Message Authentication Code):** In cryptography, a message authentication code (often MAC) is a short piece of information used to authenticate a message and to provide integrity and authenticity assurances on the message. Integrity assurances detect accidental and intentional message changes, while authenticity assurances affirm the message's origin. A MAC algorithm, sometimes called a keyed (cryptographic) hash function (however, cryptographic hash function is only one of the possible ways to generate MACs), accepts as input a secret key and an arbitrary-length message to be authenticated, and outputs a MAC (sometimes known as a tag). The MAC value protects both a message's data integrity as well as its authenticity, by allowing verifiers (who also possess the secret key) to detect any changes to the message content.

- **Magnet-URI:** The Magnet-URI scheme, defines the format of Magnet-links, a de facto standard for identifying files by their content, via cryptographic hash value) rather than by their location.

- **McEliece:** In cryptography, the McEliece cryptosystem is an asymmetric encryption algorithm developed in 1978 by Robert McEliece. It was the first such scheme to use randomization in the encryption process. The algorithm has currently not gained much acceptance in the cryptographic community but is a candidate for "post-quantum cryptography", as it is immune to attacks using Shor's algorithm and — more generally — measuring cost states using Fourier sampling. The recommended parameter sizes for the used Goppa code - which maximizes the adversary's work factor - appears to be n = 1024, t = 38, and k = 644.

- **Measurement:** process to determine a value.

- **MELODICA:** With the MELODICA feature in Spot-On Secure Messenger you call your friend and send him a new Gemini (AES-256-Key). The Key is sent over your asymmetric encryption of the RSA key. This is a secure way, as all other plaintext transfers like: email, spoken over phone or in other messengers, have to be regarded as unsafe and recorded. MELODICA stands for: Multi Encrypted Long Distance Calling. You call your friend even over a long distance of the Echo protocol and exchange over secure asymmetric encryption a Gemini (AES-256 key) to establish an end-to-end encrypted channel.

- **Meta-data:** Metadata is data [information] that provides information about other data. Many distinct types of metadata exist, among these descriptive metadata, structural metadata, administrative metadata, reference metadata and statistical metadata. In the Internet meta data often refers to the recording of when how many data has been accessed or transferred by whom to whom.

- **Monitoring:** determining the status of a system, a process or an activity.

- **Mosaic:** A mosaic is the name for a file splitted into smaller parts. These smaller parts are commonly called "blocks", "parts" or "chunks", here in the Spot-On application they are called: "links". All links build the mosaic, which can be assembled to the file, which has been transferred.

- **Multi-Encryption:** Multiple encryption is the process of encrypting an already encrypted message one or more times, either using the same or a different algorithm. It is also known as cascade encryption, cascade ciphering, multiple encryption, and superencipherment. Superencryption refers to the outer-level encryption of a multiple encryption. A hybrid cryptosystem is one which combines the convenience of a public-key cryptosystem with the efficiency of a symmetric-key cryptosystem. A hybrid cryptosystem can be constructed using any two separate cryptosystems: first, a key encapsulation scheme, which is a public-key cryptosystem, and second a data encapsulation scheme, which is a symmetric-key cryptosystem. Perhaps the most commonly used hybrid cryptosystems are the OpenPGP (RFC 4880) file format and the PKCS #7 (RFC 2315) file format, both used by many different systems. Multiple encryption is the process of encrypting an already encrypted message one or more times, either using the same or a different algorithm. Multiple encryption (Cascade Ciphers) reduces the consequences in the case that our favorite cipher is already broken and is continuously exposing our data without our knowledge. When a cipher is broken (something we will not know), the use of other ciphers may represent the only security in the system. Since we cannot scientifically prove that any particular cipher is strong, the question is not whether subsequent ciphers are strong, but instead, what would make us believe that any particular cipher is so strong as to need no added protection. Folk Theorem: A cascade of ciphers is at least as at least as difficult to break as any of its component ciphers. When a cipher is broken (something we will not know), the use of other ciphers may represent the only security in the system. Since we cannot scientifically prove that any particular cipher is strong, the question is not whether subsequent ciphers are strong, but instead, what would make us believe that any particular cipher is so strong as to need no added protection.

- **Ncat:** Netcat (often abbreviated to nc or Ncat) is a computer networking utility for reading from and writing to network connections using TCP or UDP. Netcat is designed to be a dependable back-end that can be used directly or easily driven by other programs and scripts.

- **Neighbor:** In graph theory, a neighbor of a vertex is another vertex that is connected to it by an edge.
- **Neuland:** Neuland is a German term within the context of the Internet and non-IT-savvy people, deriving as satirical designation in reference to the sentence of the year 2013 by German chancellor Angela Merkel.
- **NIST:** The National Institute of Standards and Technology (NIST) is a physical sciences laboratory, and a non-regulatory agency of the United States Department of Commerce. Its mission is to promote innovation and industrial competitiveness. NIST's activities are organized into laboratory programs that include nanoscale science and technology, engineering, information technology, neutron research, material measurement, and physical measurement.
- **NOVA:** NOVA describes a password on the to-be-transferred file. It is a symmetric encryption of the file scheduled for the transfer. It can be compared with the term of a GoldBug-Password on an E-Mail. Both are technically created with an AES-256 (or a user-defined password).
- **NTRU:** NTRU is a patented and open source public-key cryptosystem that uses lattice-based cryptography to encrypt and decrypt data. It consists of two algorithms: NTRUEncrypt, which is used for encryption, and NTRUSign, which is used for digital signatures. Unlike other popular public-key cryptosystems, it is resistant to attacks using Shor's algorithm (i.e. by "Quantum Computing") and its performance has been shown to be significantly better.
- **Objective:** result to be achieved.
- **Off-the-record (OTR):** Off-the-Record Messaging (OTR) is a cryptographic protocol that provides encryption for instant messaging conversations. OTR uses a combination of AES symmetric-key algorithm with 128 bits key length, the Diffie–Hellman key exchange with 1536 bits group size, and the SHA-1 hash function. In addition to authentication and encryption, OTR provides forward secrecy and malleable encryption.

- **One-Time-Magnet (OTM):** A One-Time-Magnet (OTM) is a Magnet, which is deployed for the File-Transfer within the StarBeam-Function. After sending the File using the cryptographic values included in the Magnet-Link, the Magnet is deleted within the Spot-On. Other Magnets for the Star-Beam-Function can be used several times – this means, several and different files can be transferred to the receiver through the symmetric Channel (including all users, knowing the specific Magnet).

- **One-Time-Pad (OTP):** In cryptography, the one-time pad (OTP) is an encryption technique that cannot be cracked if used correctly. In this technique, a plaintext is paired with a random secret key (also referred to as a one-time pad). Then, each bit or character of the plaintext is encrypted by combining it with the corresponding bit or character from the pad using modular addition. If the key is truly random, is at least as long as the plaintext, is never reused in whole or in part, and is kept completely secret, then the resulting ciphertext will be impossible to decrypt or break.

- **Open source:** Open source is a term denoting that a product includes permission to use its source code, design documents, or content. It most commonly refers to the open-source model, in which open-source software or other products are released under an open-source license as part of the open-source-software movement. Use of the term originated with software but has expanded beyond the software sector to cover other open content and forms of open collaboration. In Cryptography only open source software allows everyone to proof that the code has no backdoors implemented.

- **OpenPGP:** The OpenPGP standard (also Pretty Good Privacy) is a data encryption and decryption computer program that provides cryptographic privacy and authentication for data communication. PGP is often used for signing, encrypting, and decrypting texts, e-mails, files, directories, and whole disk partitions and to increase the security of e-mail communications. It was created by Phil Zimmermann in 1991.PGP and similar software follow the OpenPGP standard (RFC 4880) for encrypting and decrypting data.

- **OpenSSL:** In computer networking, OpenSSL is a software library to be used in applications that need to secure communications against eavesdropping or need to ascertain the identity of the party at the other end. It has found wide use in internet web servers, serving a majority of all web sites. OpenSSL contains an open source implementation of the SSL and TLS protocols. Transport Layer Security (TLS) and its predecessor, Secure Sockets Layer (SSL), both of which are frequently referred to as 'SSL', are cryptographic protocols designed to provide communications security over a computer network.

- **OTM:** See One-Time-Magnet.

- **OTR:** See Off-the-record.

- **Ozone Postbox:** The Ozone Postbox is a way to reach offline friends within the Smoke Mobile Crypto Client respective the SmokeStack Communication Server for Android. The Ozone Postbox serves as a cache for friends, which are not online. The Ozone is just a passphrase string, which must be applied in both, the client Smoke and the Server SmokeStack. The rest is done by the cryptographic keys. The Ozone can be initialized within the client by using the dyndns or IP name, port and TCP, e.g.: dyndns.org:4711:TCP. If the server administrator of SmokeStack applies this string also as one ozone within the server, the clients will automatically add the string as the ozone when entering the IP respective dyndns-string of the server.

- **P2P:** see Peer-to-Peer.

- **Pandamonium:** Pandamonium is a Web-Crawler, with which URLs of a Domain can be indexed for Spot-On. The Pandamonium Web Crawler can allocate for the URL-Search function within the Spot-On Encryption Suite a bunch of URLs over the Import-function.

- **Passphrase:** A passphrase is a sequence of words or other text used to control access to a computer system, program or data. A passphrase is similar to a password in usage but is generally longer for added security. Passphrases are often used to control both access to, and operation of, cryptographic programs and systems. Passphrases are particularly applicable to systems that use the passphrase as an encryption key. The origin of the term is by analogy with password. The passphrase in Spot-On must be at least 16 characters long, this is used to create a cryptographic hash, which is longer and stronger.

- **Pass-through:** The Pass-through method within the application Spot-On describes a function for a network path from an application, e.g. a Gopher client, over two Spot-On instances to another Gopher Client: Gopher -> Spot-On -> Internet -> Spot-On – Gopher. This function works similar as a VPN tunnel or a proxy for the external application. As the connection from a Spot-On node over the Internet to another Spot-On node is encrypted, also e.g. with the McEliece algorithm, even old applications with no encryption can communicate now secure over the Internet. The application to tie in must only meet some tolerance for chaotic transmission, a Gopher client can be ideal used for such tests.

- **Password:** A password is a word or string of characters used for user authentication to prove identity or access approval to gain access to a resource (example: an access code is a type of password), which is to be kept secret from those not allowed access. In modern times, user names and passwords are commonly used by people during a log in process that controls access to protected computer operating systems, mobile phones, cable TV decoders, automated teller machines (ATMs), etc.

- **Patch-Points:** Patch-Points describe the entry- and end-nodes of the pass-through functionality. This functionality of has been discussed in the Spot-On Developer Forum originally as Patch-Points, has then be named within the application as pass-through function. At Patch-Points two older applications without encryption can communicate over the secure connection of two Spot-On nodes.

- **Peer-to-Peer (P2P):** Peer-to-peer (P2P) computing or networking is a distributed application architecture that partitions tasks or workloads between peers. Peers make a portion of their resources, such as processing power, disk storage or network bandwidth, directly available to other network participants, without the need for central coordination by servers or stable hosts. Peers are equally privileged, equipotent participants in the application. They are said to form a peer-to-peer network of nodes.

- **Performance:** measurable result. Note: Performance can relate either to quantitative or qualitative findings.

- **PKI:** A public key infrastructure (PKI) is a set of roles, policies, and procedures needed to create, manage, distribute, use, store & revoke digital certificates and manage public-key encryption. The purpose of a PKI is to facilitate the secure electronic transfer of information for a range of network activities such as e-commerce, internet banking and confidential email. It is required for activities where simple passwords are an inadequate authentication method and more rigorous proof is required to confirm the identity of the parties involved in the communication and to validate the information being transferred. In cryptography, a PKI is an arrangement that binds public keys with respective identities of entities (like people and organizations). The binding is established through a process of registration and issuance of certificates at and by a certificate authority (CA). Depending on the assurance level of the binding, this may be carried out by an automated process or under human supervision.

- **Plain text:** In computing, plain text is a loose term for data (e.g. file contents) that represent only characters of readable material but not its graphical representation nor other objects (floating-point numbers, images, etc.). It may also include a limited number of characters that control simple arrangement of text, such as spaces, line breaks, or tabulation characters (although tab characters can "mean" many different things, so are hardly "plain"). In cryptography, plain text is the opposite of cipher text.

- **Point-to-Point:** In telecommunications, a point-to-point connection refers to a communications connection between two communication endpoints or nodes. An example is a telephone call, in which one telephone is connected with one other, and what is said by one caller can only be heard by the other. This is contrasted with a point-to-multipoint or broadcast connection, in which many nodes can receive information transmitted by one node.

- **Policy:** intentions and direction of a formal entity as formally expressed by its management.

- **POP3:** In computing, the Post Office Protocol (POP) is an application-layer Internet standard protocol used by local e-mail clients to retrieve e-mail from a remote server over a TCP/IP connection. POP has been developed through several versions, with version 3 (POP3) being the last standard in common use.

- **POPTASTIC:** POPTASTIC is a function, which enables encrypted chat and encrypted E-Mail over the regular POP3and IMAP-Postboxes of a user. The Spot-On Encryption Suite recognizes automatically, if the message has to be regarded as a Chat-Message or an E-Mail-Message. For that, the POPTASTIC encryption key is used. Once with a friend exchanged, this key is sending all E-mails between to E-Mail-Partner only as encrypted E-Mail. Third, POPTASTIC enables – respective the insertion of the POP3 / IMAP account information into the settings enables – also an old-fashioned and unencrypted E-Mail-Communication to @-E-Mail-Addresses. Spot-On extends the Instant Messaging with this function to a regular E-Mail-Client and also to an always encrypting E-Mail-Client over the POPTASTIC Key. The E-Mail-Addresses for encrypted E-Mails are indicated with a lock icon. Encrypted Chat is enabled over the free ports for E-Mail also behind more restrictive Hardware environments at any time.

- **PostgreSQL:** PostgreSQL, often simply Postgres, is an object-relational database management system (ORDBMS) with an emphasis on extensibility and standards-compliance. As a database server, its primary function is to store data securely, supporting best practices, and to allow for retrieval at the request of other software applications. It can handle workloads ranging from small single-machine applications to large Internet-facing applications with many concurrent users. PostgreSQL implements the majority of the SQL:2011 standard.

- **Privacy:** Privacy is the ability of an individual or group to seclude themselves, or information about themselves, and thereby express themselves selectively. The boundaries and content of what is considered private differ among cultures and individuals but share common themes. When something is private to a person, it usually means that something is inherently special or sensitive to them. The domain of privacy partially overlaps with security (confidentiality), which can include the concepts of appropriate use, as well as protection of information. Privacy may also take the form of bodily integrity. The right not to be subjected to unsanctioned invasions of privacy by the government, corporations or individuals is part of many countries' privacy laws, and in some cases, constitutions. All countries have laws which in some way limit privacy. An example of this would be law concerning taxation, which normally requires the sharing of information about personal income or earnings. In some countries individual privacy may conflict with freedom of speech laws and some laws may require public disclosure of information which would be considered private in other countries and cultures. The right to privacy is an element of various legal traditions to restrain governmental and private actions that threaten the privacy of individuals. Over 150 national constitutions mention the right to privacy. Since the global surveillance disclosures of 2013, initiated by ex-NSA employee Edward Snowden, the inalienable human right to privacy has been a subject of international debate. Internet privacy involves the right or mandate of personal privacy concerning the storing, repurposing, provision to third parties, and displaying of information pertaining to oneself via the Internet. Internet privacy is a subset of data privacy. Privacy concerns have been articulated from the beginnings of large-scale computer sharing.

- **Private Key:** Public-key cryptography refers to a set of cryptographic algorithms that are based on mathematical problems that currently admit no efficient solution. The strength lies in the "impossibility" (computational impracticality) for a properly generated private key to be determined from its corresponding public key. Thus the public key may be published without compromising security. Security depends only on keeping the private key private.

- **Process:** set of interrelated or interacting activities which transforms inputs into outputs

- **Public Key:** Public-key cryptography refers to a set of cryptographic algorithms that are based on mathematical problems that currently admit no efficient solution – particularly those inherent in certain integer factorization, discrete logarithm, and elliptic curve relationships. It is computationally easy for a user to generate a public and private key-pair and to use it for encryption and decryption. The strength lies in the "impossibility" (computational impracticality) for a properly generated private key to be determined from its corresponding public key. Thus the public key may be published without compromising security. Security dependes especially on keeping the private key private.

- **Pure Forward Secrecy (PURE FS):** Pure Forward Secrecy refers to a communication in the E-Mail function of Spot-On, within which the information is not sent over asymmetrical keys, but over temporary, ephemeral keys, which generate a symmetric encryption. The ephemeral keys for Pure Forward Secrecy are exchanged over asymmetric keys, but then the message is sent exclusively over the temporary symmetric key. Compare in a different approach of Instant Perfect Forward Secrecy, that the messages is encrypted and transferred with both, a symmetric key and also with a asymmetric key within the format of the Echo-protocol.

- **Qt:** Qt is a cross-platform application framework that is widely used for developing application software that can be run on various software and hardware platforms with little or no change in the underlying codebase, while still being a native application with the capabilities and speed thereof. Qt is currently being developed both by the Qt Company, a subsidiary of Digia, and the Qt Project under open source governance, involving individual developers and firms working to advance Qt.

- **Quantum Computing:** Quantum computing is the use of quantum-mechanical phenomena such as superposition and entanglement to perform computation. A quantum computer is used to perform such computation, which can be implemented theoretically or physically. The field of Quantum Computing is actually a sub-field of quantum information science, which includes quantum cryptography and quantum communication. Quantum Computing was started in the early 1980s when Richard Feynman and Yuri Manin expressed the idea that a quantum computer had the potential to simulate things that a classical computer could not. In 1994, Peter Shor shocked the world with an algorithm that had the potential to decrypt all secured communications.

- **Random:** Randomness is the lack of pattern or predictability in events. A random sequence of events, symbols or steps has no order and does not follow an intelligible pattern or combination. Individual random events are by definition unpredictable.

- **Raspberry Pi:** The Raspberry Pi is a series of small single-board computers developed in the United Kingdom by the Raspberry Pi Foundation to promote teaching of basic computer science in schools and in developing countries. The original model became far more popular than anticipated.

- **REPLEO:** With a REPLEO the own public key is encrypted with the already received public key of a friend, so that the own public key can be transferred to the friend in a protected way.

- **Requirement:** Need or expectation that is stated, generally implied or obligatory; Note: "Generally implied" means that it is custom or common practice for the organization and interested parties that the need or expectation under consideration is implied. A specified requirement is one that is stated, for example in documented information.

- **RetroShare:** RetroShare is a chat and file sharing application based on a Friend-to-Friend Network building a web of trust. Peers have been replaced in this network by trusted friends. It is in complementary the old-fashioned way to connect to a friend in regard to Echo-Accounts, which are not tied to the public key of a friend.

- **Review:** activity undertaken to determine the suitability, adequacy and effectiveness of the subject matter to achieve established objectives

- **Rewind:** Rewind describes a function within the StarBeam-File-Transfer. With this the Send-out of a file is started for a second time. It is comparable with a new play from start of a music file. In case the file has not been completely transferred, the transmission can be started new or even scheduled for a later point of time. In case only some missing block of the file should be transferred again to the receiver, the further tool StarBeam-Analyzer is able to generate a Magnet-URI-Link, which the receiver can send to the sender, so that is will send out only the missing blocks again.

- **Rosetta CryptoPad:** The Rosetta-CryptoPad uses an own Key for the encryption – as also an own key exists for E-Mail, Chat, URLs or POPTASTIC. With the Rosetta-CryptoPad a text can be converted into cipher text. It is used, to encrypt own texts before sending the text out to the internet or before you Post it somewhere into the Web. Similar to the File-Encryption-Tool for Files, Rosetta also converts plaintext into cipher text. Then the text can be transferred – either over one again secured and encrypted channel or even unencrypted as Chat or E-mail. Further messages can be posted to an Internet-Board or a Paste-Bin-Service as chipper text.

- **RSA:** RSA is one of the first practical public-key cryptosystems and is widely used for secure data transmission. In such a cryptosystem, the encryption key is public and differs from the decryption key which is kept secret. In RSA, this asymmetry is based on the practical difficulty of factoring the product of two large prime numbers, the factoring problem. RSA is made of the initial letters of the surnames of Ron Rivest, Adi Shamir, and Leonard Adleman, who first publicly described the algorithm in 1977.

- **Salt, cryptographic:** In cryptography, a salt is random data that is used as an additional input to a one-way function that hashes a password or passphrase. The primary function of salts is to defend against dictionary attacks versus a list of password hashes and against pre-computed rainbow table attacks.

- **SCTP:** In computer networking, the Stream Control Transmission Protocol (SCTP) is a transport-layer protocol (protocol number 132), serving in a similar role to the popular protocols Transmission Control Protocol (TCP) and User Datagram Protocol (UDP). It provides some of the same service features of both: it is message-oriented like UDP and ensures reliable, in-sequence transport of messages with congestion control like TCP. RFC 4960 defines the protocol. RFC 3286 provides an introduction.

- **Secret Streams:** Secret Streams are a function within the Spot-On client and describe a pool of keys, which are provided by a function deriving ephemeral keys created by the SMP – Socialist Millionaire Protocol – Process for authentication of two users. With this zero-knowledge proof at both user sides keys are generated, which need not to be transferred over the internet. This invention by the Spot-On development solved the key transmission problem over the internet.

- **Security:** Security is freedom from, or resilience against, potential harm (or other unwanted coercive change) caused by others. Beneficiaries (technically referents) of security may be of persons and social groups, objects and institutions, ecosystems or any other entity or phenomenon vulnerable to unwanted change by its environment. Security mostly refers to protection from hostile forces, but it has a wide range of other senses: for example, as the absence of harm (e.g. freedom from want); as the presence of an essential good (e.g. food security); as resilience against potential damage or harm (e.g. secure foundations); as secrecy (e.g. a secure telephone line); as containment (e.g. a secure room or cell); and as a state of mind (e.g. emotional security).

- **Server:** In computing, a server is a computer program or a device that provides functionality for other programs or devices, called "clients". This architecture is called the client–server model, and a single overall computation is distributed across multiple processes or devices. Servers can provide various functionalities, often called "services", such as sharing data or resources among multiple clients, or performing computation for a client. A single server can serve multiple clients, and a single client can use multiple servers. A client process may run on the same device or may connect over a network to a server on a different device. Typical servers are database servers, file servers, mail servers, print servers, web servers, game servers, and application servers.

- **Session Management:** Related to the identification of authenticated users

- **SHA-3:** SHA-3 (Secure Hash Algorithm 3) is the latest member of the Secure Hash Algorithm family of standards, released by NIST on August 5, 2015. Although part of the same series of standards, SHA-3 is internally different from the MD5-like structure of SHA-1 and SHA-2. SHA-3 is a subset of the broader cryptographic primitive family Keccak. Keccak's authors have proposed additional uses for the function, including a stream cipher, an authenticated encryption system, a "tree" hashing scheme for faster hashing on certain architectures, and AEAD ciphers Keyak and Ketje. Keccak is based on a novel approach called sponge construction. Sponge construction is based on a wide random function or random permutation and allows inputting ("absorbing" in sponge terminology) any amount of data, and outputting ("squeezing") any amount of data, while acting as a pseudorandom function with regard to all previous inputs. This leads to great flexibility.

- **Signature:** A digital signature is a mathematical scheme for demonstrating the authenticity of a digital message or documents. A valid digital signature gives a recipient reason to believe that the message was created by a known sender, that the sender cannot deny having sent the message (authentication and non-repudiation), and that the message was not altered in transit (integrity).

- **Simulacra:** The Simulacra function is a similar function compared to the Impersonator While Impersonator is simulating a chat of two participants with messages, Simulacra is just sending out a Fake-Message from time to time. Simulacra-Messages contain only random characters and have not the style or goal, to imitate a process of a conversation.

- **SIP-Hash:** SipHash is an add–rotate–xor (ARX) based family of pseudorandom functions. Although designed for use as a hash function in the computer science sense, SipHash is fundamentally different from cryptographic hash functions like SHA in that it is only suitable as a message authentication code: a keyed hash function like HMAC. That is, SHA is designed so that it is difficult for an attacker to find two messages X and Y such that SHA(X) = SHA(Y), even though anyone may compute SHA(X). SipHash instead guarantees that, having seen X_i and SipHash(X_i, k), an attacker who does not know the key k cannot find (any information about) k or SipHash(Y, k) for any message $Y \notin \{X_i\}$ which they have not seen before.

- **Small world phenomenon:** Small world phenomenon refers to a a hypothesis, according to which every human being (social actor) is connected to the world with each other over a surprisingly short chain of acquaintance relationships. The phenomenon is often referred to as Six Degrees of Separation. Guglielmo Marconi's conjectures based on his radio work in the early 20th century, which were articulated in his 1909 Nobel Prize address, may have inspired

Hungarian author Frigyes Karinthy to write a challenge to find another person to whom he could not be connected through at most five people. This is perhaps the earliest reference to the concept of six degrees of separation, and the search for an answer to the small world problem. The small-world experiment comprised several experiments conducted by Stanley Milgram and other researchers examining the average path length for social networks of people in the United States. The research was groundbreaking in that it suggested that human society is a small-world-type network characterized by short path-lengths.

- **Smoke Crypto Chat App**: Smoke Crypto Chat is a mobile Software Echo Client Application currently for Android, which is open source, and provides with SmokeStack an easy to configure and open source server software. The user ID is not based on phone numbers and no friends list is uploaded to any server. As it provides the secure algorithm McEliece, Smoke is regarded as worldwide the first mobile McEliece Messenger.

- **SmokeStack:** SmokeStack is the name of the server software for encryption communication over the Smoke Crypto Chat App. It functions also as a key server and a Postbox for offline user via the Ozone function. The server is provided for the operating system Android for mobile devices.

- **SMP:** See Socialist Millionaire Protocol.

- **SMP-Calling:** SMP-Calling is some modus for Cryptographic Calling, which sends temporary symmetric keys for end-to-end encryption, which are derived from the Socialist-Millionaire Protocol for Authentication. SMP-Calling is the basis for constantly generated temporary keys called Secret Streams.

- **SMTP:** Simple Mail Transfer Protocol(SMTP) is an Internet standard for electronic mail (email) transmission. First defined by RFC 821 in 1982, it was last updated in 2008 with the Extended SMTP additions by RFC 5321—which is the protocol in widespread use today. SMTP by default uses TCP port 25. The protocol for mail submission is the same, but uses port 587. SMTP connections secured by SSL, known as SMTPS, default to port 465.

- **Socialist Millionaire Protocol (SMP):** In cryptography, the socialist millionaire problem is one in which two millionaires want to determine if their wealth is equal without disclosing any information about their riches to each other. It is a variant of the Millionaire's Problem whereby two millionaires wish to compare their riches to determine who has the most wealth without disclosing any information about their riches to each other. It is often used as a cryptographic protocol that allows two parties to verify the identity of the remote party through the use of a shared secret, avoiding a man-in-the-middle attack without the inconvenience of manually comparing public key fingerprints through an outside channel. In effect, a relatively weak password/passphrase in natural language can be used.

- **Spot-On:** Spot-On is a very elaborated Encryption Software Suite with modern encryption functions. It is based on the Echo Protocol, which sends the encrypted packets address- and target less.

- **SQLite:** SQLite is a relational database management system contained in a C programming library. In contrast to many other database management systems, SQLite is not a client–serverdatabase engine. Rather, it is embedded into the end program.

- **StarBeam:** StarBeam is the function to share a file over two Echo Clients. All packets are sent encrypted.

- **StarBeam-Analyser:** The StarBeam-Analyzer is a tool, to analyze a transferred file over the StarBeam-function in that regard, if all partially blocks of the file have been received completely. The tool investigates – in case needed – the missing blocks of a file and creates a respective Magnet-URI-Link with this information. The receiver of the file can generate the Magnet and send it over to the sender of the file, who is then able to schedule a new send-out just of the missing blocks (also named as links or chunks). Over this procedure not the complete files has to be sent or replayed new to complete the original first transfer.

- **Super-Echo:** The Echo protocol consists within these re-membered characteristics (if we summarize it short), that each node tries to encrypt each message capsule – if this succeeds in terms of the hash-comparison, this message is for the own reading, and will be not again repacked and transferred further to all other connected online neighbors. As an online attacker could recognize this, when an incoming message is not sent out again, and thus could assume, that that it is a message for the receiver at this node. With Super-Echo the message will be – even if it has been decrypted successfully for the own node – sent out again to the connected nodes and for traveling on further paths. Just in regard, as this message would not have been determined for the own readings.

- **Symmetric Calling:** Symmetric Calling is some modus for Cryptographic Calling, which sends temporary symmetric keys for end-to-end encryption. It refers to send one symmetric key (pair) through one secured channel.

- **Symmetric Encryption:** Symmetric-key algorithms are algorithms for cryptography that use the same cryptographic keys for both encryption of plaintext and decryption of ciphertext. The keys may be identical or there may be a simple transformation to go between the two keys. The keys, in practice, represent a shared secret between two or more parties that can be used to maintain a private information link. This requirement that both parties have access to the secret key is one of the main drawbacks of symmetric key encryption, in comparison to public-key encryption (asymmetric encryption).

- **Symmetric Key:** These keys are used with symmetric key algorithms to apply confidentiality protection to information.

- **TCP:** The Transmission Control Protocol (TCP) is a core protocol of the Internet protocol suite. It originated in the initial network implementation in which it complemented the Internet Protocol (IP). Applications that do not require reliable data stream service may use the User Datagram Protocol (UDP), which provides a connectionless datagram service that emphasizes reduced latency over reliability.

- **ThreeFish:** Threefish is a symmetric-key tweakable block cipher designed as part of the Skein hash function, an entry in the NIST hash function competition. Threefish uses no S-boxes or other table lookups in order to avoid cache timing attacks; its nonlinearity comes from alternating additions with exclusive ORs. In that respect, it is similar to Salsa20, TEA, and the SHA-3 candidates CubeHash and BLAKE.

- **Timing:** Related to the race conditions, locking, or order of operations

- **TLS:** Transport Layer Security (TLS), and its now-deprecated predecessor, Secure Sockets Layer (SSL), are cryptographic protocols designed to provide communications security over a computer network. Several versions of the protocols find widespread use in applications such as web browsing, email, instant messaging, and voice over IP (VoIP). Web-sites can use TLS to secure all communications between their servers and web browsers. The TLS protocol aims primarily to provide privacy and data integrity between two or more communicating computer applications.

- **Token:** A security token is a physical device used to gain access to an electronically restricted resource. The token is used in addition to or in place of a password. It acts like an electronic key to access something. Examples include a wireless keycard opening a locked door, or in the case of a customer trying to access their bank account online, the use of a bank-provided token can prove that the customer is who they claim to be. Some tokens may store crypto-graphic keys, such as a digital signature, or biometric data, such as fingerprint details. Some may also store passwords.

- **Tor:** Tor is free and open-source software for enabling anonymous communication. The name is derived from an acronym for the original software project name "The Onion Router". Tor directs Internet traffic through a free, world-wide, volunteer overlay network consisting of more than seven thousand relays to conceal a user's location and us-age from anyone conducting network surveillance or traffic analysis. Using Tor makes it more difficult to trace Internet activity of the user.

- **Turtle-Hopping:** Turtle was a free anonymous peer-to-peer network project being developed at the Vrije Universiteit in Amsterdam, involving professor Andrew Tanenbaum. Like other anonymous P2P software, it allows users to share files and otherwise communicate without fear of legal sanctions or censorship. Turtle's claims of anonymity are backed by two research papers. Technically, Turtle is a friend-to-friend (F2F) network. The RetroShare File Sharing application is based on a F2f and implemented a "Turtle-Hopping" feature which was inspired by Turtle.

- **Two-way-Calling:** Two-Way-Calling is some modus for Cryptographic Calling, which creates temporary symmetric keys for end-to-end encryption, which are defined 50:50 by each of the end-users. In a Two-way Call the user sends an AES-256 as a passphrase for the future end-to-end encryption to the friend, and the friend also sends an own generated AES-256 to the first user in response. Now the first half of the AES of the first user and the second half of the AES of the second user are taken, respectively, and assembled into a common AES-256. It refers to the method of 2-way safety.

- **UDP:** The User Datagram Protocol (UDP) is one of the core members of the Internet protocol suite. The protocol was designed by David P. Reed in 1980 and formally defined in RFC 768. UDP uses a simple connectionless transmission model with a minimum of protocol mechanism. It has no handshaking dialogues, and thus exposes the user's program to any unreliability of the underlying network protocol. There is no guarantee of delivery, ordering, or duplicate protection. Time-sensitive applications often use UDP because dropping packets is preferable to waiting for delayed packets, which may not be an option in a real-time system.

- **URL:** A Uniform Resource Locator (URL), colloquially termed a web address, is a reference to a web resource that specifies its location on a computer network and a mechanism for retrieving it. A URL is a specific type of Uniform Resource Identifier (URI), although many people use the two terms interchangeably. URLs occur most commonly to reference web pages (https) but are also used for file transfer (ftp), email (mailto), database access (JDBC), and many other applications.

- **URL-Distiller:** URL-Distillers are filter rules, with which the downloaded, uploaded or imported URLS will be filtered. For example, one can configure his URL-Distillers in such a way, that all URLs are loaded into the own Database, but only specific URLS from one defined Domain, e.g. Wikipedia, are uploaded. Also e.g. a university can distribute only URLs out of the own database to its connected students, which refer to the own web-domain. URLs and URIs of Magnets, ED2K-Links and Torrent-URLs are currently not supported in the own URL-Database respective filter rules. The distillers refer to Web-URLs and also to FTP and Gopher.

- **URN:** A Uniform Resource Name (URN) is a Uniform Resource Identifier (URI) that uses the urn scheme. URNs were originally conceived to be part of a three-part information architecture for the Internet, along with Uniform Resource Locators (URLs) and Uniform Resource Characteristics (URCs), a metadata framework. URNs were distinguished from URLs, which identify resources by specifying their locations in the context of a particular access protocol, such as HTTP or FTP. In contrast, URNs were conceived as persistent, location-independent identifiers assigned within defined namespaces, so that they are globally unique and persistent over long periods of time, even after the resource which they identify ceases to exist or becomes unavailable.

- **VEMI:** VEMI stands for Virtual E-Mail Institution. See Institution.

- **Web-of-Trust:** In cryptography, a Web-of-Trust is a concept used in PGP, GnuPG, and other OpenPGP-compatible systems to establish the authenticity of the binding between a public key and its owner. Its decentralized trust model is an alternative to the centralized trust model of a public key infrastructure (PKI), which relies exclusively on a certificate authority (or a hierarchy of such). As with computer networks, there are many independent webs of trust, and any user (through their identity certificate) can be a part of, and a link between, multiple webs.

- **Wide Lanes:** One of the many obligations of a Spot-On-Kernel process is to receive, process, and forward data to one or more nodes. The mechanism that performs this task is similar to both a network hub and a network switch. Wide Lanes allow node operators to assign listener lane widths. Let's consider a basic example, a listener having a lane width of 20,000 bytes. The kernel, if necessary, will forward packets via the listener's clients if the sizes of the forwarded packets do not exceed 20,000 bytes. Optionally, clients may negotiate different lane widths with their peers. All network communications beyond the interface and the kernel must and will adhere to the configured limits.

- **YaCy:** YaCy (pronounced "ya see") is a free distributed search engine, built on principles of peer-to-peer (P2P) networks. Its core is a computer program written in Java distributed on several hundred computers, as of September 2006, so-called YaCy-peers. Each YaCy-peer independently crawls through the Internet, analyzes and indexes found web pages, and stores indexing results in a common database (so called index) which is shared with other YaCy-peers using principles of P2P networks. It is a free search engine that everyone can use to build a search portal for their intranet and to help search the public internet clearly.

- **Zero-knowledge-proof:** A zero-knowledge proof or zero-knowledge protocol is a method by which one party (the prover) can prove to another party (the verifier) that they know a value x, without conveying any information apart from the fact that they know the value x. The essence of zero-knowledge proofs is that it is trivial to prove that one possesses knowledge of certain information by simply revealing it; the challenge is to prove such possession without revealing the information itself or any additional information. If proving a statement requires that the prover possess some secret information, then the verifier will not be able to prove the statement to anyone else without possessing the secret information. The statement being proved must include the assertion that the prover has such knowledge, but not the knowledge itself. Otherwise, the statement would not be proved in zero-knowledge because it provides the verifier with additional information about the statement by the end of the protocol. Interactive zero-knowledge proofs require interaction between the individual (or computer system) proving their knowledge and the individual validating the proof.

24 Keywords

House C
Phone

House B
Computer

New honey recipe

② You see, a message from House C, can go from House D, ther to the post office.

① Echo
takes messages from and sends them to different devices. Like a post office.

House D
Robot

⑤ Each device (house) gets same mail. It echoes to their homes. Echo can go to all sorts of devices (homes), and can echo the same mail to multiple houses*

Post Office
(Server)

House A
Tablet

Mail for
Linda!

④ Mail truck
The mail truck is what delivers mail for each device, and the same mail for certain devices.

* Message
* Devices

Spot-On Encryption Suite is a secure instant **chat** messenger and encrypting **e-mail** client that also includes additional features such as group chat, **file transfer**, and a **URL search** based on an implemented URL data-base, which can be peer-to-peer connected to other nodes. Also, further tools for file encryption or **text conversion to ciphertext** etc. are included.

The Spot-On program might currently be regarded as a very elaborated, up-to-date and diversificated open source encryption software for **Multi-Encryption** and Cryptographic Calling: As it also includes the McEliece algorithm it is thus described as the **first McEliece Encryption Suite** worldwide – to be especially secure against attacks known from Quantum Computing.

Thus, the three basic functions frequently used by a regular Internet user in the **Internet** - communication (chat / e-mail), web search and file transfer - are now secure over the Internet within one software suite: **Open source** for everyone.

This handbook and user manual of Spot-On is a practical software guide with introductions not only to this application and its innovative and invented processes, but also into Encryption, Cryptography, **Cryptographic Calling** and **Cryptographic Discovery**, **Graph-Theory**, p2p Networking, NTRU, McEliece, the Echo Protocol and the Democratization of Multiple and **Exponential Encryption** also in the regard of the context of **Privacy** and **Human Rights**.

The book covers more than 15 chapters and more than 80 figures with content for presentations within educational **tutorials** or for **self-learning opportunities** about these topics.

9 783749 435067

www.ingramcontent.com/pod-product-compliance
Lightning Source LLC
LaVergne TN
LVHW022302060326
832902LV00020B/3234